领土与海洋争端问题
研 究 丛 书

国家出版基金项目

领土与海洋争端问题研究丛书

丛书主编 张海文 吴继陆

国际法实践中的历史性所有权

徐栋 / 著

知识产权出版社
全国百佳图书出版单位
—北京—

图书在版编目（CIP）数据

国际法实践中的历史性所有权/徐栋著. —北京：知识产权出版社，2025.7.
（领土与海洋争端问题研究丛书/张海文，吴继陆主编）. —ISBN 978–7–5130–9530–3

Ⅰ. D99

中国国家版本馆 CIP 数据核字第 2024PS5009 号

责任编辑：赵利肖　庞从容　　　　　责任校对：谷　洋
封面设计：乔智炜　　　　　　　　　　责任印制：孙婷婷

国际法实践中的历史性所有权
徐　栋　著

出版发行：	知识产权出版社 有限责任公司	网　　址：	http://www.ipph.cn
社　　址：	北京市海淀区气象路 50 号院	邮　　编：	100081
责编电话：	010-82000860 转 8726	责编邮箱：	pangcongrong@163.com
发行电话：	010-82000860 转 8101/8102	发行传真：	010-82000893/82005070/82000270
印　　刷：	三河市国英印务有限公司	经　　销：	新华书店、各大网上书店及相关专业书店
开　　本：	710mm×1000mm　1/16	印　　张：	14.75
版　　次：	2025 年 7 月第 1 版	印　　次：	2025 年 7 月第 1 次印刷
字　　数：	290 千字	定　　价：	88.00 元
ISBN 978–7–5130–9530–3			

出版权专有　侵权必究
如有印装质量问题，本社负责调换。

本书出版获得国家出版基金、自然资源部海洋发展战略研究所资助

丛书编委会

（以姓氏笔画为序）

马新民　王宗来　孔令杰　朱利江

刘　超　刘新民　吴继陆　余民才

张海文　张新军　陈喜峰　易显河

罗　刚　周　健　施余兵　徐贺云

高圣惕　高健军　黄　瑶　傅崐成

GENERAL EDITOR'S PREFACE

总　序

领土与海洋问题事关国家主权、安全与发展，数百年来一直是国际关系演进、国际法发展中历久弥新的主题之一。妥善处理领土与海洋争端是世界性难题。据不完全统计，当今世界上仍存在 60 多处领土争端和 200 多条未划定的海洋边界。和平解决争端是各国的共同愿望，也是国际法的基本要求。但这类争端每每涉及久远的历史恩怨、敏感的民族情绪，数十年、上百年悬而未决，在复杂多变的外来因素催化下，反而会随时升温、激化，引发新的冲突和战争。

中国与邻国之间的领土与海洋争端在外交磋商及学界研究中经常被称为东海问题、南海问题，近十年来也成为国际舆论的热点话题。领土归属和海洋划界是国际法、海洋法中的经典问题；海上执法争端自 1990 年代开始增多。在国际法院等裁决机构的案例中，这三个问题越来越深入地联系在一起，这是一个值得重视的发展趋势。2013 年开始、2016 年结束的所谓南海仲裁案，实质上也是将这三个方面的争端经过包装后强行提起和推进的。

"领土与海洋争端问题研究丛书"围绕领土归属、海洋划界和海上执法这三个密切相连的议题，以全面、客观、深入的学术研究为基础，以解决中国面临的实际问题为导向。第一批拟出版的 10 本（卷）内容既有所侧重又相互呼应，主要包括三类：一是案例分析，逐一评析国际裁决机构关于领土与海洋争端的所有裁决，力求客观全面地反映所涉重要法律问题，为深入全面地了解相关程序问题及实体问题的发展变化提供基础性研究成果；二是专题研究，例如领土取得的国际法规则、海洋划界方法论、强制仲裁机制、国际法中的关键日期等；三是国别或综合研究，例如菲律宾领土及海洋主张研究、南海问题研究等。

本丛书具有包容性，尊重入选的每一位作者的个人学术观点，鼓励对相同议题的相互补充、质疑与启发。本丛书亦具有开放性，欢迎国内同人奉献与本套丛书相关主题的学术成果，不断丰富本丛书的学术内涵，拓展领土与海洋问题研究的广度和深度。我们期待本丛书的陆续出版能促进中国国际法研究，并为实务部门的工作提供有益的参考。

本丛书从策划、组织至出版历经近5年。在丛书即将出版之际，我们对各位著作者慨然同意将个人成果纳入丛书表示感谢！本丛书是在大量研究成果基础上形成的，相关研究得到多个部门单位的长期指导与大力支持，在此特别感谢自然资源部国际合作司（原国家海洋局国际合作司）和自然资源部海洋发展战略研究所（原国家海洋局海洋发展战略研究所）！

本丛书2018年由知识产权出版社申报"'十三五'国家重点图书出版规划"并顺利入选，2020年成功获得国家出版基金资助。知识产权出版社领导给予了大力支持，丛书责任编辑庞从容女士、薛迎春女士及其团队其他编辑付出了大量的辛劳，在此谨表谢意！

张海文　吴继陆

2020年3月8日

FOREWORD

前　言

作为一项习惯法规则，历史性所有权在国际法体系内占有稳固的位置。虽然历史性所有权首次独立出现是在20世纪初，但其规则的内涵渊远流长。其在长期发展中与国际法实践不断交融，这种发展在赋予历史性所有权丰富法律内涵的同时，也给司法机构和国际法律师在应用和解释时带来种种困惑。本书的研究目的就是尝试通过考察相关的国际法实践厘清历史性所有权的内涵和适用。

历史性所有权在实践中最初起源于海洋法，是沿海国家在缺乏海洋法规则或者不被一般海洋法规则许可时获取海洋主权的方式。用于陆地领土的取得时，历史性所有权一方面填补先占和时效之间的规则空白，用于取得归属权不明的土地；另一方面也被用于替换时效，成为取得其他国家领土的方式。除此以外，国家在特定历史时期对土地的占有，也被赋予历史性所有权的法律含义，从而在确定领土的最终归属时发挥作用。

面对如此广泛的适用，学界认为，历史性所有权应尽可能保留精简的内涵以保证概念的一致性，即有效管理和相关国家的同意。这两项要件代表了关于历史性所有权要件构成不同学说间的最大公约数，与此同时，代表"历史性"的时间要素不再成为独立的要件，而是蕴含在证据是否满足要件要求的影响因素中。即便如此，这两个基本要件随着适用范围的扩展，其规定已经被更多国家在实践中采用并获得国际法实践的认可，要件之间的相互关系也随着具体争议的不同，进行着相应的调整。

照拂实践中维护国家主权权益的需要，是本书起笔时的最大初心。对中国来说，悠久的历史为我们在处理与周边国家的主权和海洋争议时提供了丰富的证据来源，然而，作为国际法体系的后来参与者则意味着我们缺乏制定和利用国际法规则的机会和优势。在解决这一矛盾的过程中，历史性所有权的内容和适用上的弹性提供了将历史事实转化为国际法权利的宝贵机会。实践中，无论是巩固中国对无争议的内水海域的主权，还是强化周边岛礁领土主权问题中的历史和法理依据，历史性所有权都有独特的用武之地。

中国国际法学界对历史性所有权的认识随着实践需要不断深化。20世纪90年代，学者首先关注的是历史性所有权及其密切相关的权利是什么，主要视角在于透过国外前辈学者的论述、国际司法的前例和《联合国海洋法公约》（以下简称《公约》）相关条款的缔约过程，弄清历史性所有权的权利形成要求和适用条件及范围。2010年前后，随着周边海洋权益争议的日益白热化，特别是在海洋大国和周边邻国纷纷质疑和否定中国在南海长期生产、生活、管辖所形成的权利时，我国的相关学者更多地将目光聚集到如何将中国丰富的历史证据转化为历史性所有权和历史性权利的工作中。2016年后，为了回应南海仲裁案仲裁庭对中国在南海历史性权利的全盘否定，中国学者的研究视角进一步打开，对历史性所有权（历史性权利）与《公约》的关系、中国在南海主张（或者应当主张）的是何种类型的历史性所有权（历史性权利）进行了深入的研究，取得了丰富的理论成果。

囿于各种原因，本书在建构历史性所有权的要件框架和适用场景后，未能对这一理论与中国的现实需求进行回应。此外，作者在思考时还形成了两个尚在萌芽期的观点：一是历史性所有权及历史性权利并不是海洋法上特有的制度，而是习惯国际法上持续反对制度在海洋法领域的具体适用，其权利基础来源是一般国际法上以国家主权为基础的普遍存在的救济权。二是关于历史性所有权与《公约》的关系，并不以其是否属于主权性问题而形成不同处理方式，而是以是否需要个案审查为不同的处理标准。只要需要个案审查，无论是否属于主权性或非主权性问题的历史性权利，《公约》均对其采取尊重态度。以上问题，作者将在未来研究时进一步探讨深化，以期能再有所得。

限于研究水平，本书还存在不少问题与不足，恳请理论和实务界同人提出宝贵意见。

主要案例名称对照表

原　名	中译名
Affaire de L'ile de Clippertion	克利伯顿岛仲裁案
Alabama and Mississippi Boundary Case	亚拉巴马州和密西西比州边界案
Argentine-Chile Frontier Case	阿根廷—智利边界仲裁案
British Guiana-Venezuela Boundary Dispute	英属圭亚那和委内瑞拉边界仲裁案
Case Concerning the Indo-Pakistan Western Boundary (Rann of Kutch)	印度和巴基斯坦之间西部边界案（卡其沼泽案）
Case Concerning Sovereignty over Pedra Branca/Pulau Batu Puteh, Middle Rocks and South Ledge	白礁岛案
Continental Shelf Case	大陆架划界案
Delimitation of the Maritime Boundary in the Gulf of Maine Area	缅因海湾划界案
Eritrea-Yemen Arbitration	厄立特里亚—也门仲裁案
Fisheries Case	英挪渔业案
Frontier Dispute Case	边界争议案
Island of Palmas Case	帕尔玛斯岛仲裁案

Land, Island and Maritime Frontier Dispute	陆地、岛屿和海洋边界案
Land and Maritime Boundary between Cameroon and Nigeria	喀麦隆和尼日利亚间陆地和海洋边界案
Legal Status of East Greenland	东格陵兰岛法律地位案
Louisiana Boundary Case	路易斯安那州边界案
Military and Paramilitary Activities in and against Nicaragua	尼加拉瓜军事和准军事行动案
Temple of Preah Vihear Case	隆端寺案
Territorial and Maritime Dispute	领土和海洋争议案
The Grisbadarna Case	格里斯巴达纳仲裁案
The North Atlantic Coast Fisheries Case	北大西洋渔业仲裁案
The Republic of El Salvador v. The Republic of Nicaragua	萨尔瓦多诉尼加拉瓜案
The Minquiers and Ecrehos Case	敏基埃岛和艾科俄斯岛案
Sovereignty over Pulau Ligitan and Pulau Sipadan	利吉丹岛、西巴丹岛主权案
Western Sahara Advisory Opinion	西撒哈拉法律地位咨询案

重要人名对照表

原　名	中译名
Charles de Visscher	查理·德·维舍
R. Y. Jennings	罗伯特·Y. 詹宁斯
Ian Brownlie	伊恩·布朗利
Surya P. Sharma	苏里亚·P. 沙尔玛
D. P. O'Connell	丹尼尔·P. 奥康纳
L. J. Bouchez	利奥·布谢
Gilbert Gidel	吉尔贝特·吉德尔
D. H. N. Johnson	D. H. N. 约翰逊
Georg Schwarzenberger	乔治·施瓦曾博格
A. L. W. Munkman	A. L. W. 蒙科蔓
Yehuda Z. Blum	耶胡达·Z. 布鲁姆
M. W. Clark. Jr	小威廉·克拉克
Clive R. Symmons	克里夫·R. 西蒙斯
Philip C. Jessup	菲利普·C. 杰赛普
Gerald Fitzmaurice	杰拉德·菲茨莫里斯
C. H. M. Waldock	克劳德·H. M. 沃尔多克
I. C. MacGibbon	伊恩·C. 麦克吉本
Mitchell P. Strohl	米切尔·P. 斯特罗尔
Donat Pharand	多纳特·法朗德

Henry Wheaton	亨利·惠顿
Arther Nussbaum	阿瑟·努斯鲍姆
Hugo Grotius	雨果·格劳秀斯
John Selden	约翰·塞尔登
Emmerich De Vattel	埃默瑞克·德·瓦泰尔

CONTENTS

目　录

第一章　绪　论 · 001
　　第一节　研究背景 /001
　　第二节　概念厘清 /002
　　　　一、权源的含义 /002
　　　　二、权源的类别 /003
　　　　三、传统的领土取得方式 /004
　　　　四、作为主权取得方式的历史性所有权 /005
　　第三节　本书结构 /009

第二章　历史性所有权的演进 · 010
　　第一节　历史性所有权的"历史"背景 /010
　　　　一、罗马法中的土地取得 /010
　　　　二、欧洲以外的土地取得方式 /012
　　　　三、领土取得规则的变化 /017
　　第二节　海洋法上历史性所有权的演进 /020
　　　　一、1930 年前的历史性所有权 /021
　　　　二、第一次联合国海洋法会议前后的
　　　　　　历史性所有权 /025

　　　　　三、第三次联合国海洋法会议与当代历史性
　　　　　　所有权的发展 /030
　　第三节　与领土取得相关的历史性所有权 /035
　　　　　一、历史上的长期占有 /036
　　　　　二、所有权的历史性巩固 /037
　　第四节　小　结 /041

第三章　历史性所有权的构成 · 043
　　第一节　时际法、关键日期和证明责任 /043
　　　　　一、时际法 /043
　　　　　二、关键日期 /048
　　　　　三、证明责任 /055
　　第二节　有效管理 /058
　　　　　一、有效管理的意图和主张 /058
　　　　　二、展示权利的行为 /062
　　　　　三、行为的持续性及和平性 /067
　　　　　四、行为的地理范围 /073
　　　　　五、地　图 /075
　　第三节　相关国家的同意 /077
　　　　　一、相关国家 /078
　　　　　二、认　知 /080
　　　　　三、同意的形式 /084
　　　　　四、抗　议 /089
　　第四节　小　结 /093

第四章　领土取得中的历史性所有权 · 095
　　第一节　历史上的长期占有 /095

　　　　一、法律基础 /095
　　　　二、对主权归属的影响 /103
　　第二节　所有权的历史性巩固 /109
　　　　一、取得主权不明但不属于无主地的土地 /110
　　　　二、取代原持有国的领土主权 /112
　　　　三、作为法律权源的解释工具 /115
　　第三节　小　结 /116

第五章　海洋法上的历史性所有权 · 118
　　第一节　历史性水域的法律基础 /119
　　　　一、权利来源 /119
　　　　二、历史性所有权的发现方式 /123
　　第二节　相关因素的影响 /131
　　　　一、自然因素 /132
　　　　二、利益因素 /136
　　　　三、影响因素不能独立成为取得历史性
　　　　　　水域的理由 /143
　　第三节　小　结 /145

结　论 · 146

参考文献 · 148

附录　联合国秘书处关于包括历史性海湾在内的
　　　历史性水域法律制度的研究报告 · 159

后　记 · 215

第一章 绪 论

第一节 研究背景

领土取得是国际法永恒的焦点之一。在传统的领土取得方式的基础上，比利时学者查理·德·维舍（Charles de Visscher）提出"历史性所有权的巩固"（Consolidation by Historic Titles）作为一种领土取得的方式，引起了国际法理论和实践的广泛关注。同时，在有关领土主权和海洋划界的争议中，争议方主张将本国对某一土地在历史上的管控证据，视为历史性所有权，并将其作为该国主权依据的实践也并不鲜见。一些重要的国际法判例，也对历史性所有权的内涵和适用有过一定程度的论述。但由于实践的发展和理论的纷争，在当前的国际法实践背景下，继续在国际法实践基础上研究历史性所有权，仍然具有很强的现实意义。

首先，历史性所有权的内涵以及在国际司法实践中的适用尚未厘清。一个国家长期稳定的实践，且这一实践得到其他国际社会成员的容许，那么就构成该国继续维持这一实践的历史性所有权。历史性所有权的巩固过程只是时间因素的简单积累，还是根据需要对领土取得方式做内涵上的调整，需要进一步的研究。另外，所谓领土取得方式本身是学者对司法实践的归纳，是构建起来的。也就是说，历史性所有权的适用，同样需要我们在厘清其内涵后，将实践与内涵进行比对和归纳才能得到。

其次，各国在领土和边界争议中的实践是否发展了历史性所有权有待考察。一国的实践要符合不断演化的国际法规则的要求，同时，国家实践也可以推动习惯国际法规则的发展。实践中，各国主张的历史性所有权与学理上的最初含义不尽相同。因此，有必要考察各国实践，确定实践中是否存在着共同趋势，这个趋势是什么，能否达到发展国际法规则的程度。

最后，对这一领域清晰界定对我国和平解决领土问题和划界争议有实践意义。当前，我国与周边国家之间存在着一系列领土和边界争议。在历史事实的基础上，根据国际法，通过谈判协商和平解决与邻国间的领土和边界问题是我国的一贯立场。因此，如果历史性所有权这一问题能够得到清晰的梳理，一方面可以为我国的主张提供坚实的法律基础，另一方面也为和平解决争议的策略选择提供参考。

第二节 概念厘清

一、权源的含义

主权是国家有权实施其职能的身份标志。对国际法来说，主权就其本身而言是先验的。国际法更关心的是，怎样才能确定国家对特定土地享有领土主权。将国家和领土主权联系在一起的是权源（Title）。

权源有着广泛的含义，基于本书的研究目的，仅对抽取国际司法机构和国际法学者在处理领土主权和海洋划界议题中的相关论述予以考虑。在司法实践中，国际法院提供了两种对它的理解，确定权利存在的证据以及权利的实际来源。[1]前者是事实，后者是法律。罗伯特·Y. 詹宁斯（R. Y. Jennings）认为权源的存在与否最终依赖于特定事实是否存在，因此权源的首要含义是被法律承认可以创造权利的事实。[2] 在"厄立特里亚—也门仲裁案"中，仲裁庭认为权源不是正在发展中的主张，而是业已确立的权利；不是是否占有的问题，而是可以脱离占有的法律问题。[3]对权源的两种不同理解并不意味着分别存在两种都叫作权源的不同事物，事实上，它们是对权利确定过程中不

---

[1] Frontier Dispute Case (Burkina Faso v. Mali), International Court of Justice Reports, 1986, p. 564.

[2] R. Y. Jennings, *The Acquisition of Territory in International Law*, Manchester University Press, 1963, p. 4.

[3] Eritrea-Yemen Arbitration (First Stage), International Legal Materials, Vol. 40: 900, p. 917 (2001).

同阶段的认识。

权源的产生和维持依赖于被国际法规范所认可的事实,但是拥有权源不一定产生权利。国内法中,如果法律不同意将权利授予某人,那么意味着此人不具有产生权利的事实。国际法上的权源不只是有或者无那么简单,伊恩·布朗利(Ian Brownlie)认为权源的实质是一国的领土主权主张相对其他国家的有效性。[1]实践中,这种有效性既可能来自对权源产生方式优先程度的比较,也可能来自对权源产生的事实证据强弱的比较。总之,法律上规定有优先权的权源产生方式,以及在同等权源产生方式中更强的证据,决定权利的归属。因此,国际法上的权源可能是相对的,如果只存在单方面主张,权源作为事实和法律是同一的。反之,如果存在相互竞争的主张,事实产生权源,通过比较后较强的权源方才产生领土主权。[2]

二、权源的类别

按照权源的产生方式,布朗利对领土权源做了更为细致的分类,形式上的权源包括条约、殖民时期国内法、司法判决以及当事国家的单方面意思表示或国家间合意等;当不存在形式上权源时,国家对希望占有的土地实施有效管理的行为(Effectivité)也构成领土主权的来源,比如在无主地或者归属不明的土地上实施本国的立法。[3]简单地说,权源在领土主权范畴内可以分为通过意思表示产生的法律权源和通过国家有效管理产生的行为权源。这两种权源在法律效力上并非可以等量齐观。在"布基纳法索和马里间的边界争议案"中,国际法院指出当存在法律权源的时候,有效管理的作用在于确认法律上的权源,当两者不一致时,有效管理服从法律权源。[4]这也是国际法代表国家

---

[1] Ian Brownlie, *Principles of Public International Law*, 7th editon, Oxford University Press, 2008, p. 119.
[2] Title 的多重含义不仅带来理解上的问题,也带来翻译中的困难。权源,权利,所有权都是常见的中文译法。本书在 Title 作为主权或权利来源时翻译为权源,而在 Historic Titles 用作主权的取得方式时将其翻译为历史性所有权。
[3] Ian Brownlie, *Principles of Public International Law*, 7th editon, Oxford University Press, 2008, p. 128 – 134.
[4] Frontier Dispute Case (Burkina Faso v. Mali), International Court of Justice Reports, 1986, p. 586.

合意这一基本性质的体现。

根据国家获取权源时的土地所处的法律状态，可以将权源分为原始权源（Original Title）和继受权源（Derivative Title）。[1] 两者的区别在于国家取得特定土地权利时，这块土地上是否已经有其他国家的权利存在。如果没有，此时权源便是原始的；如果是通过权源将原先属于其他国家的土地纳入本国主权，那么此时权源就是继受的。由于一片争议土地可能先后与不同国家的权源联系在一起，这一分类有助于发现土地权利的最初持有者。当然需要注意的是，原始权源和继受权源的分类对权源自身有效性的判定不产生影响[2]，但是会对土地的最终归属起到特定的作用。

三、传统的领土取得方式

国家通过权源确立主权的最直观方式就是将某一块土地纳为领土。这一过程的实现方式是多样的。先占（Occupation）、时效（Prescription）、让与（Cession）、添附（Accretion）和征服（Conquest）作为领土取得的五种模式得到了广泛的认可，同时这五种关于取得的分类也被认为无法完整地反映国际法领域的实践。[3] 这种感觉一方面来自国际社会变化对领土取得规则的影响，例如伴随着"禁止使用武力或以武力相威胁"成为强行法（Jus Cogens）的是单纯意义上的武力征服已经无法合法取得领土，而随着前殖民地国家独立风潮的涌动，民族自决成为新独立国家领土主权的来源。[4] 更重要的是，一系列与领土取得相关的证据很难分门别类归入某一个特定的类型，也很难见到国家将领土主张完全建立在某一种领土取得模式上。正如苏里亚·P. 沙尔玛（Surya P. Sharma）指出的，国际社会要求和渴望以单一新方法解决所有领土取

---

[1] Ian Brownlie, *Principles of Public International Law*, 7th editon, Oxford University Press, 2008, p.130.

[2] Ian Brownlie, *Principles of Public International Law*, 7th editon, Oxford University Press, 2008, p.130.

[3] R. Y. Jennings, *The Acquisition of Territory in International Law*, Manchester University Press, 1963, p.6-7.

[4] Malcolm Shaw, *Title to Territory in Africa*, Clarendon Press, 1986, p.17. 民族自决是否成为权源存在争议，布朗利认为新独立国家的领土是没有权源的，领土是国内法行为的副产品。

得问题。[1]

国家也可以以领土取得的方式将公海的一部分纳入领土。这一行为的有效性基础通常被认为来自时效取得，理由是公海不是无主物（res nullius），而是人类的共同财产（res communis）。[2] 但是国际法委员会指出时效适用于陆地和海洋时的区别，通过时效取得的是原本属于另一国家或原有主权不明的土地，而沿海国在主张对一部分海域的主权时，相关国家的抗辩不是他们也拥有主权，而是这片海域不属于任何国家。

因此，无论是陆地领土的取得还是将海洋纳入国家主权范围，都需要一种不同以往的领土取得理论作为支撑。国际法院前法官、比利时法学家德·维舍的研究在这个方向上指出了可能的新路径，他认为"经证实的长期利用，……代表着包含关系和利益的集合，这一集合自身能产生将某一片陆地或者海洋归属某一国家的效力"，并将这一模式称为"所有权的历史性巩固"。[3]

四、作为主权取得方式的历史性所有权

（一）研究现状

虽然适用于陆地和海洋取得的历史性所有权统一的概念由德·维舍第一次提出，事实上在此之前，作为沿海国以历史性所有权为法律基础取得超过国际法规则许可水域已经在实践中得到了认可。因此，历史性所有权的界定也与海洋法上的特殊水域制度联系在一起。丹尼尔·P.奥康纳（D. P. O'Connell）认为历史性所有权的适用最早可追溯到1887年，在确定康塞普申海湾（Conception Bay）主权时，历史性所有权得以克减一般规则的条件已经被提出，即权利的主张和对方的

---

[1] Surya P. Sharma, *Territorial Acquisition, Dispute and International Law*, Martinus Nijhoff Publishers, 1997, p. 185.
[2] R. Y. Jennings, *The Acquisition of Territory in International Law*, Manchester University Press, 1963, p. 23.
[3] Charles de Visscher, *Théories et Réalités en Droit International Public*, 4th edition, Editions A. Pedone, 1970, p. 226.

默认。[1] 吉尔贝特·吉德尔（Gilbert Gidel）认为历史性水域就是"那些经由其他国家同意而取得特殊法律地位的水域，这些水域法律地位的取得不同于一般国际法规则"[2]。利奥·布谢（L. J. Bouchez）将历史性水域定义为："沿海国在一段时间内清晰、持续、有效行使主权权利的水域，虽然权利的行使不符合一般国际法但是得到了国际社会的默认。"[3]

在讨论历史性所有权能否成为陆地领土的取得方式时，学者们已经普遍接受海洋法语境下历史性所有权的定义，而将争议的焦点放在历史性所有权要件与其他领土取得方式的关系上。例如，D. H. N. 约翰逊（D. H. N. Johnson）认为，历史性所有权通过将"直接占有"（Straightforward Possession）和"逆权占有"（Adverse Possession）包含在巩固的过程中[4]，从而使"时效"的概念或者被放弃，或者只保留"逆权占有"的含义。[5] 詹宁斯认为历史性所有权的内涵不只是一次术语上的改革，他指出传统意义上的"时效"强调的仍是长时间的和平占有，而其他国家态度的作用仅仅在于为和平占有提供证据。而对历史性所有权来说，仅凭其他国家的态度就可以成为是否产生领土权源的决定性因素。[6] 乔治·施瓦曾博格（Georg Schwarzenberger）则把历史性巩固（Historic Consolidation）视为一种对权源的完善，随着时间的推移，一种起初不完善的权源由于被多数国家承认而成为"对世权"（erga omnes）。[7]

---

[1] D. P. O'Connell, Edited by I. A. Shearer, *The International Law of the Sea*, Clarendon Press, 1982, p. 423.

[2] Historic Bays: Memorandum by the Secretariat of the United Nations, A/CONF. 13/1, 1957, p. 19.

[3] L. J. Bouchez, *The Regime of Bays in International Law*, Sythoff, 1964, p. 199.

[4] 普通法在移植罗马法的特定制度时，将占有他人物权的时效制度称为"逆权侵占"或者"逆权占有"。由于国际法的领土取得拟制于私法上的占有规则，因此早期的英国学者直接借用了本国法律中的术语，随后这一术语被普遍接受用于描述领土主权属于特定国家，但是被另一个国家或地区和平占据的情形。需要注意的是，国际法中的逆权占有只是描述现象，是某种领土取得方式适用的情形，而不是规则本身。

[5] D. H. N. Johnson, *Acquisitive Prescription in International Law*, British Yearbook of International Law, Vol. 27: 332, p. 332 (1950).

[6] R. Y. Jennings, *The Acquisition of Territory in International Law*, Manchester University Press, 1963, p. 26–27.

[7] Georg Schwarzenberger, *Title to Territory*, *Response to a Challenge*, American Journal of International Law, Vol. 51 (2): 308, p. 310 (1957).

通过先前国际法学者的研究，我们可以初步确定历史性所有权的特征：它既是历史性水域的唯一法律基础，也是陆地领土主权的取得方式之一。它由两部分要件构成，包括国家对土地有效管理的行为以及国际社会的认同态度。

历史性所有权的另一个重要特征是，无论针对陆地或海域，取得的结果都是排他性的主权，这使得历史性所有权在根本上区别于非排他性的历史性权利（Historic Rights）。非排他性的历史性权利，无论是传统捕鱼权，还是历史性通行权利，都是在他国主权或管辖范围内保留本国实践的权利。非排他性的历史性权利和历史性所有权在构成要件上具有一定的相似性，也依赖于长期稳固的实践和受影响国家的同意或容忍，但是非排他性的历史性权利无论如何不能产生排他的法律效果。[1]由于本书意在探讨取得主权的历史性所有权，因此非排他性的历史性权利将不在本书的讨论范围之内。

（二）当前历史性所有权研究存在的问题

第一，对历史性所有权的认识尚不明确。詹宁斯承认历史性所有权对其他国家态度的重视符合现实的要求，但是也看到了这一概念对其他国家态度的看重将减少人们对最初权利取得是否合法的考虑[2]，因此他认为如果不加限制地适用这一领土取得方式将是极其危险的。奥康纳从概念区分的角度也提出了类似的问题，质疑除了要求其他国家的态度外，历史性所有权和有效占领之间缺乏实质的区别[3]。最强烈的反对声音来自 A. L. W. 蒙科蔓（A. L. W. Munkman），她批评德·维舍对巩固历史性所有权的阐释太模糊，认为只靠利益和关系的集合很难构成

---

[1] Max Planck Institute for Comparative Public Law and International Law, *Historic Titles*, Max Planck Encyclopedia of Public International Law (June12, 2014), http://opil.ouplaw.com/view/10.1093/law:epil/9780199231690/law-9780199231690-e705? rskey = 3CtvAW&result = 1&prd = EPIL.

[2] R. Y. Jennings, *The Acquisition of Territory in International Law*, Manchester University Press, 1963, p. 28.

[3] D. P. O'Connell, *International Law and Boundary Disputes*, Proceedings of the American Society of International Law at Its Annual Meeting (1921–1969), Vol. 54: 77, p. 79 (1960).

一种独立的领土取得方式，也无法为解决实际争议提供指导。[1] 沙尔玛同样认为这一概念的内涵太过宽泛，并且它与人权因素、民族自决等当代领土权源的关系也不确定。[2]

第二，没有反映全部的国际法实践。现代国际法的规则体系建立在西方实践的基础上，随着国际法适用范围的扩展，其中的具体规则面临如何适用于非西方国家实践的问题。非西方国家不但有着不同于西方国家的社会管理方式，有的甚至已经形成了独特的主权观和领土观，这是解决这些国家领土争议时需要面对的问题。在近年来的国际司法实践中，许多非西方国家主张本国在历史上曾经占有争议土地，虽然后来被其他国际法认可的领土取得方式所取代，但是这种历史上的占有也构成历史性所有权，并据此将本国的领土主张全部或部分地建立在历史性所有权基础上。[3] 对于如何在历史性所有权两大构成要件的法律框架内解决这些问题，事实上已超出西方理论范畴的历史实践，既有的研究还没有给出确定的回应。

第三，研究时间较早且存在比较严重的专业领域切割问题。从目前的理论成果看，对历史性所有权的研究依然围绕着海洋法上的历史性水域以及领土取得的一般国际法各自展开，前者以国际法委员"包括历史性海湾在内的历史性水域法律制度研究"为代表；后者则以德·维舍的论述为中心，对历史性所有权在术语改革、权源补充等方面的意义各持赞许或批评的态度。但是，缺少以历史性所有权为线索，贯通一般国际法和海洋法的研究，目前只有耶胡达·Z. 布鲁姆（Yehuda Z. Blum）在 1965 年出版的《国际法中的历史性权利》（*Historic Titles in International Law*）一书中，从要件的解析出发，对历

---

[1] A. L. W. Munkman, *Adjudication and Adjustment-International Judicial Decision and the Settlement of Territorial and Boundary Disputes*, British Yearbook of International Law, Vol. 46: 1, p. 103 – 104 (1972 – 1973).

[2] Surya P. Sharma, *Territorial Acquisition, Dispute and International Law*, Martinus Nijhoff Publishers, 1997, p. 185.

[3] 与此相关的国际司法实践包括：The Minquiers and Ecrehos Case (France v. The United Kingdom), International Court of Justice Reports, 1953, p. 47 – 73. Case Concerning the Indo-Pakistan Western Boundary (Rann of Kutch), United Nations Reports of International Arbitration Awards, Vol. 17, 1968, p. 1 – 576. Western Sahara Advisory Opinion, International Court of Justice Reports, 1975, p. 12 – 69. Eritrea-Yemen Arbitration (First Stage), International Legal Materials, Vol. 40: 900, p. 900 – 982 (2001)。

史性所有权从概念到在一般国际法和海洋法中应用作了全面的梳理。

上述研究的另一个问题是前人的杰出工作大多发生在 20 世纪五六十年代，新近的研究成果仅有小威廉·克拉克（M. W. Clark. Jr）的《历史性海湾和历史性水域：一项新近开始并持续使用的制度》（Historical Bays and Waters, A Regime of Recent Beginning and Continued Usage）和克里夫·R. 西蒙斯（Clive R. Symmons）的《海洋法中的历史性水域的现代再评价》（Historic Waters in the Law of the Sea, A Modern Re-Appraisal）。从上次历史性所有权研究高潮至今，不但国家实践发生了剧烈变化，许多新兴的独立国家都将历史上的占有视为本国对争议土地的主权来源；国际法特别是海洋法本身也经历从重视维护海洋自由到在维护海洋自由前提下尽可能授予沿海国权利的重大变化。这些变化都意味着历史性所有权已经处在新的国家实践和国际法规则体系的语境中，迫切需要研究在新环境中历史性所有权是如何发挥作用的。

第三节　本书结构

根据历史性所有权既有的研究成果和存在的问题，笔者对历史性所有权的研究将包含以下几个层面：首先是对历史性所有权的构成要件研究，包括各自要件的内涵以及要件之间的关系，建立起能够区别于其他领土取得方式的独立的历史性所有权概念；其次是历史性所有权在实践中的应用，包括要件成立的标准、考虑的相关因素，以及历史性所有权成立后对领土取得的整体影响。对上述两个问题的研究将贯穿全书，在此基础上，笔者还将特别关注历史性所有权对中国实践的意义。中国作为具有悠久历史同时建立过不同于西方的"国际法"体系的国家，历史对我们来说，是解决领土和海洋争议的宝贵财富，应当认真深入地研究，努力把客观的历史事实转化为具有直接法律意义的历史证据。

本书正文包括五部分内容：（1）梳理历史性所有权从背景到产生再到发展的整个历史，提出具体需要解决的问题；（2）历史性所有权的构成要件以及实践中判断要件成立的相关规则；（3）领土争议中历史性所有权对判断主权归属和对提出竞争主张国家的影响；（4）适用于历史性水域时所做的调整和需要补充的考察因素；（5）结论。

第二章 历史性所有权的演进

在讨论历史性所有权的内容和它的具体适用前,首先需要回答的是这一规则或者说制度是如何出现的,又是如何逐步变成今天人们所看到的样子。考察这段历史的寄望正如阿瑟·努斯鲍姆(Arther Nussbaum)所言,尽管"训诫并非结论性的,但至少它们显示了演化进程的大概可能之路径,消除了那些极端的看法"[1]。

第一节 历史性所有权的"历史"背景

一、罗马法中的土地取得

罗马人推崇以法律治国,在古罗马的众多文化成就中,法律居于最高地位,特别是以《优士丁尼法典》为代表的罗马私法,对后世的影响力远远超出民法的范畴,成为众多当代部门法借鉴的原型,国际法也不例外。虽然,古罗马也存在处理罗马人与外邦人关系的万民法(Jus Gentium),这一称谓甚至构成现代国际法(Law of Nations)的词源,但万民法不是现代意义上的国际法,而是适用于非罗马人的罗马私法。因此,就对国际法具体规则的实质影响而言,探讨适用于罗马人的罗马私法与现代国际法之间的关联更具有现实意义。[2]

(一)罗马法中的所有权取得

早期的罗马公法中并不存在取得无主土地或者他国土地的规则。

---

[1] [美]阿瑟·努斯鲍姆:《简明国际法史》,张小平译,法律出版社2011版,第1页。
[2] Cornelis G. Roelofsen, *Treaties between Europeans and Non-European Powers in the Early Modern and Modern Times*, in Thilo Marauhn, Heinhard Steiger, *Universality and Continuity of International Law*, 1st edition, Eleven International Publishing, 2011, p. 151.

实践中，罗马通过战争和签订臣属条约（Vassalage Treaties）扩展统治范围，此外，罗马对外族土地的取得还包括一种有特色的归降（Deditio），即在得到罗马口头承诺后，归降民族可以在一定的附加条件下并入罗马。[1] 如果坚持以现代国际法的观念评价这些实践，那么罗马不断扩张的领土无疑来自征服和让与，而不是通过有效管理的行为取得领土主权。

相比之下，罗马私法对私人所有权的讨论和编纂更值得关注。最早时期的罗马法注重家庭的结构，基本特点表现为家父权力的至高无上，这种权力的对象之一便是土地及其附属品。[2] 因此，土地所有权（Dominium）是家父统一主权的组成部分。至于这些土地的取得方式，属于罗马早期土地的取得方式，主要来自对城邦公有土地的分配。随着罗马夺取的外族土地不断增多，这些土地在罗马人看来都属于无主地，导致在除分配土地之外的一部分公有土地成为人们自由占据的对象。[3] 这种占据理论上是临时的和可撤销的，但是大量这类土地从被占有到实质上被兼并，使得所谓的临时性和可撤销性名存实亡，占有逐步成为罗马土地的所有权类型之一。[4] 罗马私法的集大成者《优士丁尼法典》编纂了这类土地取得方式，称之为"取得时效和长期占有"，其中规定不动产通过一定时间的长期占有，则被赋予取得时效。[5] 对土地来说，为了保证有限的土地资源得到充分的利用，法典进一步规定对明知是他人土地仍进行占有的，只要没有以盗窃或暴力方式占有的，仍能通过长期占有取得土地所有权并将已取得的土地交付给第三人。[6]

(二) 从罗马法的取得到一般国际法的领土取得规则

当以自然法为基础的国际法开始成为一门独立学科的时候，罗马法和神学理论一同成为学者论证国际法规则的重要依据。从16世纪直

---

[1] [美] 阿瑟·努斯鲍姆：《简明国际法史》，张小平译，法律出版社2011版，第13—14页。
[2] [意] 朱塞佩·格罗索：《罗马法史（2009年校订本）》，黄风译，中国政法大学出版社2009年版，第83页。
[3] Western Sahara Advisory Opinion, International Court of Justice Reports, 1975, p. 86.
[4] [意] 朱塞佩·格罗索：《罗马法史（2009年校订本）》，黄风译，中国政法大学出版社2009年版，第85—86页。
[5] 徐国栋：《优士丁尼〈法学阶梯〉评注》，北京大学出版社2011年版，第210页。
[6] 徐国栋：《优士丁尼〈法学阶梯〉评注》，北京大学出版社2011年版，第216页。

到 18 世纪早期，人们都尝试使用罗马时期的规则和术语解释当时国家间关系的准则以及国家与其领有土地间的关系。君主与领土的关系就是罗马家父权与土地关系的再现，从而国家的领土取得也自然可以拟制罗马法上私人取得土地所有权的规则。取得时效和长期占有由此变成了国际法的领土取得方式。同时，由于土地是君主的私人财产，那么不但可以根据君主的意志分配给下一级封建领主，还可以随着土地占有者的生丧嫁娶而产生不同的组合，并且在占有者去世后成为财产继承的对象，也就是说封建权利和私人继承在当时同样构成合法的领土来源。

然而，国际法毕竟是一个自洽的法律体系。国际法的大量具体规则虽然来源于罗马法的具体规定，但是在处理国家间关系时在实践中逐渐被赋予区别于起源时的特定含义。就领土的取得和维持而言，世俗化的民族国家体系的建立首先排除了宗教在确定领土关系中的作用，人民主权的兴起则随之将领土和君主财产脱钩。这些观念和政治现实对领土取得规则的影响使国家对领土的占有不再表现为实际的居住或者利用，而是国家主权和平持续的展示。

此时，罗马法的土地取得对国际法的借鉴意义更多体现在借助罗马法概念以描述国际法的相关规则。而借鉴自罗马法的术语，一方面是法律传统延续的客观结果，另一方面，由于无法确切对应实践中的各类领土取得方式，罗马法的术语越来越无法满足确切描述国家取得领土的需要，这就为实践中创设新的领土取得方式创造了条件。

二、欧洲以外的土地取得方式

在罗马法不断发展兴替的同时，欧洲以外的其他地区也发展出与本地区自然环境、文化、宗教意识相匹配的法律制度，其中同样包括领土的取得方式和观念。在这些文明中，以中国为中心的东方文明以及伊斯兰教文明一直延续至今，这两种文明的领土观念对今天的国际法实践仍有其特定的意义，是裁决与这些国家相关的领土争议时不可缺少的考虑因素。

（一）以中国为中心的朝贡体制

古代中国由于相对封闭的国土地理特征和以农业为主的经济生产

方式，产生了与欧洲截然不同的传统法律秩序[1]，这一秩序体现在古代中国对法律方方面面的认识中，也包括对领土秩序的认知。

要理解古代中国的领土秩序不能离开对"礼"和"法"的认识。[2]"礼"和"法"被视为中国传统法律制度的两大支柱，礼是儒家思想的重要特征，恰当的行为规则被称为"礼"，礼的内涵取决于适用者在社会中所处的身份。[3] 简言之，"礼"就是依照不同身份地位遵守不同的社会行为准则。尽管最初的儒家已经形成一套完整的社会管理理念，但是并不打算采取强制措施推行，而是通过习俗、伦理、道德来调整人们的行为使之符合礼的要求。因此，社会强制的角色被交给了"法"。法是和儒家同时代的法家的观念，法所指的不是单纯的法律，而是一套完整的中央集权社会管理制度，全国范围内有统一的法律，并由服从中央的各级政府和官吏负责实施这些法律，人们必须对中央政府承担纳税和服役的义务，某种程度上这和现代国家的管理方式并无二致。

经过周和秦的实验，从汉代早期开始，中国的统治者同时接受了这两种完全不同的法律理念，形成一套社会等级伦理和中央集权政治相结合的社会治理模式。[4]这一模式不但被用于治理国内，而且随着中国的逐步强大，历代王朝根据这一模式建立起以中国为核心的东方世界体系，也就是朝贡体系。[5]可以说，东方世界体系是一个以中国为圆心，层层扩展的同心圆，从圆心到周边分为四层，分别是郡县、羁縻、藩属以及其他国家。中国的皇帝接受上天的命令来管理这个被称为"天下"的同心圆，同时根据"礼"的要求对位于不同等级的地区采取区别性的管理和接触手段。[6]

对郡县制的部分，管理方式是建立各级政府实施中央政府的各项法令，这种管理和现代国家的管理方式已经没有本质区别。羁縻主要

---

[1] Li Zhaojie, *Traditional Chinese World Order*, Chinese Journal of International Law, Vol. 1：20, p. 24 – 25 (2002).

[2] Pan Junwu, *Towards a New Framework for Peaceful Settlement of China's Territorial and Boundary Disputes*, Martinus Nijhoff, 2009, p. 71 – 75.

[3] [德] K. 茨威格特、H. 克茨：《比较法总论》，潘汉典、米健、高鸿钧等译，法律出版社 2003 年版，第 509 页。

[4] 梁治平：《法辩：中国法的过去、现在与未来》，中国政法大学出版社 2002 年版，第 157 页。

[5] 王铁崖：《国际法引论》，北京大学出版社 1998 年版，第 365 页。

[6] 王铁崖：《国际法引论》，北京大学出版社 1998 年版，第 367 页。

针对边远地区的少数民族政权,这些政权的首领除了保有原先的政治地位外,往往还被授予中央政府地方官的称谓,中央政府也会派出部分监管官员。[1]一部分羁縻地区随着和内地交流的逐渐深化,实现"改土归流",例如现在四川、广西、云南、贵州的部分地区;另一部分虽然保留着自身的政治结构,但是须接受中央的任免和监督管理,例如西藏和内蒙古。[2]总的来说,羁縻地区被视为中国多民族统一疆域的组成部分。

藩属国是基本具有独立地位的国家,中国虽然在与它们的关系中处于优越者的地位,但是对他们的影响主要体现在文化上而不是政治管理上。[3]从管理的角度,这些国家与中国之间只是存在特定的权利义务,比如国王的法定地位需得到中国的认可,定期朝觐皇帝,同时中国向他们提供军事保护和通商许可。[4]更重要的是,中国与这些属国之间存在边界,例如,中国和琉球之间就以"黑水沟",也就是今天的冲绳海槽为界。[5]明清两代中国的藩属国曾一度包括朝鲜、琉球、越南等十余国,一般认为这些国家依旧保留了他们的主权。[6]随着反抗西方殖民主义的失败,中国到19世纪末失去了所有的藩属国。

除上述以外,其他国家并不属于中国建构的世界体系,只是和中国有联系。中国式的天下观讲究"普天之下,莫非王土",不过这并不意味着中国的统治者会狂妄地认为自己是天下所有土地的主人,比如近在咫尺的日本,绝大多数时候并没有被纳入中国的体系。[7]出于维护"礼"的需要,中国依然在和他们的交往中坚持自己的中心地位,但当需要从务实的角度出发解决实际问题时,中国政府并不会顽

---

[1] 张博泉、苏金源、董玉英:《东北历代疆域史》,吉林人民出版社1981年版,第120页。
[2] 彭建英:《中国古代羁縻政策的演变》,中国社会科学出版社2004年版,第6页。
[3] Li Zhaojie, *Traditional Chinese World Order*, Chinese Journal of International Law, Vol. 1: 20, p. 25 (2002).
[4] Wang Tieya, *International Law in China: Historical and Contemporary Perspectives*, in Hague Academy of International Law, *Hague Academy Collected Courses*, 1990, p. 220 - 222.
[5] 中华人民共和国国务院新闻办公室:《钓鱼岛是中国的固有领土》白皮书,人民出版社2012年版,第5页。
[6] 王铁崖:《国际法引论》,北京大学出版社1998年版,第366页。
[7] 王铁崖:《国际法引论》,北京大学出版社1998年版,第366页。

固地不将对手视为平等的谈判对象。[1] 因此，对于事实上并不处于中国体系内的国家，中国理论上将它置于同心圆的最外围，视其为"蛮夷"，但在实际交往中会在认识到自身实力不足以征服对方的前提下给予其相对平等的地位。[2]

综合上述，根据中国传统的"礼法"观念以及由此衍生的版图观，以中国为代表的东方式领土观念的特点应包括：首先，对于可以被视为中国领土的那部分土地，中国在"法"的基础上至少实施了一定程度的有效管理，即便按照现代国际法的领土取得规则加以评判，也符合持续有效展示主权的要求。其次，由于"普天之下，莫非王土"这一"礼"的观念，至少在中国本土、羁縻和藩属国之间不存在无主地的观念。最后，与陆地上只有边疆没有边界的认识不同，中国与特定属国之间已经形成边界的意识。边界意味着朝向各自方向的部分都是国土，也就是说不分海洋、陆地，都是主权覆盖的对象。

(二) 伊斯兰文明

《古兰经》是伊斯兰文明的圣典，也是伊斯兰法的最基本和最高的渊源。[3]《古兰经》记录了穆罕默德在神的启示下的言行，并没有提出一整套完整的法律规则体系，其中只有一小部分可以作为法律规则直接适用。但是其中记录的穆罕默德对法律适用疑难问题的看法显示出他对伊斯兰法的期待，就是要以法律为工具，以一个对真主信仰的共同体来改变古代阿拉伯各部落的分散状态。[4] 可见，《古兰经》奠定了伊斯兰文明政教合一的基本特征。

《古兰经》和其他伊斯兰法的渊源中没有提到有关土地的规定，不过我们可以根据其中对私人财产权的规定对此一窥端倪。《古兰经》

---

[1] 以中俄关系为例，清朝在《尼布楚条约》签订后一直与俄罗斯保持了实质上相对平等的外交往来。参见孙喆、王江：《对1689—1727年中俄外交关系的考察》，载《中国边疆史地研究》2006年1期，第9—16页。
[2] 王铁崖：《国际法引论》，北京大学出版社1998年版，第374页。
[3] [德] K. 茨威格特、H. 克茨：《比较法总论》，潘汉典、米健、高鸿钧等译，法律出版社2003年版，第422页。
[4] [德] K. 茨威格特、H. 克茨：《比较法总论》，潘汉典、米健、高鸿钧等译，法律出版社2003年版，第422页。

承认私人可以占有并使用财产,并在财产中受益,但同时宣布一切财产归真主所有,穆斯林被称作财产的受托人,只有使用财产的权利。[1] 这一观念同样适用于伊斯兰国家对土地的占有,"厄立特里亚—也门仲裁案"的当事双方历史上都信仰伊斯兰教,仲裁庭认为应该在岛屿主权裁决中加入这一历史性的考虑因素。[2] 最终仲裁庭裁决根据伊斯兰教传统的"共有"观念,双方在取得争议岛屿的同时,应当继续维持对方渔民对岛屿及其周边水域的传统利用,并为这种利用提供相应的便利。[3] 这事实上体现了《古兰经》对穆斯林财产利用方式的要求。

除了宗教以外,另一个对伊斯兰国家土地占有方式产生影响的是他们所生存的自然环境。伊斯兰教的发源地阿拉伯半岛多为沙漠草原,降水量少,自然环境难以满足定居的农耕生活。因此传统阿拉伯人多以"逐水草而居"的游牧为业。[4] 以丝绸之路为代表的东西方交通线打通后,正好位于这条交通线必经之路的伊斯兰国家开始广泛从事商业活动,同样也属于流动性很强的社会经济活动。与这种流动性相符合的国家管理模式强调个人的政治效忠而不是常态化的行政管理措施。"西撒哈拉法律地位咨询案"中,摩洛哥提出居住撒哈拉的游牧部落和摩洛哥苏丹间存在宗教和政治上效忠关系,请求法院将效忠关系和其他民族、文化和宗教的纽带一起,视为代表地方与中央关系的主权展示。[5]

总之,伊斯兰国家的政教合一的政治传统和流动性强的社会经济方式同样产生了独特的领土观念:首先,必须将宗教因素影响下共有观念纳入判断领土归属的考虑范围;其次,在考虑土地与人的联系时,不能简单以定居生活方式的管理标准作为评价依据。

---

[1] 高鸿钧:《伊斯兰法:传统与现代化》(修订版),清华大学出版社 2004 年版,第 29 页。

[2] Eritrea-Yemen Arbitration (First Stage), International Legal Materials, Vol. 40: 900, p. 920-921 (2001).

[3] Eritrea-Yemen Arbitration (First Stage), International Legal Materials, Vol. 40: 900, p. 920 (2001).

[4] 高鸿钧:《伊斯兰法:传统与现代化》(修订版),清华大学出版社 2004 年版,第 6 页。

[5] Western Sahara Advisory Opinion, International Court of Justice Reports, 1975, p. 44.

三、领土取得规则的变化

（一）公海自由和海洋法的独立

罗马人面对的海洋主要是地中海，因此罗马的海洋观念与地中海结合在一起。在彻底战胜迦太基人后，罗马取得了地中海的控制权，当罗马进一步取得地中海沿岸的全部土地时，地中海成为罗马事实上的内海。罗马将地中海作为粮食和货物在帝国各个行省间流转的通道，因此在法律上将海洋视为"共有物"，而不是可以成为取得对象的"无主物"。[1]

航海大发现时代的海洋和陆地没有区别，都成为大国争相主张所有权的对象，葡萄牙和西班牙甚至在教皇的见证下将全球水域一分为二。[2] 16 世纪末，英国取代了葡萄牙和西班牙在海上的霸主地位，也仍坚持垄断海洋的立场，而此时，海峡对岸的荷兰逐渐兴起，带动了航行和捕鱼自由的呼声。[3] 17 世纪初，荷兰人胡果·格劳秀斯（Hugo Grotius）提出了"海洋自由论"，主张海洋应向所有国家和人民开放，供他们自由使用，不适用领土取得的规则，不得征收通航税或禁止渔业。[4] 格劳秀斯的主张立刻受到英国学者约翰·塞尔登（John Selden）的反击，塞尔登针锋相对地提出了"海洋取得论"，并在当时获得多数学者的支持。[5]

格劳秀斯的理论虽然输在争论的起跑线上，但赢得了这场赛跑的最终胜利。随着全球范围内交通运输的日益频繁，海洋有了完全不同于陆地的利益产生方式。各国没有必要，也不可能再将海洋视为本国的禁脔，事实上到 17 世纪末，各国船只已经可以自由航行在海洋上。

---

[1] Mitchell P. Strohl, *International Law of Bays*, Martinus Nijhoff, 1963, p. 19.

[2] D. P. O'Connell, Edited by I. A. Shearer, *The International Law of the Sea*, Clarendon Press, 1982, p. 2.

[3] D. P. O'Connell, Edited by I. A. Shearer, *The International Law of the Sea*, Clarendon Press, 1982, p. 3.

[4] D. P. O'Connell, Edited by I. A. Shearer, *The International Law of the Sea*, Clarendon Press, 1982, p. 9.

[5] D. P. O'Connell, Edited by I. A. Shearer, *The International Law of the Sea*, Clarendon Press, 1982, p. 4.

最终在19世纪，英、美、法、荷等当时主要海洋大国一致确认公海自由的原则。[1] 由此建立起来的稳固实践就是海洋从此脱离主权主张的对象范围。而现代海洋法也在公海自由原则上滥觞，不再接受一般国际法的调整，成为国际法的独立规则体系。

（二）领土取得规则适用地域的扩展

在国际法内部规则体系不断完善的同时，国际法也走出它的发源地，在适用范围上由欧洲中心法逐步转变成为真正意义上的国际法。明确非欧洲地区在何时开始接受国际法的观念和规则不单单具有辨明历史的意义，实践中还影响到领土争议中适用规则的选择，从而影响最终的裁决结果。"厄立特里亚—也门仲裁案"中，仲裁庭承认红海两岸的传统渔业机制所反映的经济社会结构体现了伊斯兰法没有"领土主权"的特点。但是，仲裁庭进一步指出在1856年克里米亚战争后，争议双方的宗主国奥斯曼土耳其帝国就已经放弃了伊斯兰体系的国际法，并且在1875年接受现行国际法的适用，从而接受了"领土主权"的观念。[2] 换句话说，如果双方在1856年前行为的效力需要参考传统伊斯兰法的规定，那么评价双方1875年之后的行为准则则完全是现行国际法的领土取得规则了。

历史上不同地区接受现代国际法的时间、方式和态度都有所不同，学者可以描述特定国家从接触国际法的某些规则到全面接受国际法的历程，但是也难以抽象界定该国到底在何时接受了现行的国际法体系。因此，只能在特定的具体环境中得出当事国对待某一具体国际法规则的态度。

首先，接触国际法的时间不等于接受国际法的时间。特别是对本身已经存在稳定法律体系文明的国家来说，它们可能断断续续地根据现代国际法的某些理念处理与西方国家间的关系，但并不意味着他们同意接受现代国际法规则的拘束。以中国为例，中国最早在17世纪中叶因为使节豁免权问题的争议开始接触到国际法，甚至在1689年中俄

---

[1] Ian Brownlie, *Principles of Public International Law*, 7th editon, Oxford University Press, 2008, p. 224–225.

[2] Eritrea-Yemen Arbitration (First Stage), International Legal Materials, Vol. 40：900, p. 920 (2001).

《尼布楚条约》的签订过程中遵照了条约法的程序和规则，但是不能认为中国在当时接受了国际法并以此替代以中国为中心的朝贡体系。[1] 而此时这类由西方国家和非西方国家间签订的条约，也只能被视为多元影响下的混合条约，而不是平等国家间的现代条约。[2]

其次，接受国际法规则并不意味着放弃本国原有的国际法体系。仍以中国为例，中国在 1864 年发生的渤海湾丹普捕获事件中首次主动适用国际法的规则维护中国在内水的主权，这代表中国正式在实践中适用国际法的相关规则，但中国并未就此放弃原有的周边秩序体系。[3] 可以说，中国当时同时适用两套不同的国际法制度，一方面适用来自欧洲的国际法处理与西方国家间的关系，另一方面用传统的国际法体系（朝贡体系）处理与原来藩属国间的关系，这一双重体制一直延续到中国失去全部的藩属国为止。

可见，多线索的"历史"背景已经暗示了现代国际法框架内的历史性所有权从产生之日起，就不可避免地包含了复杂的法律内涵。首先，这一概念承担了领土取得的术语规则从拟制于罗马私法到成为自洽的国际法体系的转变任务。其次，历史上的占有对当代领土争端的效果需要借由历史性所有权作出评价。最后，海洋法规则体系的独立和公海自由原则的确定并不彻底排除国家取得海洋的可能，而历史性所有权是这种可能的唯一法律基础。因此，在结束对历史性所有权背景整理后，我们需要将目光投向这一权利本身，探寻历史性所有权在产生后的发展历程。

---

[1] 王铁崖：《国际法引论》，北京大学出版社 1998 年版，第 374—375 页。
[2] Cornelis G. Roelofsen, *Treaties between Europeans and Non-European Powers in the Early Modern and Modern Times*, in Thilo Marauhn, Heinhard Steiger, *Universality and Continuity of International Law*, 1st edition, Eleven International Publishing, 2011, p. 416.
[3] 在渤海湾事件交涉成功后，清政府虽然在对外交往中开始主动适用国际法，但更多地关注其为中国争取权利的实用价值，并未将中国自身看作国际法的规范对象。林学忠：《从万国公法到公法外交——晚清国际法的传入、诠释与应用》，上海古籍出版社 2008 年版，第 201 页。

第二节 海洋法上历史性所有权的演进

在公海自由成为一般原则后,随之而来的问题是:自由是不是绝对的,如果不是,它的边界在哪里?沿海国需要一定宽度的海域以保护他们免受其他国家海军侵袭并保证捕鱼和航行的经济利益。格劳秀斯在主张海洋自由的同时承认沿海国有权主张一定程度的海洋主权(Imperium),埃默瑞克·德·瓦泰尔(Emmerich De Vattel)也在承认公海不可取得的前提下,坚持国家有权以占有陆地的方式对部分海洋行使管辖权。班克舒克(Bynkershoek)则提出将"岸炮射程"(Cannon Range)作为划分海洋上自由和沿海国管辖的界线,这一理论后来成为领海制度的雏形。[1]国家实践逐步为"岸炮射程"拟制出一个确定的距离,即由海岸低潮线向海延伸3海里为沿海国领海。[2]

但是,从低潮线开始计算领海宽度不适用海岸线凹入陆地的海湾或其他水体。基于保护原则的要求,被一国领土包围的海湾在特定条件下被视为该国领土,领海宽度从连接海湾岬角(Headlands)的直线即海湾封口线起算。[3]特定条件就是对封口线长度的限制,对此国际法长期缺乏统一的规定,实践中主要存在6海里、10海里及不限制三种做法。[4]但是沿海国在主张不限制封口线宽度的海湾为本国领土时,所持的依据并不是海洋法对湾口封口线的规定,而是主张海湾长期在沿海国的占有下,并且这种占有得到国际社会的默认,也就是沿海国对海湾拥有历史性所有权。

历史性所有权的概念源于领土取得规则在海洋法框架内的应用,它的演变也伴随着现代海洋法在各个历史阶段的发展。本节选取的三个时间点,与其说对应着历史性所有权本身的发展,不如说是代表了海洋法整体发展的关键时刻。通过观察这些时间点前后的国家实践和

---

[1] Philip C. Jessup, *The Law of Territorial Waters and Maritime Jurisdiction*, G. A. Jennings Co., Inc., 1927, p. 5–6.

[2] Philip C. Jessup, *The Law of Territorial Waters and Maritime Jurisdiction*, G. A. Jennings Co., Inc., 1927, p. 10.

[3] John P. Grant, J. Craig Barker, *Harvard Research in International Law: Original Materials*, W. S. Hein, 2008, p. 253.

[4] Mitchell P. Strohl, *International Law of Bays*, Martinus Nijhoff, 1963, p. 187.

司法判例，本节将尝试梳理和归纳历史性权利的内涵和适用对象在海洋法框架下的发展脉络。

一、1930 年前的历史性所有权

（一）早期司法实践

有关海湾的历史性所有权实践最早发生在国内司法中。1793 年英国卷入法国革命战争，此时一艘英国船"格兰杰"号在美国特拉华河河口处被法国护卫舰捕获，酿成"格兰杰号事件"。美国认为捕获发生地是作为中立国的美国领土，因此捕获是侵害美国主权的事件。总检察长兰多夫（Randolgh）提出特拉华湾（Delaware Bay）作为入海口两侧都是美国领土，且美国继承英国在海湾内排他性的航行权，该海湾应当视为美国领土。[1]

在 1877 年的"直美电缆有限公司诉美国英美电报公司案"中，英国上议院枢密院主张康塞普申海湾是英国领土。枢密院先是长篇大论地论证国际法理承认只要海湾的自然构造符合岬角理论，那么此时无论海湾封口线宽度为何，沿海国都可以将其纳入主权范围。之后却话锋一转指出，英国根本无须借助这一地理便利，因为长时间的主权控制以及各国对英国主权主张的默认已经使康塞普申湾成为英国领土的一部分。[2]

1885 年，负责处理美国南北战争引起的相应赔偿事务的亚拉巴马赔偿委员会第二法庭认定，内战中南方邦联政府击沉"阿勒格尼安"号所在的切萨皮克湾（Chesapeake Bay）属于美国领土，因此法庭具有管辖权。法院首先分析了海湾的地形，指出海湾入口处宽度仅 10 余海里而进深达到 200 海里，封闭性很强且不是供国际航行的水道。随后，法院又提出海湾两侧的土地分别于 1609 年和 1632 年被授予弗吉尼亚和马里兰

---

[1] Historic Bays: Memorandum by the Secretariat of the United Nations, A/CONF. 13/1, 1957, p. 5–6.
[2] 在枢密院眼中，康塞普申湾成为英国领土的根本原因是该湾比布里斯托尔海道（Bristol Channel）具有更明显的深入陆地的特征，而后者在"Cunningham"案中已经被视为英国领土。参见 Philip C. Jessup, *The Law of Territorial Waters and Maritime Jurisdiction*, G. A. Jennings Co., Inc., 1927, p. 384–385.

州殖民当局，并随两个州一起加入美国。国会分别在1789年、1790年和1799年的立法中确认了对海湾的管辖权，美国的管辖也得到了英、法两个海洋大国的默认。因此，切萨皮克湾是美国领土而不是公海。[1]

1910年的"北大西洋渔业仲裁案"是与历史性所有权相关的第一例国际司法实践。英美两国在1818年签订协议规定美国渔民有在加拿大北大西洋沿岸的捕鱼权利，并划定了行使权利的具体地域范围，规定美国渔民可以进入这些区域特定的海湾、河口和港口。此后，英国开始通过严格立法缩减美国渔民的权利，矛盾在1905年达到顶点。美英两国在1910年建立仲裁庭，请求澄清1818年协议的内容，双方共请求仲裁庭对7个问题作出回应，其中第5条提出"对条款中涉及的任何海岸、海湾、河口和港口的3海里"应从何处起算？

仲裁庭认为当时的国际法规则中没有关于海湾封口线宽度的规定，而在缺乏现存规则的前提下，可以根据条约和业已确定的惯例主张海湾为沿海国领土，并明确将这类海湾称为"历史性海湾"。[2]迭戈（Drago）法官在反对意见中明确指出，支持历史性海湾的法律基础是沿海国的主权主张以及特殊情况，如，地理构造、长期使用，特别是自卫的需要，都为沿海国主权主张提供了合理理由。[3]

1917年，萨尔瓦多向中美洲法院起诉尼加拉瓜，要求法院认定丰塞卡海湾（Gulf of Fonseca）处于沿海各国共管（Condominium）的状态，从而判定尼加拉瓜将海湾内港口租借给美国的条约无效。[4]法院分析了丰塞卡海湾的自然构造和战略价值，也回溯了萨尔瓦多摆脱西班牙殖民之后，海湾被周边国家占有的历史，指出在所有的历史时期，周边国家都公开确认并和平持有海湾的所有权。沿海各国在没有发生矛盾和受到抗议的情况下在海湾内实施警察、卫生、财政执法活动，而国际社会不但默认沿海国的执法行为，甚至在海湾内从事商业行为前应事

---

[1] Historic Bays: Memorandum by the Secretariat of the United Nations, A/CONF. 13/1, 1957, p. 4.
[2] The North Atlantic Coast Fisheries Case (Great Britain v. United States), United Nations Reports of International Arbitration Awards, 1910, Vol. 11, p. 197.
[3] The North Atlantic Coast Fisheries Case (Great Britain v. United States), United Nations Reports of International Arbitration Awards, 1910, Vol. 11, p. 206.
[4] The Republic of El Salvador v. The Republic of Nicaragua, The American Journal of International Law, Vol. 11 (3), p. 675 – 767 (1917).

先寻求沿海国家的同意。[1]基于上述原因的综合考虑,中美洲法院认定丰塞卡海湾是沿海三国共同行使主权的"封闭的历史性海湾"。

(二)历史性海湾规则的首次编纂

一战结束后,国际联盟(以下简称"国联")着手编纂当时存在的习惯国际法规则,其中也包括海洋法规则。1924年,由国联任命的专家委员会编列了适于编纂海洋法的21项主题,其中第8项是"国际法上时效概念的适用",但送交成员国的问卷中并未包含这一问题,只是在领海制度中涵盖了历史性海湾。[2]作为专家委员会的结论,修正后的《舒金草案》(Schücking Draft)第4条规定,持续而长期地使用可以使得封口线宽于10海里的海湾取得比照内水的国际法地位。[3]

响应国联编纂海洋法的号召,各个国际法研究机构都提出了自己的草案,而在起草海湾制度时,各个研究机构都以但书形式对一般海湾规则的适用范围做了例外规定,构成例外的法律基础普遍被认为是业已确定的惯例。[4]其中有两个草案值得特别关注,一个是美国国际法学会(American Institute of International Law)草案,它解释了惯例的具体内涵,即沿海国或他们的组成部分以传统方式行使或维持他们的主权所有权,具体方式是国内立法和管辖、行为或权威学说。[5]另一个则是《哈佛草案》,其第12条规定前述领海范围的条款不排除业已确定的惯例对领海的划分,评论中提到该条的必要性来自国家对特定水体或特别水域的历史性主张和其他国家的默认。《哈佛草案》首次明确了默认也是惯例内涵的一部分,同时将例外规则的适用拓展到海湾之外的其他水域。[6]

---

[1] The Republic of El Salvador v. The Republic of Nicaragua, The American Journal of International Law, Vol. 11 (3), p. 700 – 704 (1917).
[2] R. R. Churchill, A. V. Lowe, *The Law of the Sea*, 3rd edtion, Manchester University Press, 1999, p. 14.
[3] Mitchell P. Strohl, *International Law of Bays*, Martinus Nijhoff, 1963, p. 313.
[4] Historic Bays: Memorandum by the Secretariat of the United Nations, A/CONF. 13/1, 1957, p. 14 – 16.
[5] M. W. Clark Jr., *Historical Bays and Waters, A Regime of Recent Beginning and Continued Usage*, Oceana Publication, 1994, p. 41 – 43.
[6] John P. Grant, J. Craig Barker, *Harvard Research in International Law: Original Materials*, W. S. Hein, 2008, p. 288.

1929年，继承专家委员会工作的准备委员会在收到各国政府对"计划要点"的回复后，对其中涉及历史性海湾部分做出总结，认为各国接受超过10海里封口线的基础是沿海国需证明存在满足这一地位（历史性海湾）的惯例。[1]在这一观察的基础上，准备委员会起草了讨论"要点8"作为1930年海牙国际法编纂会议第二委员会讨论历史性海湾领海宽度测量方式的起点：

> 如果惯例表明海湾处于沿海国的排他权力之下，无论连接海湾入口两端的直线的宽度是多少，领海都从该直线开始测量，惯例存在的举证责任归于沿海国。[2]

在回复准备委员会的"计划要点"和第二委员会讨论"要点8"的过程中，有关国家表达了他们对历史性海湾的国际法基础的观点。澳大利亚认为"默认"是历史性海湾被视为领海的依据。比利时认为历史性海湾主张的可接受性建立在特殊地理环境基础上的无可争议的国际惯例。德国、波兰和日本的观点同时强调沿海国长时间的实践和其他国家普遍接受。加拿大认为使海湾被视为沿海国内水的基础包括历史或者地理的原因。挪威和葡萄牙结合解释本国实践，主张应当综合历史、地理和经济因素，特别是渔业考量作为判断的依据。希腊也认为"历史性"背后的原因是多样化的，包括军事、经济和国防因素。[3]英国认为首先必须存在地理上的海湾，沿海国还必须证明通过惯例或时效的方式取得了水域的主权。此外，各国的默认也是重要的因素。[4]美国认为所谓"历史性"反映的不仅是历史问题，更是沿海国实施国家管辖的问题。[5]

第二委员会经历长时间讨论，对历史性海湾的法律基础，即定义，没有形成一致意见。在递交大会的报告中，特别报告员表示编纂工作

---

[1] Mitchell P. Strohl, *International Law of Bays*, Martinus Nijhoff, 1963, p. 314.
[2] Historic Bays: Memorandum by the Secretariat of the United Nations. A/CONF. 13/1, 1957, p. 16.
[3] Historic Bays: Memorandum by the Secretariat of the United Nations, A/CONF. 13/1, 1957, p. 20 - 21.
[4] L. J. Bouchez, *The Regime of Bays in International Law*, Sythoff, 1964, p. 205.
[5] 美国代表团从整体上否定讨论"历史性海湾"的必要，认为"历史性"和"海湾"都是不准确的表达。沿海国主权的基础并不只是历史，适用的对象也不限于海湾。Mitchell P. Strohl, *International Law of Bays*, Martinus Nijhoff, 1963, p. 314 - 315.

不影响沿海国已取得的海洋权利，同时承认确定或定义这些权利是解释报告内容的必要前提。[1]

二、第一次联合国海洋法会议前后的历史性所有权

（一）海洋法的发展趋势

尽管海牙国际法编纂会议未能取得实质成果，但这并不阻碍建设国际法治的进一步努力。在战争迷雾消散后的 1947 年，联合国国际法委员会成立。1949 年，国际法委员会第一次会议决定首先开始制定公海制度，1950 年联合国大会建议将领海制度纳入考虑范围，1951 年这一议题正式进入国际法委员会的日程。[2] 与海牙国际法编纂会议相比，国际法委员会不但被赋予编纂的职能，更要承担起逐步发展国际法的任务。[3] 在一系列标志和推动着战后海洋法发展新趋势的实践中，"杜鲁门宣言"和"英挪渔业案"对历史性所有权的影响最为突出。如果说前者为历史性所有权的发展提供了政治背景，那么后者就是为历史性所有权的内涵和适用添加了最直白的注脚。

"杜鲁门宣言"的影响并不在于宣言的内容本身。领海范围外的大陆架长期适用公海自由原则，作为沿海国第一次对领海以外区域提出实质性主张，这一宣言引发一连串反应，许多国家开始单方面向公海扩展管辖权。[4] 更重要的是，由于国际社会的默认，大陆架原则被视为"即时的习惯国际法"[5]（Instant Customary International Law）。这意味着，在海洋科技发展和沿海国经济需要的不断推动下，沿海国权利在与海洋自由原则博弈中的扩张趋势得到了国际法的认可。这一趋势不但为沿海国新主张提供合法性基础，也为既存海洋法规则

---

[1] Mitchell P. Strohl, *International Law of Bays*, Martinus Nijhoff, 1963, p. 316.
[2] Donald R. Rothwell, Tim Stephens, *The International Law of the Sea*, Harting Publishing, 2010, p. 5 – 6.
[3] D. P. O'Connell, edited by I. A. Shearer, *The International Law of the Sea*, Clarendon Press, 1982, p. 22.
[4] M. J. Jewett, *The Evolution of the Regime of Continental Shelf*, The Canadian Yearbook of International Law, Vol. 22: 153, p. 159 – 164 (1984).
[5] H. Lauterpacht, *Sovereignty over Submarine Area*, British Yearbook of International Law, Vol. 27: 377, p. 431 (1950).

的解释和适用创造了新的空间,"英挪渔业案"也是在这一背景下发生的。[1]

(二) 英挪渔业案

英国与挪威同是北海沿海国,挪威沿岸遍布浅滩和岩礁,地形复杂,渔业资源丰富,自19世纪末期开始,两国之间存在长达40多年的渔业争议。1935年,挪威王室颁布的新捕鱼法令生效,双方冲突进一步加剧,这一法令规定以直线连接基点的方式构成挪威专属渔区的基线。英国认为这与一般国际法上的基线确定方式相冲突,请求国际法院明确适用确定基线的国际法原则。[2]双方在主张中分别提出对历史性所有权的不同理解,法院的回应和双方主张一起,在三个方面促进了历史性所有权理论的发展。

首先,法院给出了历史性水域的明确定义,肯定了历史性所有权是历史性水域的法律基础,排除了沿海国单纯依靠地理原因、国防需要和经济利益取得历史性水域的可能。[3]在具体论述历史性所有权内容时,法院认为经济因素是挪威直线基线的有效性的部分基础,但是经济因素的存在需要长期惯例(long usage)来证明,而长期惯例的存在可以继续分解为对三个问题的肯定回答:挪威的主张内容是否明确;实践是否一贯;这一实践是否拘束英国。[4]也就是说历史性所有权的内涵包括沿海国的主张和实践以及相关国家态度三个方面。

其次,历史性所有权的适用范围扩展到海湾以外。挪威沿岸的地形不止海湾,还包括河口、沿岸群岛以及这些地形之间供渔民通行的航道。英国坚持只有在上述地形符合海湾的定义时,它们所包围的水域才能根据历史性所有权被视为挪威内水。[5]法院认为这些地形都构

---

[1] Fisheries Case (The United Kingdom v. Norway), International Court of Justice Reports, 1951.

[2] Fisheries Case (The United Kingdom v. Norway). International Court of Justice Reports, 1951, p. 124 – 127.

[3] Fisheries Case (The United Kingdom v. Norway). International Court of Justice Reports, 1951, p. 130.

[4] Jens Evensen, *The Anglo-Norwegian Fisheries Case and Its Legal Consequence*, American Journal of International Law, Vol. 45: 609, p. 623 – 625 (1951).

[5] Fisheries Case (The United Kingdom v. Norway). International Court of Justice Reports, 1951, p. 131.

成挪威沿岸整体的一部分，因此这些地形周围和之间的水域，只要位于挪威直线基线内，都应当视为内水。[1]

最后，对历史性所有权与一般国际法之间的关系出现新的理解。英国承认挪威的历史性所有权，但仅限于4海里领海宽度及封口线宽度10海里的海湾，这延续了长久以来对历史性所有权适用范围的理解。[2]而在挪威看来，历史性所有权的概念和一般国际法并不冲突，历史与其他相关因素一起，证明挪威适用一般国际法的方法是合理的。[3]由于与解决争议本身没有直接关系，法院在这里没有讨论历史性所有权是否具有例外的属性。但是法院确认适用于本案的习惯法规则是基线不能偏离海岸的一般走向，而由于特殊的地理构造和沿岸居民长期利用水域形成了依存关系，挪威有权采用直线基线作为一般国际法的特别适用。[4]从这个角度看，法院在某种程度上接受了挪威的意见。

（三）第一次联合国海洋法会议上的历史性所有权

1956年，国际法委员会第八次会议通过了海洋法公约草案，其中关于直线基线的规定全盘接受"英挪渔业案"的法理，间接将历史性所有权引入正在编纂中的海洋法公约。[5] 当然，草案中与这一权利关系最为密切的仍然是历史性海湾制度。草案第7条第4款规定关于海湾制度的前三款不适用于"历史性"海湾。[6]1957年，为了向即将在日内瓦召开的联合国海洋法大会提供有关"历史性"海湾的资料，联合国秘书处准备了题为"历史性海湾"的备忘录。[7]备忘录继承了国

---

[1] Fisheries Case (The United Kingdom v. Norway). International Court of Justice Reports, 1951, p. 132.
[2] Fisheries Case (The United Kingdom v. Norway). International Court of Justice Reports, 1951, p. 123.
[3] Fisheries Case (The United Kingdom v. Norway). International Court of Justice Reports, 1951, p. 133.
[4] Fisheries Case (The United Kingdom v. Norway). International Court of Justice Reports, 1951, p. 129–131.
[5] Articles concerning the Law of the Sea, Reports to General Assembly, International Law Commission Yearbook, 1956 (2), p. 287.
[6] Articles concerning the Law of the Sea, Reports to General Assembly, International Law Commission Yearbook, 1956 (2), p. 257.
[7] Historic Bays: Memorandum by the Secretariat of the United Nations, A/CONF.13/1, 1957, p. 1–2.

际法院在"英挪渔业案"中的观点,肯定国际法上存在依据历史性所有权主张除海湾以外历史性水域的趋势。[1]此外,备忘录全面整理了学说和实践中对历史性所有权要件的解读,包括国家使用(National Usage)、重大利益(Vital Interest)、多种因素考虑(Various Elements Considerations),以及取得历史性所有权所需的举证责任、证明要件以及时间因素和持续性因素。[2]由于目的所限,备忘录没有对历史性所有权的定义和内涵给出自己的观点。

在1958年的日内瓦联合国海洋法会议上,历史性海湾并没有引起充分的讨论。[3]对于设立一个专门委员会讨论历史性海湾的动议,特别报告员的回复认为在"英挪渔业案"对历史性水域定义基础上进一步说明取得历史性所有权的条件会引发关于时效取得的整体问题,备忘录所做的准备工作尽管优秀,仍不足以为全面研究这一问题提供答案。因此,会议只使用"历史性海湾"这个称谓,而它的内涵将在具体的争议中留给法院结合每个案件的特征加以考虑。[4]尽管如此,在随后的会议进程中,日本代表团在修正案中仍然坚持定义"历史性海湾"应该成为编纂工作的组成部分。日本在参考有效性、长期性和默认三个要件基础上提出历史性所有权的定义,但由于其他与会国家认为这三个要件都充满争议,日本的建议未能获得支持。为了明确与历史性水域相关的法律问题,巴拿马和印度提出联合草案决议,建议将这一问题提交联合国大会,请求联大做出适当安排研究历史性水域法律制度,并将结论交予所有会员国。[5]

在第一次海洋法会议通过的4个公约和1个任择议定书中,与历史性所有权相关的条款共有3项[6],包括:

---

[1] Historic Bays: Memorandum by the Secretariat of the United Nations, A/CONF.13/1, 1957, p.1-2.
[2] Historic Bays: Memorandum by the Secretariat of the United Nations, A/CONF.13/1, 1957, p.28-37.
[3] 参加日内瓦会议的各国代表团对草案中有关历史性海湾规定的意见并不一致。Strohl认为会议可能采取一些预备措施将这一议题排除在辩论之外。Mitchell P. Strohl, International Law of Bays, Martinus Nijhoff, 1963, p.318.
[4] Mitchell P. Strohl, International Law of Bays, Martinus Nijhoff, 1963, p.322.
[5] L. J. Bouchez, The Regime of Bays in International Law, Sythoff, 1964, p.206.
[6] Geneva Convention on Territorial Sea and Contiguous Zone, United Nations Treaty Series, 1958, Vol.516.

(1)《领海与毗连区公约》第4条第4款规定,在海岸线地形适用直线基线法的情况下确定特定基线时,应特别注意关系区域内经由长期惯例证明之特殊经济利益;

(2)《领海与毗连区公约》第7条第6款规定,"历史性"海湾不适用普通海湾规定;

(3)《领海与毗连区公约》第12条第1款规定,海岸相邻或相向国家间领海划界,如存在历史性所有权可排除适用中间线法。

此外,会议还决议通过了巴拿马和印度的提案,请求联合国大会安排对包括历史性海湾在内的历史性水域法律制度展开研究。[1]

(四)"包括历史性海湾在内的历史性水域制度"研究

1959年,联大通过1453(XIV)号决议,请求国际法委员会研究包括历史性海湾在内的历史性水域法律制度。[2]这次研究的目的是讨论适用于调整"历史性水域"制度的国际法原则以及由此产生的如何确定这些原则的问题。[3] 1962年,国际法委员会公布了研究报告,其中依次陈述了"历史性水域"的概念;构成"历史性水域"权利来源的要件;证明存在"历史性水域"的举证责任分配、"历史性水域"的法律地位以及争端解决机制的研究结果。与秘书处备忘录的根本不同在于,报告在讨论上述问题的基础上提出了结论。

报告首先认为对待"历史性水域"的现实态度应当是独立考虑它权源的实质内容而不是考虑这一制度是否构成一般国际法的例外。确定"历史性水域"的权源需要满足三个要素:(1)国家在主张"历史性水域"区域实施基于主权的管理;(2)管理需持续足够长时间以至于发展为惯例;(3)其他国家对该国实践的态度需达到普遍容忍。证明国家实践满足上述三个因素从而取得"历史性水域"的责任由主张拥有这一权利的国家承担。至于"历史性水域"在法律地位上被视为内水还

---

[1] Study of the Juridical Regime of Historic waters, including Historic Bays, United Nations General Assembly Resolution 1143 (XIV), A/CONF. 13L. 56, 1958.

[2] Study of the Juridical Regime of Historic waters, including Historic Bays. United Nations General Assembly Resolution 1453 (XIV), A/PV. 847, 1959.

[3] Juridical Regime of Historic Waters, Including Historic Bays, International Law Commission Yearbook, 1962 (2), p. 5.

是领海，则根据该国在主张的水域内实施的主权行为来确定。[1]基于上述结论，尽管国际法委员会谨慎地表示报告并未穷尽对这一命题的研究而仅是提供进一步讨论和修改的基础[2]，报告事实上勾勒出了历史性所有权的理论内涵并为这一理论在实践中的应用提供了指引。

三、第三次联合国海洋法会议与当代历史性所有权的发展

（一）第二次联合国海洋法会议和海洋法实践的新发展

为解决第一次海洋法会议遗留的问题，联合国于1960年在日内瓦召开第二次海洋法会议，这次会议的议题仅有两项：确定领海宽度和沿海国在领海范围外的渔业区域，主要关注领海扩展带来的安全、航运以及沿海国和渔业国在领海内外的互惠权利。[3]与会国对领海宽度持有6海里和12海里两种意见，作为对两方观点的协调，美国和加拿大联合提出联合方案，内容包括：一是沿海国共享有6海里领海加6海里专属渔业区；二是在专属渔业区内，对享有历史性渔业权的渔业国在特定年限内有权继续作业。[4]上述提案都没能取得通过所需的三分之二的多数同意，会议没有达成任何成果。[5]坦率地说，随后的国家实践表明，第二次海洋法会议的成功与否都不可能阻挡沿海国扩展海洋权利和管辖的步伐。

1960年代后期至1970年代，不但12海里领海宽度被多数国家实践接受[6]，超过20个国家主张12海里以外宽度不等的渔业专属管辖

---

[1] Juridical Regime of Historic Waters, Including Historic Bays, International Law Commission Yearbook, 1962 (2), p. 25.

[2] Juridical Regime of Historic Waters, Including Historic Bays, International Law Commission Yearbook, 1962 (2), p. 25.

[3] Arthur H. Dean, *The Second Geneva Conference on the Law of the Sea*, American Journal of International Law, Vol. 54: 751, p. 752 (1960).

[4] D. W. Bowett, *The Second United Nations Conference on the Law of the Sea*, International and Comparative Law Quarterly, Vol. 9: 415, p. 422 - 427 (1960).

[5] Arthur H. Dean, *The Second Geneva Conference on the Law of the Sea*, American Journal of International Law, Vol. 54: 751, p. 767 - 770 (1960).

[6] 至1969年已有64个国家提出12海里及以上的领海宽度，1972年，仅有27个国家继续坚持3海里领海宽度。R. Y. Jennings, *Changing International Law of the Sea*, Cambridge Law Journal, Vol. 31 (1): 32, p. 33 (1972).

区（EFZ）、承袭海（Patrimonial Sea）和专属经济区（EEZ），更重要的是，各国不止通过单方面行为扩展权利，而且经由双边和地区协议的确认使扩展权利有成为习惯国际法的趋势，传统海洋法下领海/公海双重体制面临严峻的挑战。[1]尤其在国际社会结构因为大量新独立国家的出现而发生根本性改变的情况下，这些新国家对主权的关心使得逆转沿海国权利扩展注定是徒劳无功的。与其墨守公海绝对自由的成规，不如承认这一事实并将其纳入国际法的规则之中。[2]由此，沿海国不断向公海扩展的权利和管辖的趋势，与其他因素一起，共同推动第三次联合国海洋法会议的召开和《联合国海洋法公约》（以下简称《海洋法公约》）的制定。[3]

(二)《海洋法公约》框架内的历史性所有权

1968年，联大通过第2467（XXIII）A号决议设立"和平利用国家管辖范围以外的海床洋底委员会"，委员会的职责之一是确定第三次联合国海洋法会议需要讨论的议题列表。在1972年由委员会批准的列表中，"历史性水域"被包含在"领海"部分议题之内列入海洋法会议的日程，交由会议第二委员会讨论。[4]第二委员会于1974年通过题为"第二委员会工作文件：主导方向"的报告，其中与历史性所有权直接相关的条款包括：有关"历史性水域"定义的第2条和第3条；采用直线基线划界法时使用低潮高地作为基点的第7条B款，采用直线基线法时可以考虑区域内经由长期惯例证明之特殊经济利益的第8条，有关"历史性"海湾和其他历史性水域的第17条，历史性所有权

---

[1] Carolyn Hudson, *Fishery and Economic Zones as Customary International Law*, San Diego Law Review, Vol. 17：661，p. 663（1979-1980）.
[2] R. Y. Jennings, *Changing International Law of the Sea*, Cambridge Law Journal, Vol. 31（1）：32，p. 33（1972）.
[3] Reservation Exclusively for Peaceful Purposes of the Sea-Bed and the Ocean Floor, and the Subsoil Thereof, Underlying the High Seas Beyond the Limits of Present National Jurisdiction and Use of their Resources in the Interests of Mankind, and Convening of A Conference on the Law of the Sea, United Nations General Assembly Resolution 2750（XXV），A/PV. 1933，1970.
[4] Shabtai Rosenne, *Historic Waters in the Third United Nations Conference on the Law of the Sea*, in Leo J. Bouchez, Terry D. Gill, Wybo P. Heere, *Reflection on Priciples and Practice of International Law：Essays in Honour of Leo J. Bouchez*, Martinus Nijhoff Publishers, 2000，p. 501-502.

排除领海划界中间线规则的第 21 条，领海最大宽度限制不适用于历史性海湾的第 22 条 A 款等。[1]经过非正式协商后，历史性水域问题没有被列为第二委员会正式讨论的议题，上述条款仅有少数在最后的条约文本中得到保留。[2]

与第一次海洋法会议不同，联大在召开第三次海洋法会议的决议中就赋予会议以"一揽子方式"编纂和发展海洋法的职能。最后通过的《海洋法公约》共有 17 部分、446 条和 9 个附件，其中既包含有关海洋制度的实体规则，也包括解决海洋纠纷的程序性规则。[3]在实体规则中，有关直线基线的第 7 条第 5 款，历史性海湾的第 10 条第 6 款以及海岸相向和相邻国家领海划界的第 15 条与《领海和毗连区公约》中关于历史性所有权的规定一致。

《海洋法公约》第 46 条（b）项对"群岛"的定义包括历史上被视为同一实体的一群岛屿、水域或其他自然地形。条文本身和缔约谈判记录都没有明示定义中的"历史"就是指历史性所有权，但是考虑到菲律宾和印度尼西亚等积极支持群岛国制度的国家从第一次联合国海洋法会议开始就以历史性水域为法律根据，主张各自国家群岛水域的直线基线，可以认为历史性所有权构成了群岛国制度的一部分法律基础。

从整体上看，尽管《海洋法公约》增减了与历史性所有权相关的实体和程序条款，新海洋法体系下的历史性所有权依然被认为是对第

---

[1] Statement of Activities of the Conference during Its First and Second Sessions Prepared by the Rapporteur-General: Mr. Kenneth O. Rattray, Annexes II, Appendix I. A/CONF. 62/L. 8/REV. 1, 1958, p. 106–111.

[2] Shabtai Rosenne, *Historic Waters in the Third United Nations Conference on the Law of the Sea*, in Leo J. Bouchez, Terry D. Gill, Wybo P. Heere, *Reflection on Priciples and Practice of International Law: Essays in Honour of Leo J. Bouchez*, Martinus Nijhoff Publishers, 2000, p. 504.

[3]《海洋法公约》的程序规则同样涉及历史性所有权，第 298 条第 1 款（a）项（1）目规定涉及历史性海湾或所有权的争端，缔约国可以声明不接受公约第 15 部分第 2 节规定的强制程序。由于该条涉及与历史性权利有关的程序规则，与本文无密切联系，故不作讨论。

一次海洋法会议成果的确认和延续。[1]但如果就此得出新的海洋法体系对历史性所有权毫无影响或者说历史性所有权的发展陷入停滞的结论,显然不符合国际法与国家实践发展的真实情况。一方面,海洋法原有规则的改变和新制度的创设会改变先前各国基于历史性所有权主张的必要性和有效性;另一方面,根据《海洋法公约》实施的国家实践和国际司法实践表明,历史性所有权的适用范围并不仅限于公约中有明示规定的条款。

(三) 当代国家和国际法实践的现状

长期以来,对历史性所有权的讨论围绕着国家有权实施排他性主权的历史性水域展开,其中最重要的是历史性海湾,另外也涉及历史性海峡和历史性群岛水域。通过采纳"用于国际航行的海峡"制度、"群岛国"制度和直线基线法,沿海国对"历史性海峡"和"历史性群岛水域"的主张已经融入国际海洋法的一般法律规范中,不再依赖一般国际法的调整。就历史性海湾而言,《海洋法公约》对一般海湾封口线的规定沿袭了《领海和毗连区公约》24 海里的规定,这意味着许多历史性海湾可以成为《海洋法公约》认可的一般海湾。[2]再加上由于大陆架制度的完善和专属经济区的建立,过去需要依靠历史性所有权主张的经济权利和管辖权转而由《海洋法公约》直接赋予缔约国,在某种程度上削弱了沿海国主张历史性水域的必要性。因此,海洋法的上述发展似乎在理论和实践上都削弱了历史性水域的重要性,甚至将历史性水域理论导向过时和多余。[3]

实践表明这种担忧可能并不切实。截至 2000 年,有 19 个国家提出或维持原有的历史性水域主张,另有一部分国家虽然没有明确提出

---

[1] M. W. Clark Jr. , *Historical Bays and Waters*, *A Regime of Recent Beginning and Continued Usage*, Oceana Publication, 1994, p. 44. Also see Shabtai Rosenne, *Historic Waters in the Third United Nations Conference on the Law of the Sea*. in Leo J. Bouchez, Terry D. Gill, Wybo P. Heere, *Reflection on Priciples and Practice of International Law*: *Essays in Honour of Leo J. Bouchez*, Martinus Nijhoff Publishers, 2000, p. 502.

[2] 1957 年《备忘录》列举有关历史性海湾的国家实践中,只有加拿大、挪威、澳大利亚和突尼斯主张的历史性海湾入口宽度超过 24 海里。

[3] Clive R. Symmons, *Historic Waters in the Law of the Sea*, *A Modern Re-Appraisal*, Martinus Nijhoff, 2008, p. 292.

历史性主张,但以直线基线方式确立超过24海里的海湾封口线。[1]其中,多米尼加和危地马拉等国主张的历史性海湾已经符合《海洋法公约》对一般海湾的地理要求,但这些国家并未因此撤回对历史性海湾的诉求。这一观点得到国际司法实践的认可,国际法院在"陆地、岛屿和海洋边界案"中指出,丰塞卡海湾的地理条件满足"法律"上海湾的要求并不取代它的历史地位。[2]事实上,国家实践表明历史性水域理论没有被抛弃。

第一,沿海国向大体量水体提出历史性水域主张。加拿大除了坚持哈德逊湾(Hudson Bay)为历史性海湾外,还在第三次海洋法会议上主张北极群岛水域属于加拿大,随后于1985年确立北极群岛基线并宣布基线内为该国历史性内水。[3]利比亚于1973年主张入口宽度超过140海里的锡德拉湾(Gulf of Sidra)为历史性海湾,由此引发的争议成为第一次"锡德拉湾事件"的导火索。[4]

第二,沿海国以双边条约形式确认多沿海国历史性海湾。对历史性水域的习惯法编纂仅限于单一沿海国的水体,《海洋法公约》第10条第6款对历史性海湾的规定也被设置在该条第1款"海岸属于一国的海湾"框架内。1982年,柬埔寨和越南签订历史性水域协议,宣布临近两国陆地边界的水域为两国的"共同历史性水域"(Joint Historic Water),由两国共同行使内水管辖权。[5]此前,印度和斯里兰卡已经通过缔结条约,完成了对两国之间历史性水域的划界。[6]

如果说大体量的历史性水域主张仅是违反历史性水域制度的这一初衷,并未超出历史性水域不考虑海域地理情形的习惯法规则,那么

---

[1] 数据来源:Untied States Department of State Bureau of Ocean and International Environmental and Scientific Affairs, Limits in the Sea No. 36, National Claims to the Maritime Jurisdiction, 8th Revision, 2000。

[2] Land, Island and Maritime Frontier Dispute (El Salvador v. Honduras Nicaragua Intervening), International Court of Justice Reports, 1992, p. 593.

[3] Donat Pharand, *The Arctic Waters and the Northwest Passage: A Final Revisit*, Ocean Development and International Law, Vol. 38: 3, p. 4 - 5 (2007).

[4] Yehuda Z. Blum, *The Gulf of Sidra Incident*, American Journal of International Law, Vol. 80: 668, p. 668 (1986).

[5] Jonathan I. Charney, Lewis M. Alexander, *International Maritime Boundaries*, Martinus Nijhoff, 2004, p. 2357.

[6] Jonathan I. Charney, Lewis M. Alexander, *International Maritime Boundaries*, Martinus Nijhoff, 2004, p. 1409.

多国沿岸历史性水域的实践应该对条约和习惯法发展产生影响。当然，上述实践能否得到国际法的肯定，还要经过历史性所有权的有效实践、延续性和其他国家态度等标准的测试。

可见，早期的典型案例和有关历史性海湾的法规编纂过程表明国际法对究竟是哪些因素使得沿海国有权利将主权延伸到超过领海范围以外的水域有着不同理解。实践中既存在认为水域的自然地理构造表明取得水域适合的说辞，也有强调水域由于其地理或者经济条件对沿海国具有特别重大意义的声音。但是，基本上所有的国家实践和司法实践都提及沿海国实际上已经长期占有他们提出主张的水域，并且这一占有方式得到了国际社会的明示或默示认可，这一共识也为历史性所有权的下一步发展打下了基础。

"英挪渔业案"和随后的第一次联合国海洋法大会及其成果奠定了历史性所有权在海洋法上的稳固地位。这一阶段的历史性所有权不但经由编纂习惯法在海洋法规则体系中占据一席之地，更通过典型的国际司法实践和国际法委员会的权威研究明确了权利的构成要件。而在实践中，历史性所有权作为权利扩展的法律基础，成为沿海国向公海扩展管辖权的有力法律工具，得到广泛的主张和应用。

《海洋法公约》再次确认了历史性所有权在海洋法中的位置，但是随着大陆架和专属经济区制度被纳入海洋法的规则体系，沿海国似乎理论上没有必要再将扩展管辖的权利主张建立在历史性所有权的基础上。即便如此，历史性所有权由于能够产生排他主权，那么对周边水域有特定需求的国家，特别是对关心本国主权独立和安全的新独立国家来说，仍有吸引力。

第三节 与领土取得相关的历史性所有权

即便科技已经可以实现从远海获得生存所需的物质和贸易沟通所需的通道，陆地依然是人类最重要的活动场所。因此，无论对国内法还是国际法，领土问题在现代国际关系中都处于核心地位，在很长一段时间内，国际法的任务和目的就是在领土基础上划分主权行使的边界。[1] 相

---

[1] R. Y. Jennings, *The Acquisition of Territory in International Law*, Manchester University Press, 1963, p. 1-2.

比当代海洋法经历两次编纂并拥有包括《海洋法公约》在内的一系列条约体系,有关陆地领土的国际法规则一直交由一般国际法调整,规则的归纳主要来自对国际司法实践的观察和公法家学说的整理。在国际司法实践中,国家使用"历史性所有权"时往往赋予其不同的内涵,使得对历史性所有权的解读不可避免表现出碎片化的倾向。就本节的目的而言,这种碎片化表现为理论上存在着两种与领土取得相关的历史性权利。[1]

一、历史上的长期占有

正如前文所述,以国家合意或持续展示主权为基础的领土取得习惯法规则成形于19世纪至20世纪之交的欧洲,在此之前,形形色色的领土取得和移转实践早已存在于世界各个时代的文明中。几乎所有现存国家的版图都经历过大大小小或缩减或扩张的变动,当代每一块的争议土地在历史上都可能先后出现过相互取代的两个甚至更多的占有者,为当代的领土争端留下了可称之为"历史"的遗迹。

尽管一般国际法已经确立了领土取得的规则,仍然不能阻止争议的双方尽可能寻找有利于本国主张的"历史"证据,自然包括与争议土地相关的全部历史事实,主张这些事实构成该国对争议领土的历史性所有权。[2] 因此,如何认定历史上存在国家确实占有过特定土地,这种占有对根据现代国际法规则确定的领土归属产生怎样的影响,是领土取得规则不能回避的问题。

国际司法实践中的历史性权利根据案情表现为不同的具体形式,可以肯定的是,被适当证据证明已经众所周知的历史事实可以影响当代的领土争端。[3] 需要进一步回答的是,这类在领土取得规则被普遍

---

[1] Ian Brownlie, *Principles of Public International Law*, 7th editon, Oxford University Press, 2008, p.142, 156-158.

[2] 在具体案件中对历史性权利的称呼并不相同,在"敏基埃岛和艾科俄斯案"中,英国和法国分别称自己的权利为古老权利(Ancient Title)和原始权利(Original Title),在"西撒哈拉法律地位咨询案"中,摩洛哥称其为长期占有(Immemorial Possession),在"印度和巴勒斯坦之间西部边界案"(以下简称"卡其沼泽案")和"也门—厄立特里亚仲裁案"中,巴基斯坦和也门的主张被仲裁庭称为历史性所有权。

[3] Ian Brownlie, *Principles of Public International Law*, 7th editon, Oxford University Press, 2008, p.148.

接受之前发生的历史事实,在何种情况下具备领土权源的地位,又以何种方式影响现代国际法体系下对领土主权的确定。

二、所有权的历史性巩固

(一)传统领土取得方式的不足

另一种形式的历史性所有权源于对传统领土取得方式中存在问题的回应。起源于罗马私法的五种领土取得方式,尽管已经在新的语境下完成了从国内法概念向国际法概念的转变,成为"自治"的概念体系,但仍然没有摆脱每个案件的事实可以排他性地列入其中的一类这个假设前提。[1]伴随着20世纪50年代后越来越多的领土争端提交国际司法,这种严格分类方式的缺点日益明显,而在以国家有效行为为基础建立领土权源的两种模式,即"先占"和"时效"上,问题表现得尤为突出。

首先是"时效"这一术语涵盖的内容不清。国内法意义上的时效是指他人通过一段合理时间的和平持有,从而推断原物所有人放弃该物,继而取得物权的方式。然而,即便承认国际法上存在以时效取得领土的可能[2],时效在两个法域中的含义是否相同依然存疑。约翰逊采用普通法中的逆权占有概念描述取得原属他国领土的时效取得方式,同时将长期占有的方式(Immemorial Possession)以获得原先权利不明的土地也纳入时效范畴[3],因此他提出将"取得时效"(Acquisitive Prescription)作为统一两类时效的新概念。

取得时效对原来时效概念的扩展模糊了其与先占之间的界限。国内法中时效和先占之间泾渭分明,除了取得对象不同之外,占有只要通过一个带有占有意识的行动即可结束对象的无主状态,而时效的基

---

[1] D. P. O'Connell, *International Law and Boundary Disputes*, Proceedings of the American Society of International Law at Its Annual Meeting (1921 – 1969), Vol. 54: 77, p. 78 (1960).

[2] 国际法上是否存在时效取得领土是自格劳秀斯起就开始争论的问题,国际司法实践中多回避直接使用时效一词来判断领土归属。

[3] D. H. N. Johnson, *Acquisitive Prescription in International Law*, British Yearbook of International Law, Vol. 27: 332, p. 353 – 354 (1950).

础则在于持续一段时间控制的事实。[1]而在国际法上，无论先占还是时效，基础都是"和平持续展示主权"，这种情况下将时效的对象扩展到原权利不明的土地，无疑时效的产生如奥康纳所说"一方面，长期占有无主地；另一方面，长期占有真正主权者的土地"的效果，在模糊自身的同时，侵夺了先占的适用范围。[2]

对先占和时效理论最严重的挑战还是来自实践。国际司法机构在做出与领土相关的判决时，既慎于对时效表达自己的看法[3]，也不愿意将判决结果的法律基础置于时效还是先占的分类方式中。总之，理论没有得到实践的遵从或回应。施瓦曾博格将原因归结为影响领土取得的国际法规则的改变，应当从国际法的基本原则中抽象出相互影响的法律规则体系。[4]奥康纳则认为关于领土取得的法律本身没有问题，问题出在移植自罗马私法的术语体系。[5]很难说是因为国际司法实践让理论变得模糊，还是理论的模糊使得国际司法机构在实践中不得不采取谨慎的态度。现实就是，国际法迫切需要归纳实践中存在的规则以补充或更替原有的领土取得方式，而"英挪渔业案"判决为解决上述困境提供了一种新思路。

（二）巩固理论的提出

在"英挪渔业案"中，挪威沿岸渔民对峡湾内渔业资源的依赖所形成的经济关系是挪威直线基线划界法不违反国际法的理由之一。存在这种经济关系的证据是挪威颁布的划界法令和根据法令实施的实践，没有引起其他国家的反对。法院认为由于规定直线基线划界法的法令本身构

---

[1] D. P. O'Connell, *International Law and Boundary Disputes*, Proceedings of the American Society of International Law at Its Annual Meeting (1921 – 1969), Vol. 54：77, p. 78 (1960).

[2] D. P. O'Connell, *International Law and Boundary Disputes*, Proceedings of the American Society of International Law at Its Annual Meeting (1921 – 1969), Vol. 54：77, p. 79 (1960).

[3] Surya P. Sharma, *Territorial Acquisition*, *Dispute and International Law*, Martinus Nijhoff Publishers, 1997, p. 167 – 168.

[4] Georg Schwarzenberger, *Title to Territory*, *Response to a Challenge*. American Journal of International Law, Vol. 51 (2)：308, p. 308 (1957).

[5] D. P. O'Connell, *International Law and Boundary Disputes*, Proceedings of the American Society of International Law at Its Annual Meeting (1921 – 1969), Vol. 54：77, p. 78 (1960).

成完善而统一的体系，并且对体系的适用证明其他国家普遍容许的存在，而以普遍容许为基础的历史性巩固（Historical Consolidation）使划界体系对所有国家产生效力。[1]

德·维舍将这种权利巩固的理念引申为一种领土取得模式——"历史性所有权的巩固"（La Consolidation par Titres Historiques），并赋予其超出传统领土取得方式的内容。作为"英挪渔业案"的法官之一，德·维舍认为领土在国家地位中具有的客观性和绝对性，以及国际关系对稳定和安全的重视，使得多数学者关注的是领土作为国家行使权力和职能的空间。这是对领土性质抽象且脱离现实的认识，既没有反映领土形成的历史过程，也无法在领土占有、划分和完整性的概念中展示出有关民族纽带和国家整体的人类精神。只有给人类和民族保留重要地位的领土概念才能反映国际关系中有关领土的真实情况。[2] 对多重联系和过程的强调反映在"历史性所有权的巩固"的定义中，即"经证实的长期利用……代表着包含关系和利益的集合，这一集合自身能产生将某一片陆地或者海洋归属某一国家的效力"[3]。

（三）围绕巩固理论的争议

在德·维舍看来，是否存在历史性所有权的巩固应当由法官考虑每个案件所不同的利益和关系来决定，而不是根据国际法上并无定论的"一段特定时间"。从这一点出发，一方面，历史性所有权的巩固获得了它相对于取得时效的独立性。[4] 而相对于国际承认，历史性所有权的巩固不需要严格意义上的默认，只需相关国家长时间没有抗议

---

[1] Fisheries Case (The United Kingdom v. Norway), International Court of Justice Reports, 1951, p.130. 法院的这段判决并不是简单套用了历史性水域理论中持续有效管理和其他国家默认的要件分解，而是在承认历史性所有权的基础上再对这一权利作出是否巩固的评价。这可能也是布朗利建议仔细阅读该段判决的原因。

[2] Charles de Visscher, *Théories et Réalités en Droit International Public*, 4th edition. Editions A. Pedone, 1970, p.222.

[3] Charles de Visscher, *Théories et Réalités en Droit International Public*, 4th edition. Editions A. Pedone, 1970, p.226.

[4] 由于德·维舍将时效取得的对象限制为原属其他国家的领土，因此指出历史性所有权的巩固与时效的区别还在于适用于所有权不明的土地。Charles de Visscher, *Théories et Réalités en Droit International Public*, 4th edition. Editions A. Pedone, 1970, p.226.

足矣。[1] 一方面,詹宁斯赞同"巩固"概念的提出打开了新的领土取得通道,"广为人知"这一因素不再仅仅是时效存在的证据,它本身就是权利创造过程中的决定性因素。另一方面,詹宁斯出于对未来实践的担忧,明确了巩固的过程所发生的前提是实际的占有。[2] 尽管对巩固的理解有差异,两人都认为这类历史性所有权可以成为新的领土取得方式。[3]

约翰逊从"历史性所有权的巩固"中看到了消除时效术语内涵不清的可能,既然时效内涵不清是由"时效"术语无法容纳长时间占有和逆权占用造成的,而历史性所有权的巩固由于强调维持现有国际关系的稳定,并不将领土原始的所有情况作为考虑内容,用巩固取代时效就回避了对取得对象的限制,简化了问题。[4] 布鲁姆从国际法上是否存在时效入手,然后从构成要件的相似性转而讨论历史性所有权,在不改变实质的情况下以历史性所有权取代时效从而回避争议的意味也是明显的。可见,两人都重视历史性所有权在术语改革上的意义。[5]

施瓦曾博格认为理解"英挪渔业案"中的"历史性巩固"不能和其他国际法领土取得方式一样,代入一个国内法的语境中。在该案的语境中,它指的是权源的完善,一开始的权源是有缺陷的,在实践的过程中和认同国家的发展中不断完善,最终甚至成为普遍的权利。[6] 从历史的角度看,领土权源的巩固表现出三个明显的特征:第一,权

---

[1] Charles de Visscher, *Théories et Réalités en Droit International Public*, 4th edition. Editions A. Pedone, 1970, p. 226 - 227.

[2] 詹宁斯对德·维舍定义的担忧表现为两点:"利益"关系被明确置于定义中,以及不同形式的承认被赋予重要的地位但是缺乏界定。实践中这两点可能模糊法律上的权利和政治主张的区别,使巩固这种领土取得方式可能蜕变为一般意义上的禁止反言效果。R. Y. Jennings, *The Acquisition of Territory in International Law*, Manchester University Press, 1963, p. 26 - 27.

[3] 德·维舍的定义更加开放而詹宁斯的解释保证了和国际法上传统领土取得方式的衔接。此外,德·维舍的定义似乎没有脱离"英挪渔业案"的语境,这可能也是德·维舍提出"历史性所有权的巩固"而詹宁斯修改为"所有权的历史性巩固"的原因。

[4] D. H. N. Johnson, *Acquisitive Prescription in International Law*, British Yearbook of International Law, Vol. 27: 332, p. 332 (1950).

[5] 两人都肯定了历史性所有权不仅是术语的改革,约翰逊认为引入历史性巩固在实践中统一了权利的创造和维持的概念,而布鲁姆提出默认是历史性所有权的法律基础已经接近于詹宁斯对时效和历史性所有权进行区别的观点。

[6] Georg Schwarzenberger, *Title to Territory, Response to a Challenge*, American Journal of International Law, Vol. 51 (2): 308, p. 310 (1957).

源的巩固通常是一个逐步的过程。第二，每一个权源从一开始都是相对的，而权源的持有者总是渴望把它转化成绝对的权利。第三，权源越巩固，越依赖于多重的基础。[1] 国际法的七个基本规则是主权、承认、同意、善意、自卫、国际责任和海洋自由，如果将国际司法机构的实践归入这七个类别中，领土权源首先是由和主权、承认、同意和善意相关的规则调整，在这些规则的相互作用下，相对的权源成为绝对的主权。主权越绝对，构成基础的相关因素越多。在特定案件中，这样一个逐渐演变的过程被法院描述为历史性权利的巩固。[2] 因此，与其将历史性所有权视为一种领土主权的来源，不如将它看作是指导判断主权归属的操作规则更符合实际。

可以确定的是，无论被称为历史性所有权的巩固还是所有权的历史性巩固，这一类型的权利在构成要件方面，和沿海国家取得公海所依赖的历史性所有权是一致的。至于国际司法实践是否回应了学者们对所有权的历史性巩固概念的构造，以及这类历史性所有权在领土取得中所扮演的角色，究竟是一种介于占领和时效的补充性的权源，还是对两者在术语上的统一，抑或是国际司法机构在判断主权归属时的操作性规则，需要对国际司法实践的进一步观察。

第四节 小　结

本章梳理了历史性所有权的背景、起源和发展现状，初步得出以下结论：

1. 现代国际法的历史性所有权概念起源于海洋法维持沿海国家既得权利的需要，是一项习惯法规则。

2. 历史性所有权由两部分法律内容组成，包括主张国实际的占有和国际社会对占有状态的认可。

3. 随着海洋法中扩展沿海国权利的趋势和原有领土取得方式不足的暴露，比利时法学家德·维舍提出了统一海洋和陆地取得的新方式，

---

[1] Georg Schwarzenberger, *Title to Territory*, *Response to a Challenge*, American Journal of International Law, Vol. 51 (2): 308, p. 311 (1957).

[2] Georg Schwarzenberger, *Title to Territory*, *Response to a Challenge*, American Journal of International Law, Vol. 51 (2): 308, p. 324 (1957).

所有权的历史性巩固。

4. 在国际法被用于解决非欧洲国家间的领土和边界过程中，历史性所有权在实践中被用来描述历史上曾经存在过的占有事实。

5. 因此，历史性所有权在实践中既用于取得水域，也可用于取得陆地领土；既可主张归属不明土地，也可作为取得原属他国领土的法律基础。

粗略回顾历史性所有权的发展历史，笔者发现尚待解决的问题远远多于已经获得解答的问题。尚待解决的问题包括：

1. 就历史性所有权要件的要件而言，怎样才能满足占有状态，相关国家的何种反应足以表明同意的态度？

2. 海洋法和领土取得的不同起点对历史性所有权的要件是否满足国际法要求，产生怎样的影响？

3. 两个要件在适用于不同的实践环境中时，相互间的关系是固定的还是变动的？

4. 历史上曾经发生过的占有，在现代的领土取得中扮演怎样的角色？

5. 所有权的历史性巩固理论的作用是统一现有的领土取得方式，还是补充现有方式的不足，抑或是单纯替代时效这一在国际法领土高度争议的概念？

回答上述疑问的最好办法是回到国际法的实践中去，首先我们要解析的是历史性所有权作为法律概念本身的含义，也就是历史性所有权的构成。

第三章 历史性所有权的构成

通过对历史性所有权演进的描述,这一概念本身包含的内容已经得到明确,即有效管理和相关国家的同意,问题是如何在实践中判定两项要件满足习惯国际法的要求,并进而得出主张国确实持有历史性所有权的结论。这需要考察要件成立的标准以及影响因素。本章将尝试从规则和证据两个角度入手,讨论历史性所有权的两大构成要件。

第一节 时际法、关键日期和证明责任

胡伯法官在"帕尔玛斯岛仲裁案"中指出领土主权包括展示国家活动的排他性权利,以及随之而来的保护领土内国民的义务。如果国家没有以当时环境所要求的方式展示主权,就无法完成它的义务。[1]在国家行为和国际法规则都在不断变化的环境下,评价国家行为的法律意义首先要明确的是国家在什么时候的行为,当时环境所要求的方式是什么,以及由谁提供行为的证据。因此,时际法(Intertemporal Law)、关键日期(Critical Date)和证明责任(Burden of Proof)是讨论历史性所有权构成的先决问题。

一、时际法

任何行为只能由行为发生时有效的法律规则评价,这一原则维系法律变革的发展性与社会成员行为期待的稳定性之间的平衡。"法不溯及既往"作为一般法律原则在国际法上的适用,一方面体现在条约解

---

[1] Island of Palmas Case (Netherlands v. The U.S.A.), United Nations Reports of International Arbitration Awards, 1928, Vol.2, p.839.

释的方法[1]，另一方面则表现为影响领土取得的实质性规则[2]，时际法是"法不溯及既往"原则在领土取得中的体现，也是与选择领土取得规则相关的习惯法。

(一) 领土取得中的时际法

在1908年的"格里斯巴达那仲裁案"中，时际法的原则首次被用于解决领土和边界争议。案中挪威和瑞典请求常设仲裁法院决定1661年条约及其附属地图是否全部或部分确立了双方海洋边界，并应以何种方式建立边界线，如果条约和地图没有确立边界，那么请求仲裁庭根据环境事实和法律原则确立双方边界。[3]仲裁庭认为1661年条约及其附属地图没有完全划定领海边界，但基于"陆地统治海洋"原则，双方领海界线其实在1658年丹麦通过的《罗斯基勒和约》将布胡斯地区割让给瑞典时已经自动做了划分，而为了确定这条由1658年和约自动形成的边界线，应当追寻条约缔结时，也就是1658年时的划界规则。[4]基于这一判断，仲裁庭拒绝采用"中间线"（Median Line）或"航道中心线"（Thalweg）规则而选择了被认为在当时已经失去法律效力的"海洋边界沿海岸一般走向"作为该案划界的法律原则。[5]

胡伯（Huber）法官在"帕尔玛斯岛仲裁案"中明确引用了时际法的概念。案件中美国主张本国对争议岛屿的主权来自西班牙的割让，而证据表明西班牙仅仅是在16世纪发现了该岛屿而没有实施事实或象征性的占有。[6]胡伯法官认为，从中世纪到19世纪末，有关发现以及取得无人区域权利的国际法规则经历了巨大的变化。争议双方也都同

---

[1] Aegean Sea Continental Shelf Case (Greece v. Turkey), International Court of Justice Reports, 1978, p. 34 – 38. 另见李浩培：《论条约法上的时际法》，载《武汉大学学报（社会科学版）》1983年第6期，第61页。

[2] T. O. Elas, The Doctrine of Intertemporal Law, American Journal of International Law, Vol. 74: 285, p. 285 (1980).

[3] The Grisbadarna Case (Norway v. Sweden), United Nations Reports of International Arbitration Awards, 1909, Vol. 11, p. 157.

[4] The Grisbadarna Case (Norway v. Sweden), United Nations Reports of International Arbitration Awards, 1909, Vol. 11, p. 159.

[5] The Grisbadarna Case (Norway v. Sweden), United Nations Reports of International Arbitration Awards, 1909, Vol. 11, p. 160.

[6] Island of Palmas Case (Netherlands v. The U. S. A.), United Nations Reports of International Arbitration Awards, 1928, Vol. 2, p. 843 – 845.

意法律上的事实应当根据事实发生时的法律，而不是以解决争议时的法律来理解。因此，西班牙发现岛屿的意义应由 16 世纪前半叶的国际法规则来决定。[1]

随后的分析沿着"发现"在 16 世纪足以产生主权和"发现"即便在当时也只能产生"原初权利"（Inchoate Title）两条路径分别展开。假定承认"发现"能够产生领土主权，那么问题是这一主权在西班牙向美国割让时是否仍然存在，胡伯法官认为这涉及对时间上前后相继不同法律体系的适用。在特定案件中，应当区分权利的创设和权利的存在，如果说存在权利的产生应符合产生权利时的法律这样一条法律原则，那么该原则的内容也应当包括权利的存在同样要符合法律演变所提出的要求。

而从 18 世纪中叶开始，有效占领已经成为领土主权主张的基础。由于西班牙没有采取任何后续的占有行为，那么即便曾经通过"发现"取得过主权，这一权利在西班牙向美国割让时已经因为不符合当时的国际法要求而不复存在。另外，假设"发现"只能产生"原初权利"，根据 19 世纪的国际法，"发现"所产生的"原初权利"必须在合理的期限内通过有效占有才能形成完整的主权。因此适用权利的存在必须符合法律演变的要求这一时际法原则，同样得到没有实际占有行为的西班牙不享有主权的结论。如果说西班牙向美国让与的是帕尔玛斯岛的原初权利，那么这一权利显然不能超越另一国家通过持续有效展示主权而获得的权利。[2]

至此，胡伯法官通过将取得领土主权的过程区分为权利的产生和权利的维持两个阶段，将时际法的内涵作了延展。一方面，权利的产生要符合权利产生时法律的要求；另一方面，权利的维持要符合不同阶段法律演变的要求。前者代表了对时际法的传统理解，因此得到普遍支持。后者则由于被认为改变了时际法规则的含义而引起争议。

菲利普·C. 杰赛普（Philip C. Jessup）批评对时际法的这一理解将使国际法规则产生溯及力效果，从而干扰现存的领土秩序，因为国

---

[1] Island of Palmas Case (Netherlands v. The U.S.A.), United Nations Reports of International Arbitration Awards, 1928, Vol. 2, p. 845.

[2] Island of Palmas Case (Netherlands v. The U.S.A.), United Nations Reports of International Arbitration Awards, 1928, Vol. 2, p. 845–846.

家不得不持续检验本国领土各个部分的主权来源是否符合法律变化的要求。[1]由于国际法上的领土权源来源于私法,杰赛普进一步假设如果将这一原则反向推衍到私法中,结论是必然会引起混乱,物权的保证将成为镜花水月。[2]詹宁斯在围绕"帕尔玛斯岛仲裁案"展开讨论中支持权利产生和维持的区分,国际法上的领土取得和民法上的占有毕竟不同,土地不是被纳为所有物而是实施领土主权的对象。如果对同一块土地存在相互竞争的领土主张,那么无法维持最低限度的主权行为可能被视为放弃了主权。[3]詹宁斯考虑到了杰赛普所指出的风险,因此强调权利持有国不需要表现出和提出竞争主张的国家同等程度的主权行为,只要表现出没有默示放弃主权或默认对方主张即可。[4]布鲁姆也不认为区分权利的产生和维持会产生杰赛普所描述的结果。他指出时际法的第一个原则目的在于维持国际关系的稳定和安全,而第二个原则意在满足不断变化的国际环境对国际法适应性的要求。时际法的两个原则确实存在根本的区别,但是两者相互依赖而不能单独援引其中的一个方面。[5]

尽管质疑不能被完全排除,但观察后续国际法实践可以发现,时际法的两方面内容,即要求领土的取得要符合当时国际法的要求,同时领土主权的维持需要符合国际法规则变化的要求,已经构成稳定的习惯国际法规则。[6]

(二)时际法与历史性所有权

权利的产生和维持必须符合各自时期的国际法,这一原则对历史

---

[1] Philip C. Jessup, *The Palmas Island Arbitration*, American Journal of International Law, Vol. 22: 735, p. 740 (1928).

[2] Philip C. Jessup, *The Palmas Island Arbitration*, American Journal of International Law, Vol. 22: 735, p. 740 (1928).

[3] R. Y. Jennings, *The Acquisition of Territory in International Law*, Manchester University Press, 1963, p. 30.

[4] R. Y. Jennings, *The Acquisition of Territory in International Law*, Manchester University Press, 1963, p. 30.

[5] Yehuda Z. Blum, *Historic Titles in International Law*, Martinus Nijhoff, 1965, p. 207.

[6] 相应的国际司法实践包括:The Minquiers and Ecrehos Case (France v. The United Kingdom), International Court of Justice Reports, 1953, p. 47 - 73. Western Sahara Advisory Opinion, International Court of Justice Reports, 1975, p. 12 - 69. Eritrea-Yemen Arbitration (First Stage), International Legal Materials, Vol. 40: 900, p. 900 - 982 (2001).

性所有权有特别的意义。在国际法的适用从欧洲国家扩展到全球的过程中，非欧洲国家领土主权的来源也被逐步纳入国际法中领土取得规则的评价范围。在这种情况下，时际法不但承担解决不同时间段法律冲突的任务，还扮演调和不同法律体系间冲突的角色。

在"厄立特里亚—也门仲裁案"中，也门主张对争议岛屿的历史性所有权，认为这些岛屿在历史上构成伊玛目管理下也门的组成部分，同时还列举了也门大陆和争议岛屿之间的经济和社会联系作为历史性所有权的补充证据。[1]仲裁庭认为也门的主张应当在相关时期的历史和法律环境中来分析，也门主张中描述的经济、社会和文化模式确实符合经典伊斯兰法律的概念，因此这些因素构成具有法律意义的历史性考虑。[2]但是，自克里米亚战争结束后，奥斯曼帝国作为当时也门的控制者已经放弃了伊斯兰体系的国际法而采用现代的西方国际法规则，自此以后对红海两岸的情势判断必须建立在新的现实上。[3]也就是说，也门为历史性所有权主张提供经济与社会方面的证据效力将交给伊斯兰法律评价，而假设历史性所有权存在，那么这一权利在19世纪中叶之后是否保持有效性则交给现代的领土取得规则来判断。

在此，有必要重温布鲁姆的告诫，时际法的两部分内容相辅相成，共同承担着维护国际法和国际领土秩序的稳定和发展的任务。在判断主权归属的司法过程中，不能将时际法的两方面内涵分割开来使用。事实上，仲裁庭最后的判决也充分调和国际法和伊斯兰法的领土观念，仲裁庭根据伊斯兰法对土地共有的观念和当地业已形成的传统渔业机制，认为主权的分配不能终结传统渔业机制，双方渔民仍然享有自由进出传统渔业活动水域、自由使用岛屿从事与传统渔业相关活动的权利。而也门在取得岛屿主权以及相应领海权利的同时，有义务采取措施保证双方渔民继续享有传统渔业活动带来的利益。[4]

---

[1] Eritrea-Yemen Arbitration (First Stage), International Legal Materials, Vol. 40: 900, p. 905-907 (2001).

[2] Eritrea-Yemen Arbitration (First Stage), International Legal Materials, Vol. 40: 900, p. 917 (2001).

[3] Eritrea-Yemen Arbitration (First Stage), International Legal Materials, Vol. 40: 900, p. 921 (2001).

[4] Eritrea-Yemen Arbitration (First Stage), International Legal Materials, Vol. 40: 900, p. 979 (2001).

总的说来，领土权源的产生和维持，都是国家行为根据当时当地适用的国际法规则评价的结果。但是由于国家行为的连续性并不因为争议发生或提交第三方解决而终止，那么这时候我们首先要为争议情形的变化和国家行为的考虑范围设定时间点，才能由此出发寻找争议国家的行为和适用的国际法规则，从而评价这些行为的法律效果。这时就牵涉到另一个领土取得的相关规则——关键日期。

二、关键日期

（一）关键日期的含义与作用

关键日期第一次进入领土争议的视野也是在"帕尔玛斯岛仲裁案"中。美国主张西班牙通过《巴黎条约》已将争议岛屿让与美国，因此案件的要点在于美国和西班牙之间的《巴黎条约》缔结或生效时帕尔玛斯岛是荷兰的还是西班牙的领土组成部分。只有得到在条约缔结这个关键时刻，岛屿主权或属荷兰或属西班牙的结论，才能进一步回答条约的缔结及告知荷兰对争议岛屿的权利主张是否产生影响以及产生怎样的影响。[1]尽管双方争议始于1906年，胡伯法官仍然选择1898年《巴黎条约》缔结的时刻作为分析争议岛屿法律情况的最后日期。

在不久以后的"东格陵兰岛法律地位案"中，常设国际法院认为挪威1931年6月颁布的王室法令引发了这场争议。如果依丹麦主张，挪威对东格陵兰地区的占有在这一行为发生时是无效的，那么必须证明丹麦对该地区的主权在当时已经存在，这个时间点就是1931年6月10日。[2]然而，法院梳理的案件基本情况表明，最晚在1921年丹麦向挪威政府请求承认丹麦在格陵兰岛主权时，双方之间的争议已经发生并在此之后以外交通信方式持续讨论这一争议。[3]从这两个早期案例

---

[1] Island of Palmas Case (Netherlands v. The U.S.A.), United Nations Reports of International Arbitration Awards, 1928, Vol.2, p.843.

[2] Legal Status of East Greenland (Denmark v. Norwegian), Permenent Court of International Justice, Series A./B. 1933, p.45.

[3] Legal Status of East Greenland (Denmark v. Norwegian), Permenent Court of International Justice, Series A./B. 1933, p.37-38.

中可以看出，关键日期并不是争议发生的日期，而是由于发生了影响争议领土后续法律地位的事件，使得争议领土法律地位必须得到明确的时刻。

然而，并不是每个案件都存在一个特定的事件让关键日期显而易见，更多时候关键日期并不是明白无误的选择而是一个谨慎的决定。[1] 在"敏基埃岛和艾科俄斯岛案"中，围绕关键日期的讨论不但影响了岛屿主权的最终归属，也形成了对关键日期概念的典型理解。法国主张根据1259年《巴黎条约》取得海峡群岛主权，其中也包括敏基埃和艾科俄斯两个小岛[2]。1839年8月2日，英法两国签订渔业条约，规定泽西岛低潮线3海里线和条约第1条规定的特别线之间为双方的共同渔业区。敏基埃岛和艾科俄斯岛以及它们的附属岩礁都位于共同渔业区内，根据双方建立共同渔业区的目的，条约不影响岛屿的主权地位。[3] 因此，法国主张将1839年8月2日作为本案的关键日期，双方在此之后的行为不能作为行使主权的证据从而产生确定主权的效果。

英国代表杰拉德·菲茨莫里斯（Gerald Fitzmaurice）在口头辩论中拒绝法国的关键日期主张并陈述了英国在这一问题上的观念。他认为关键日期的理论基础在于时间终止于当时。领土争端往往经过长时间的发酵，在此期间，双方以谈判、抗议等形式交换不同意见，这是争议的预备阶段。如果争议继续，双方会放弃说服对方而选择站定立场维护本国的权利，此时不同意见已经明晰化为一个正式的争端。因此，领土争议中的关键日期应当是指参考当时存在的情况，而使争议双方主张的实质可以得到决断的时刻。[4] 此时，案件的情况已经明晰了，或者说冻结了，双方此后的行为不能改变或伤及任何一方的立场。如果确立1839年8月2日为关键日期，那么至少应当发现双方对争议岛屿主权存在一定程度上的争议。

---

[1] R. Y. Jennings, *The Acquisition of Territory in International Law*, Manchester University Press, 1963, p. 30.

[2] The Minquiers and Ecrehos Case (France v. The United Kingdom), International Court of Justice Reports, 1953, p. 51.

[3] The Minquiers and Ecrehos Case (France v. The United Kingdom), International Court of Justice Reports, 1953, p. 51.

[4] Gerald Fitzmaurice, *The Law and Procedure of International Court of Justice*, 1951 – 1954: *Points of Substantive Law. Part* II, British Yearbook of International Law, Vol. 32: 21, p. 61 – 67 (1955 – 1956).

法院观察到1839年条约缔结时，关于敏基埃岛和艾科俄斯岛的主权争议还没有发生。虽然双方对专属渔业捕捞权有诸多争议，但是无一涉及岛屿的归属问题，直到1886年和1888年，法国才分别主张艾科俄斯岛和敏基埃岛的主权。法院提出鉴于案件的特殊情况，在这两个时间点之后的行为也将被纳入考虑的范围，除非双方采取措施的目的是改善处境，争取有利位置。[1]法院在此过程中没有明确提及关键日期的选择，但是从关键日期之后的行为不能改变当时法律地位的角度看，应该认为法院将1886年和1888年视作本案的关键日期。但是，从选择法国第一次提出主权主张的时刻作为关键日期来看，法院似乎也没有接受关键日期是案件明晰或者冻结点的观点，布鲁姆认为法院是将争议产生的起始点作为关键时刻，更确切地说，法院将关键日期放在争议为双方所明确知晓的时间点上。[2]

在上述三个案件中，"帕尔玛斯岛仲裁案"的关键日期早于争议发生的日期，"东格陵兰岛法律地位案"的关键日期可以被视为是双方已经充分了解对方主张后的时刻，而根据菲茨莫里斯的阐释，"敏基埃岛和艾科俄斯岛案"的关键日期还处于争议的发酵期而不是明晰的阶段。由此可见，无论将关键日期认定为争议的发生还是争议的明晰时刻都会与实践产生一定偏差。[3]因为关键日期的选择并不是固定的形式程序，而要受到案件事实和双方主张的实质内容的制约。相对于具体时间点的差异，关键日期对案件裁决的效果则是一致的，即双方在关键日期之后的行为不对关键日期时争议的法律地位产生影响。

需要注意的是，不产生影响并不意味着双方在关键日期以后的全部行为与案件无关。前文已经提到在"敏基埃岛和艾科俄斯岛案"中，法院在选择法国第一次提出主权主张的时刻作为关键日期后立刻表态此后的双方的行为，除非意在改变本国在争议中的法律地位，否

---

[1] The Minquiers and Ecrehos Case (France v. The United Kingdom), International Court of Justice Reports, 1953, p. 59 - 60.
[2] Yehuda Z. Blum, *Historic Titles in International Law*, Martinus Nijhoff, 1965, p. 217.
[3] Gerald Fitzmaurice, *The Law and Procedure of International Court of Justice, 1951 - 1954: Points of Substantive Law. Part* II, British Yearbook of International Law, Vol. 32: 21, p. 23 - 24 (1955 - 1956).

则仍将被法院纳入证据的考虑范围。[1]这一实践甚至可以追溯到"帕尔玛斯岛仲裁案",胡伯法官指出1898年至1906年发生的事件本身不能证明《美西巴黎条约》签订时争议岛屿的法律情况,但对揭示关键日期之前的情况具有特定的间接利益。[2]

考虑关键日期之后行为的理由同样建立在领土争议的发酵是一个长时间过程的基础上。由于争端的持续性,那么争议一方在关键日期确定后仍持续和稳定地行使主权则会产生一个强烈的假设,即主权的行使已经存在了相当一段时间并很可能上溯到关键日期以前。这种间接的指示作用类似于条约缔结后缔约国行为对条约的解释作用。[3]此时,关键日期之后的行为事实上被视为在此之前行为的证据。

围绕"帕尔玛斯岛仲裁案"、"东格陵兰岛法律地位案"和"敏基埃岛和艾科俄斯岛案"中关键日期选择的讨论构成了对关键日期的传统理解,即关键日期是指此后各方行为不再影响双方在争议中所处的法律位置的时刻,每个争议中都存在且只存在一个能够确定主权的关键日期,时间上至少不晚于解决争议的法律程序开始之时,对关键日期以后的双方行为,如果延续了之前行为的特征,则视为推断关键日期前争议情况的证据,如果没有延续,则不纳入考虑范围。[4]后来的国际法实践基本遵循了这些原则,包括对关键日期的选择和对新现象的界定。

(二)无关键日期和多个关键日期

在"阿根廷—智利边界仲裁案"中,争议双方都同意关键日期以后的行为不作为证据。由于双方都认为本国的主张是确认业已存在的主权而对方则提出新的主权要求,仲裁庭认为它们各自提出关键日期

---

[1] The Minquiers and Ecrehos Case (France v. The United Kingdom), International Court of Justice Reports, 1953, p. 60.

[2] Island of Palmas Case (Netherlands v. The U.S.A.), United Nations Reports of International Arbitration Awards, 1928, Vol. 2, p. 866.

[3] Gerald Fitzmaurice, *The Law and Procedure of International Court of Justice*, 1951–1954: Points of Substantive Law. Part Ⅱ, British Yearbook of International Law, Vol. 32:21, p. 90 (1955–1956).

[4] Gerald Fitzmaurice, *The Law and Procedure of International Court of Justice*, 1951–1954: Points of Substantive Law. Part Ⅱ, British Yearbook of International Law, Vol. 32:21, p. 21 (1955–1956).

的目的在于排除对方行为的证据效力,而且双方提出的关键日期相差并不多。[1]另外,仲裁庭认为对不同的目的来说,关键日期是不一样的。就仲裁庭被请求解释和完成1902年仲裁而言,关键日期应当是1902年,最晚不超过1903年划界开始时。同时对请求法庭关于1902年仲裁未解决的部分进行划界这一议题来说,关键日期就是将争议递交仲裁的时刻,也就是1964年。基于上述两个理由,法院认为关键日期这个概念对该案没有重大意义,法庭将考虑双方提交的所有证据,不管这些证据相关行为发生的时间点。[2]

此案中,法庭对关键日期的讨论出现了两种新思路:第一,对不同的法律问题设定不同的关键日期,使得一个案件中可能存在多个关键日期。第二,由于案件中存在多个关键日期,不管是来自案件包含的多个法律议题还是争议方主张不同的关键日期,法庭在裁决过程中不再选择关键日期而是将双方所有行为纳入考虑范围。从表面上看,这两点都突破了原来对关键日期的理解。

实践中,不选择关键日期的也发生在"厄立特里亚—也门仲裁案"中,由于争议双方提出关键日期的目的在于确定争议涉及的岛屿范围,而不是岛屿主权权源的实质问题,因此仲裁庭决定遵从"阿根廷—智利边界仲裁案"的做法,检视双方向仲裁庭提交的全部证据而不考虑相关行为发生的时间。[3]其实,不选择关键日期只能说明在争议提交裁决之前不存在双方法律立场明晰的时间点,而不是不存在关键日期。事实上,仲裁庭在两个案件中实际选择的关键日期都很明确,就是菲茨莫里斯主张的最晚时间点,也就是争议提交裁决的日期。

相比之下,在一个案件中存在多个关键日期则涉及对关键日期法律作用的理解,从而影响对关键日期的定义。菲茨莫里斯设想过在一个争议中出现多个关键日期的情况,在他的设想中多个关键日期是因为争议双方的主张各自需要一个关键日期来评价,因此就争议本身而

---

[1] Argentine-Chile Frontier Case, United Nations Reports of International Arbitration Awards, 1966, Vol. 16, p. 165.

[2] Argentine-Chile Frontier Case, United Nations Reports of International Arbitration Awards, 1966, Vol. 16, p. 166 - 167.

[3] Eritrea-Yemen Arbitration (First Stage), International Legal Materials, Vol. 40: 900, p. 915 (2001).

言，他坚持与主权相关的关键日期有且只有一个。[1]而在"阿根廷—智利边界仲裁案"中，仲裁庭实际上是为争议涉及的两部分边界各自确定一个关键日期[2]，也就是说，如果仲裁庭最后的决定是选择关键日期，那么对不同地段的边界争议来说，关键日期仍然只有一个。因此，这两种情况下的多个关键日期并没有脱离一个法律议题、一个关键日期的范畴。

多个关键日期的另一种情况是一个争议中包括一个绝对意义上与权源相关的关键日期和另一个用以证明权源的相对的关键日期。这种情况最早出自詹宁斯的假设，在以"帕尔玛斯岛仲裁案"为例，推演以明晰作为确定关键日期的依据，并以此来定义关键日期过程中，詹宁斯提出一个争议将会牵涉两个甚至更多关键日期的可能，并具体设想了这种可能性包括一个绝对意义上与权利相关的关键日期和另一个在案件中用以证明权利存在的相关日期。[3]实践证实了这一设想，在"白礁岛案"中，法院认为新加坡对马来西亚1979年出版的地图提出抗议的日期，也就是1980年2月14日，双方对白礁岛的争议已经明晰了。[4]同时，由于马来西亚主张自古以来长期占有白礁岛而新加坡主张白礁岛在1847年时还是无主地，法院又选取1840年代这个时间段讨论马来西亚在此前是否拥有对白礁岛的原始权利以及这种权利是否维持到那时。[5]这样一来，法院在确定1980年2月14日为本案关键日期的同时，选择了1840年代作为证明权源的相关日期。可能是为了避免概念的争议，法院在白礁案中没有使用关键日期这个术语，即使是对1980年2月14日这个真正具有关键日期意义的时间点，法院使用的也是"争议在那时已经明晰"的表达方式。在更早的"卡其沼

---

[1] Gerald Fitzmaurice, *The Law and Procedure of International Court of Justice*, 1951 – 1954: Points of Substantive Law. Part Ⅱ, British Yearbook of International Law, Vol. 32: 21, p. 40 – 43 (1955 – 1956).

[2] Argentine-Chile Frontier Case, United Nations Reports of International Arbitration Awards, 1966, Vol. 16, p. 166.

[3] R. Y. Jennings, *The Acquisition of Territory in International Law*, Manchester University Press, 1963, p. 34 – 35.

[4] Case Concerning Sovereignty over Pedra Branca/Pulau Batu Puteh, Middle Rocks and South Ledge (Malaysia v. Singapore), International Court of Justice Reports, 2008, p. 28.

[5] Case Concerning Sovereignty over Pedra Branca/Pulau Batu Puteh, Middle Rocks and South Ledge (Malaysia v. Singapore), International Court of Justice Reports, 2008, p. 31.

泽案"中，印度和巴基斯坦双方都同意在1819年10月13日卡其成为英国的附庸国后，双方在该地区的边界保持不变。同时由于对1819年边界的位置无法达成一致意见，双方也都同意以1947年7月18日印度独立法案通过的日期作为最终确定边界的日期。在这里，仲裁庭在术语上甚至没有区分绝对意义的关键日期和证明意义的关键日期，而是将两个时间点都定为争议的相关日期（Relevant Dates）。[1]

如果严格遵循关键日期的传统内涵，一方面，可以看到"白礁岛案"和"卡其沼泽案"也没有突破争议中确定主权的关键日期有且只有一个这一规则，其他的日期可以被视为协助理解案情的相关时间点，这两案的裁决机构也小心翼翼地回避了关键日期的提法。另一方面，如果从观察实践入手，则不妨将关键日期的内涵扩大，正如布朗利所看到的，在每个案件中都有一个或几个日期在评价事实的过程中承担突出的角色。[2]关键日期的选择在某些环境中依靠适用于特定事实的必然法律逻辑，而在另外一些环境中，则是出于将决策过程限制在相关和关键事实的实际需要，这类事实因此可能体现为争议存在之前的行为。如果把关键日期必须与主权的最终确定联系在一起的说法看作狭义的关键日期，那么布朗利的解释无疑可以被视为广义的关键日期，后者包含了前者。而对关键日期之后的行为不能改变当时双方法律地位的效果来说，两者没有区别。

(三) 关键日期与历史性所有权

事实上，对关键日期的广义和狭义理解可以被认为仅存在理论上的争议，至于关键日期对争议的影响和如何选择关键日期的操作原则，双方的见解并无不同。无论是对领土取得的整体规则体系还是对历史性所有权这一特定权利取得方式来说，关键日期的作用都表现在两个方面：首先，由于关键日期确定了争议发生的最后时刻，争议的裁决机构可以根据时际法的原则确定当时适用的领土取得规则；其次，关键日期的确定自动排除了之后可能影响关键日期时双方法律地

---

[1] Case Concerning the Indo-Pakistan Western Boundary (Rann of Kutch), United Nations Reports of International Arbitration Awards, 1968, p. 18 - 19.
[2] Ian Brownlie, *Principles of Public International Law*, 7th editon, Oxford University Press, 2008, p. 125 - 126.

位的行为。[1]

对案件的裁决来说，不同的关键日期不但意味着证据数量的变化，更可能造成评价规则适用的不同。可以说，关键日期的选择在某种程度上可以决定主权归属的迥异结果。正因如此，关键日期的选择原则才显示出重要性。在案件裁决过程中，争议的双方都会提出有利于本方的关键日期，但这绝不意味着关键日期的确定是律师辩护艺术的体现。无论是菲茨莫里斯还是詹宁斯都强调关键日期选择的证据决定原则，即裁决机构根据双方提供的证据选择关键日期，而不是先选择关键日期再去寻找证据。

由此可见，无论关键日期的确定还是主权归属的判断，决定性因素都在于证据。在考虑什么样的证据可以证明历史性所有权存在之前，还有一个问题有待解决，就是谁应当负责向争议的裁决机构提供这些证据，也就是举证责任。

三、证明责任

时际法和关键日期被作为先决问题讨论并不是因为它们在案件裁决的过程中先于实体问题，在特定案件中时际法和关键日期的决定都与双方提交的证据密切相关。相比之下，证明责任才是审理实体问题前必须明确的先决问题。

"白礁岛案"中，国际法院认为提出存在相关事实支持其主张的一方必须证明该事实，这是国际法院判决法理确认的一般法律原则。[2] 国际法院在"尼加拉瓜军事和准军事行动案"中提出寻求确立事实的诉讼参与方承担举证责任，在没有伴随相应证据的情况下，与判决相关的主张会因为未能得到证明而被驳回。[3] 这个简要的论述可以被视作国际法层面的证明责任包含提供证据和承担失败结果两个层面。提供证据的责任由争议双方各自承担，各自负责提供足以证明本

---

[1] L. F. E. Goldie, *The Critical Date*, International and Comparative Law Quarterly, Vol. 12: 1251, p. 1266 (1963).
[2] Case Concerning Sovereignty over Pedra Branca/Pulau Batu Puteh, Middle Rocks and South Ledge (Malaysia v. Singapore), International Court of Justice Reports, 2008, p. 31.
[3] Military and Paramilitary Activities in and against Nicaragua (Nicaragua v. The U. S. A.), International Court of Justice Reports, 1984, p. 437.

方观点的证据。

对承担证明失败的结果责任来说，国际法没有确定由哪一方承担证明责任的统一规定。这种不明确提供两种解释的可能：一是不管是否存在特殊类型的国际法案件，都适用证明责任分配的一般规则即由提出积极主张的一方承担证明责任；二是司法机构在具体案件中判定到底由谁承担证明责任。联合国秘书处在向第一次海洋法大会提交的备忘录中，就历史性水域的证明责任引用了吉德尔的观点，主张由"紧邻该国海岸的特定海域具有通常情形下不具备的内水特征的国家承担证明责任。沿海国是这类行为的请求者，其主张构成了对公海的侵夺，且不符合目前仍是国际法必要基础的公海自由原则。因此由于公海减少而受害国家的证明责任应当转移到历史性水域的主张国"[1]。这段论述意味着，沿海国提出历史性水域的积极主张时，既承担提供证据的责任，也承担证明失败的结果责任，这并不超越一般的证明责任分配原则。另外，"由于公海减少而受害国家的证明责任应当转移到历史性水域的主张国"，表明在其他国家主动质疑历史性水域的案件中，证明责任发生倒置，结果责任仍然由历史性水域的主张国承担。这种情况下，证明责任的分配与主张国在诉讼中所处的地位没有关系，统一由历史性水域的主张国承担证明责任，当主张国是原告时，由原告承担，当其是被告时，由被告承担。

在"包括历史性海湾在内的历史性水域法律制度"研究中，国际法委员会考虑了历史性水域的主张国承担通常意义上的举证责任还是特殊举证责任的问题。委员会认为作出一个由主张海洋历史性所有权的国家承担证明责任的一般性结论并没有太大意义。如果这一论断意味着，在无法向法官证明全部要件时，由主张历史性所有权的国家承担证明失败的责任，那么这个结论并不来自历史性水域的例外特性，而是因为证明责任的一般逻辑结果就应是如此。任何案件的裁决中，双方都以说服法官接受本方观点为目标，那么就无法成功说服的部分，显然应各自承担失败的责任。因此，国际法委员会认为对历史性水域制度的证明责任作出一般性规定是没有必要的，甚至是误导性的，更适当的

---

[1] Historic Bays: Memorandum by the Secretariat of the United Nations, A/CONF.13/1, 1957, p. 31.

做法是将证明责任的分配交给适用具体案件的程序规则来解决。[1]

可以说，对由主张历史性水域的国家承担证明责任这一点，吉德尔和国际法委员会之间没有区别。区别在于吉德尔试图将历史性水域的证明责任融入与原被告地位联系在一起的结果责任分配体系，对主张者作为原告时承担通常意义上的证明责任和作为被告时承担的特殊证明责任进行区分。国际法委员会则不把证明责任和主张国作为原被告的身份相联系，而是在承认"谁主张，谁举证"原则的基础上，将原告或被告承担责任的问题交给司法做个案处理。两者的根本立场是一样的，无论作为原告还是被告一方，提出历史性水域主张的一方既要承担证明存在相关事实支持其主张的证据提供责任，也要承担在证明不力时诉讼失败的结果责任。

理解这一点同时也解决了陆地领土取得和边界争议中历史性所有权主张的证明责任问题。前面讲过与历史性水域被视为公海自由原则的例外不同，陆地本身就是领土取得的对象，不存在例外一说，但这不意味着证明责任分配没有特殊之处。在"隆端寺案"中，国际法院认为从形式上看，柬埔寨是启动诉讼程序的原告，但泰国也对同样一片土地提出了主权主张，两国都将各自的主张建立在一系列事实，以及针对对方主张提出的反对论点之上，因此证明责任当然由提出这些主张的双方各自承担。[2]领土取得和边界争议中的诉讼双方，对事实并不总是持一方肯定另一方否定的态度，更多情况下是双方都坚持领土属于本方的主张并提供相应的肯定性证据，由第三方比较证据的相对强弱决定主权的归属。由于双方都是肯定性事实的主张者，如规定证明失败的风险由原告或者被告承担都太过僵化，不符合证明责任分配的一般法律原则，由各自在其主张的范围内承担证明责任是适合的。

总的来说，历史性所有权的主张者应当承担能够证明权利存在的证据，并在证据不足时承担无法取得权利的后果。这种责任既不因主张者在诉讼中所处的位置而有所区别，也不因为其主张的是海洋法上历史性所有权或是领土取得和边界争议中的历史性所有权而有所不同。

---

[1] Juridical Regime of Historic Waters, Including Historic Bays, International Law Commission Yearbook, 1962 (2), p. 22 – 23.

[2] Temple of Preah Vihear Case (Cambodia v. Thailand), International Court of Justice Reports, 1962, p. 15 – 16.

第二节 有效管理

传统的领土取得方式分类中，先占、时效和征服，甚至添附都以占有土地为基础，历史性所有权也不例外。詹宁斯主张领土主权的巩固过程中可能包含着各种各样重要的因素，但这一权利的基础和必要条件仍然是占有的事实。如果占有这个条件不能得到满足，那么巩固的过程根本就不会开始。[1]

由于国际法的领土取得规则最早源于私法的所有权取得规则，早期的领土占有表现为本国国民的居住，以及排他性的利用和开发。在领土主权与所有权脱离的过程中，国际司法实践和公法家学说将观察领土占有的重点从是否完成物质占有转向是否以执行政府职能的方式展示主权的存在。因此，对所主张的土地实施有效管理成为占有领土的最有力证据。

是否存在有效管理的判断取决于是否满足胡伯法官在"帕尔玛斯岛仲裁案"中主张的和平而持续地展示主权的要求[2]，但是"和平而持续地展示主权"本身不是一项国际法原则，作为相关国家单方面行为的表达方式，它的最终法律效果需要结合具体的条件才能准确评价。

一、有效管理的意图和主张

在"东格陵兰岛法律地位案"中，常设国际法院申明主权的主张只能来自持续展示的权利，其中必须存在两个要件：主权者实施行为的意志和意识；实际行使和展示权利的行动。[3] 国际法对取得领土的要求包括占有的意图（animus occupandi）和占有实体的行为（corpus occupandi），分别构成有效管理的主客观要件。通常认为，主客观要件在实践中起到评估双方主张和排除相关证据的作用。没有客观要件支

---

[1] R. Y. Jennings, *The Acquisition of Territory in International Law*, Manchester University Press, 1963, p. 26.
[2] Island of Palmas Case (Netherlands v. The U. S. A.), United Nations Reports of International Arbitration Awards, 1928, Vol. 2, p. 839.
[3] Legal Status of East Greenland (Denmark v. Norwegian), Permenent Court of International Justice, Series A./B. 1933, p. 45 - 46.

持的主观认识只能被认为是抽象的主张,在效力上无法对抗有效管理的证据。另外,主观要件所包含的行为应当具备建立或维持主权的主观目的,这一含义则将主张国与这一主题无涉的证据排除在法庭的考虑范围之外。

在领土取得的争议中,法院评价占领的主观意图并不基于国家的主张,而是根据主张国的行为来推测其占领意愿的范围和程度,这就带来占领的认识是否脱离占领的行为而存在的问题。例如,在"领土和海洋争议案"中,尼加拉瓜主张对所有争议岛屿的主权,但是未能提供任何实施有效管理的证据。[1]这貌似是尼加拉瓜占领这些岛屿的主观意识没有得到客观行为的支持,而如果回顾"东格陵兰岛法律地位案"对两个要件的描述,更为适当的结论应该是既然没有对争议岛屿采取任何有效管理的措施,那么尼加拉瓜不但缺乏取得这些领土的客观行为,同时也不应被认为具有占领这些岛屿的主观意图,在法庭面前的主张仅仅是出于利益考虑的政治渴望而不是具备法律基础的主观意图。

通常情况下由于争议双方都实施了一定的主权行为,这时双方的主观认识有两种可能:一是笼统认定双方都具备占领的主观意图,那么两者在比较中可相互抵消。二是根据双方行为的强弱程度来比较主观意图,那么结果和直接比较双方客观行为毫无差异。在这两种可能性下,管理的意图都不脱离管理的行为而存在。

事实上,只有当管理意图在扮演消极角色时,即在展示主权性质行为的一方不主张主权的情况下,它独立于客观要件的必要性才展现出来。由于实施了有效管理的行为,正常情形下应当推论实施行为方具备占领的认识,而实际上由于某种原因,行为方没有取得主权的意思,这时他需要通过主张表明自己没有取得领土的主观意愿,从而使行为不产生占领的实际效果。布朗利举例说,如果行为得到另一国家或除行为国外的国家——即被认为是合法主权国——的许可,那么行为国任何数量的有效管理行为都无法成熟至可认定为主权的行为。[2]

---

[1] Territorial and Maritime Dispute (Columbia v. Nicaragua), International Court of Justice Reports, 2012, p. 652.
[2] Ian Brownlie, *Principles of Public International Law*, 7th editon, Oxford University Press, 2008, p. 135.

这时，通过得到许可的意思表示，行为国申明占领的行为不具有占领的认识。

此外，行为方单方面表示不主张主权的例子在国际法实践中也并不鲜见。第一次世界大战期间，英国军事占领了红海中靠近阿拉伯半岛沿岸原本属于奥斯曼土耳其帝国的岛屿，但是在战争结束缔结的一系列条约中，英国都表示这些岛屿的主权依然属于土耳其。[1]当土耳其通过1923年的《洛桑条约》宣布放弃这些岛屿主张时，英国对这些岛屿的管理已经满足取得这些岛屿主权的要求，但英国仍然决定维持这些岛屿在《洛桑条约》中的状态，即处于主权未定的法律地位。在英国和意大利之间的"罗马对话"中，英国主张任何欧洲国家不应该寻求在红海靠近阿拉伯半岛沿岸的岛屿建立主权。根据罗马对话所达成的协议中的相关条款，"厄立特里亚—也门仲裁案"的仲裁庭认为，唯一的理解就是原本可以取得主权的行为由于协议的存在而不再具有取得主权的意义。[2]

据此似乎可以这样说，在国家具有取得领土的主观认识时，该认识的范围和程度并不单独由主张表达，而应该根据实际采取的有效占领行为来判断。反之，由于国际法默认采取有效占领行为的国家具有占领的主观意识，如果实际上实施了有效占领行为的国家无意取得主权，反而需要一个主张来证明它的消极意图。

一方面，与陆地领土的取得不同，如果沿海国试图取得海洋法上的历史性所有权，包含明确内容和范围的主张是不可缺少的。支持这种观点的理由一部分是因为海洋法中沿海国同样的管理行为既可以推定为支持排他的历史性水域主张，也可能是其他非排他的历史性权利主张。"英挪渔业案"中法院在判断挪威主张的划界规则在对英国是否存在法律效果前，首先回答的是这部分划界规则的准确内容是什么。挪威1812年王室法令宣布挪威的海洋主权范围是从最远离大陆未覆水岛礁向海延伸1里格（1里格约合3海里），随后的1869年划界法令

---

[1] Eritrea-Yemen Arbitration (First Stage), International Legal Materials, Vol. 40: 900, p. 927 (2001).
[2] Eritrea-Yemen Arbitration (First Stage), International Legal Materials, Vol. 40: 900, p. 927 (2001).

和立法理由表明了岛屿间以直线相连接的具体划界办法。[1]法院认为1812年法令虽然仅以一般形式描述挪威传统划界体系,缺乏岛屿之间是如何连接起来的说明,但其立法理由清楚地描述了挪威划界体系的内容,即以岛屿为基点,以直线相连接,以及不限制直线长度。[2]法院由此确信存在挪威主张的划界体系从而进一步考虑该体系是否在实践中得到一贯执行。

另一方面,随着海洋法的发展,沿海国被越来越多地赋予领海以外的管辖职权,在争端解决过程中很难仅依靠行为判断沿海国究竟是履行多边条约赋予的职权还是根据主权认识行使管辖权。西蒙斯认为由适当的国家机关对特定水域提出一个正式的、清楚的和一致的主张是权利为人所知的保障,否则可以成为不存在历史性所有权的抗辩理由。[3]在"大陆架划界案"中,突尼斯认为其根据自古以来采集大陆架寄居生物和相应管理形成了对大陆架的历史性所有权,利比亚并不否认突尼斯沿岸渔民从事了这些活动,但是,其认为突尼斯在一系列国内立法中表现出对权利性质的认识,并不是突尼斯在法庭上所主张的自古取得并得到广泛承认的历史性所有权。[4]在利比亚看来,突尼斯在沿岸水域中实施管理行为有可能代表着突尼斯将这片水域视为其主权覆盖的范围,但是在海洋法已经赋予沿海国大陆架权利的情况下,更大的可能性是突尼斯执行的是沿海国在大陆架上享有的专属管辖权利。由于突尼斯在争议发生提交法院之前从未提出过关于历史性水域的主张,因此,利比亚不认为突尼斯的管理行为建立在将水域视为其内水的意图之上。

无论是陆地还是海洋的历史性所有权,行使权利的行为都必须伴随着相应的主观意图。但是对这一认识的表达方式来说,陆地领土取得的推论起点是占领的行为必然伴随着的占领意识,主张并不是具有

---

[1] Fisheries Case (The United Kingdom v. Norway), International Court of Justice Reports, 1951, p. 35 – 36.

[2] Fisheries Case (The United Kingdom v. Norway), International Court of Justice Reports, 1951, p. 36.

[3] Clive R. Symmons, *Historic Waters in the Law of the Sea*, *A Modern Re-Appraisal*, Martinus Nijhoff, 2008, p. 117.

[4] Continental Shelf Case (Tunisia v. Libyan Arab Jamahiriya), Libya Counter-Memories, 1982, p. 194.

主观认识的必要条件。而对海洋排他性的历史性所有权来说，一个独立于行为的主张是表明主观认识不可或缺的条件。

二、展示权利的行为

伴随着占领认识的国家行为是对特定区域行使主权管理的证据。挪威作为历史性水域的主张国，在"英挪渔业案"的辩诉状中指出，在适用历史性水域过程中，沿海国根据其国内法采取的行为暗示了构成主权基础的历史性所有权，这些行为具体包括立法、行政管理和司法决定。[1]实践中，由于个案案情的不同，一方面无法预先穷尽权利展示行为的具体表现形式，另一方面也不可能设定一条统一的评价规范来判断个案中相关行为的性质。但是，这并不意味着国际法对评价主权展示行为采取的是实用主义的模糊策略，下面尝试将实践中代表国家行使权利的行为以及各自对有效占领的意义进行简要的归类和评价。

（一）立法行为

立法是显示国家主权最明显的方式之一。[2]布鲁姆认为国内立法是国家展示认识的通常方式，表明国家对特定地区的主张及程度。在法律条款中提及争议地区源于国家认为这些地区当然属于该国法律的管辖范围，相关立法被视为国家具有实施有效管理意图的证据。[3]

"敏基埃岛和艾科俄斯岛案"中，1875年的英国财政部授权将泽西作为海峡群岛的港口，而艾科俄斯群礁被法令规定包括在泽西港的范围内。法院认为这一立法清楚表明在主权争议尚未产生时英国主权已经涉及争议岛屿。[4]而对无人定居区域或者远离大陆的岛屿来说，英国的立法不仅展示取得主权的意图，甚至足以代表对该主权的实际展示。在"东格陵兰法律地位案"中，1721年探险者在东格陵兰建立两块殖民地，并获得当时丹麦-挪威联合王国颁发的贸易垄断许可，王

---

[1] Fisheries Case (The United Kingdom v. Norway), Norway Counter-Memories, 1951, p. 567-568.
[2] Legal Status of East Greenland (Denmark v. Norwegian), Permenent Court of International Justice, Series A./B. 1933, p. 48.
[3] Yehuda Z. Blum, *Historic Titles in International Law*, Martinus Nijhoff, 1965, p. 114.
[4] The Minquiers and Ecrehos Case (France v. The United Kingdom), International Court of Justice Reports, 1953, p. 66.

国以立法的形式保护和实施贸易垄断权。由于立法规定对贸易垄断的保护不仅限于既存的殖民地而是整个格陵兰岛上未来可能建立的全部殖民地，法院认为此时丹麦-挪威联合王国对格陵兰岛的主权并不局限在岛上的殖民地范围内而是覆盖全岛。[1]

立法作为主权展示行为的优点在于其确定性和公开性。立法中明确提及争议地点代表了国家意图实施主权的明确主张，同时是否得到立法授权也是判断行政和社会管理行为是否代表国家真实意图的重要证据。同时，由于国家立法的公开性特点，相关争议国和第三方国家对相应地区的主权存在情况的认知成为判断相关国家态度的起始点。评价立法行为效力的复杂因素在于它的效力在绝大多数情况下依赖于法律实施行为的存在，尤其是在争议的另一方提供实际管理的证据时，单纯的立法行为将在争议解决中处于不利的位置。

(二) 执法和实施经济、社会管理的行为

主权争议中，主张国总是尽可能多地向裁决机构提供本国对争议地区实施管理行为的证明，冀望在证据强度的比较中占据优势地位。在司法实践中出现过的相关行为有：维持政治秩序，包括建立行政和司法机构维护秩序，登记人口和土地，征收土地、农业和海关税，派遣军事巡逻和建设军事设施，移民管理，发放入境和访问许可；提供公共服务，包括发布航行和飞行公告，开展搜索和救援行动，建设和维护海上信号设施，提供邮政、公共健康和教育服务；管理经济活动，包括组织自然资源调查，填海造陆，规范渔业和其他产业经营，签订特许专营合同和授予排他经营权利；等等。国际法实践环境的多样性决定行为的类型和内容是无法穷尽列举的，我们需要关心的是两部分内容，一是如何确定这些行为与主权展示的相关性，二是不同类型行为的主权展示效果。

确定相关性的判断有三个要素。

一是主体的身份。即以主权者的身份采取行动（à titre de souverain）。首先将政府作为主体与私人相互分立，但也不是每一层级的政府或者政府的每个组成部门都被视为具有主权者的身份。领土取

---

[1] Legal Status of East Greenland (Denmark v. Norwegian), Permenent Court of International Justice, Series A./B. 1933, p. 48 - 51.

得的习惯法规则并没有像《维也纳条约法公约》一样明确规定代表国家对外行为的主体,但在实践中依然发展出一些识别主体是否适格的规则。一方面,一般来说,代表主权者采取行动的应当是中央政府。除非地方政府的行为是基于实施国家立法的认识,否则受职能所限,地方政府的行为一般情况下由于不具备取得领土的主观意图,因此不能被视为主权的展示行为。在联邦制国家中,享有部分主权的联邦成员可能以自己的行为构成全联邦的主权展示,这取决于联邦和成员之间的法律关系。[1]另一方面,即便对中央政府来说,也只有有权作出与领土主权相关决定的职能机构和个人,其行为才当然构成主权的展示。[2]

二是行为的类型。对于司法管辖和行政管理的行为,除非有证据证明与领土取得的目的无关,都会被纳入检验有效管理的考虑范围。经济和社会管理事务与主权展示之间的关系则是中立的。这类行为即便由官方组织实施,由于行为的根本目的是经济性的,除非有证据证明在特定地区实施行为是基于该地区属于行为国主权范围的认识,这种情况下,经济和社会管理属性的行为也不能直接产生权源,但是可以作为主权存在的证据。

三是行为发生时的客观环境。管理行为是否与展示主权相关还需要结合行为所处的具体环境加以评价,同类行为在不同的案件中会产生不同的法律效果。以争议岛屿上修筑和维护灯塔为例,由于修筑和维护灯塔的直接目的一般是保证水道的航行安全,国际司法处理这类证据的一般原则是不认为在争议岛屿上建设和维护这类设施与取得岛屿主权间有必然关联[3],但是,如果争议对象是非常小的岛屿,那么在这样的岛屿上建设航行辅助设备会与主权展示产生一定法律上的关联。[4]

司法实践的不同处理方式往往和争议地点的情况以及是否存在其

---

[1] Clive R. Symmons, *Historic Waters in the Law of the Sea, A Modern Re-Appraisal*, Martinus Nijhoff, 2008, p. 122.

[2] The Minquiers and Ecrehos Case (France v. The United Kingdom), International Court of Justice Reports, 1953, p. 80.

[3] The Minquiers and Ecrehos Case (France v. The United Kingdom), International Court of Justice Reports, 1953, p. 71.

[4] Maritime Delimitation and Territorial Questions between Qatar and Bahrain (Qatar v. Bahrain), International Court of Justice Reports, 2002, p. 99 – 100.

他证据密切相关。"敏基埃岛和艾科俄斯岛案"所涉都是海峡群岛中有人定居的岛屿,前者甚至还有一个小型渔港,英法两国特别是英国对岛上居民实施了种类繁多的管理行为[1],而建设灯塔无论从行为目的和行为主体上都无法与实施有效管理产生必然联系,那么在拥有其他更加有力证据的情况下,法院选择不考虑灯塔的建筑和维护有自己的道理。反之,对于较小且重要性不突出的岛屿来说,与其直接相关的管理行为很少,甚至没有,此时建设灯塔虽然只具有较小的有效管理意义,但是在这种情况下对岛屿主权归属的判断已经是弥足珍贵了。

至于不同类型行为的主权展示效果,由于同样的行为在不同案情中也会扮演不同的角色,因此除一般情况下立法、司法和执法所代表的政治管辖的行为在效力上高于展示经济与社会管理职能的行为以外,很难脱离具体案情分析不同类型行为的效果。更重要的是,司法机构在作出主权归属的裁决时,并不是依赖某个特定时刻的特定行为给裁决者带来的深刻印象,而是根据在一定时间段内囊括所有证据在内的整体行为,比较这些证据力度上的相对优势得出最后的结论。从这个角度来看,寻找有关特定行为效果的一般结论既不现实,也缺乏实践中的必要性。

总的来说,对行为的相关性及其法律效果的总结可以归纳为以下三点:一是行为只能来自国家,或被授权或被追认代表国家的机关和个人。二是行为在相应的环境中至少能够被解释为具有取得和维持领土主权的认识,而不存在与领土主权无关的合理解释。三是最重要的一点,司法机构在对争议主权的归属作出最终评判时,考虑的并不是判断单个行为对主权归属的影响,而是就行为的总体数量和质量作出评价。

(三)私人行为

"私人行为不是主权展示的行为"是国际法对这类行为效力的基本判断。麦克奈尔(McNair)法官在"英挪渔业案"的反对意见中提出,历史性所有权要求国家行使管辖的证据,而个人行为在这方面的价值微乎其微,除非能够表明他们是根据国家颁发的证照或国家授予

---

[1] The Minquiers and Ecrehos Case (France v. The United Kingdom), International Court of Justice Reports, 1953, p. 66–67.

的权利行事,抑或政府通过他们以其他方式主张管辖。[1]这一观点也得到后来国家实践和司法实践的持续遵从。私人行为可以再细分为三类:第一类,私人行为完全由个人组织实施,并且以获取私人利益为行为目的,这类行为也许持续很长时间而且实施过程中也没有受到其他国家人民的干扰,但是仅凭自身并不足以产生主权。[2]第二类,国家通过私人主张管辖的行为。这时私人行为带有为主权取得的认识,也采取了实际的行动,而国家的授权或追认弥补了私人在主体资格上的瑕疵。这时,私人作为国家权力的直接行使者,他的行为类似私法上的代理[3],其行为的私人性质已经终止,因而可以被视为代表国家的有效管理行为。第三类,私人行为没有代替主权者主张管辖的认识,其行为的目的是获取个人利益,但是行为者因为某种原因确信自己的行为发生在本国领土范围内。这类行为与使他产生主权确信的国家行为结合在一起所产生的主权展示效果,是国际司法实践中时常需要评价的内容。

"卡其沼泽案"中信德牧民在达哈拉班尼和查德贝特两片地带的放牧行为是仲裁庭讨论的焦点之一。证据表明信德的牧民在这两片争议地带有着超过一百年的放牧历史,控制信德的英国当局向这些牧民征税并鼓励他们不向卡其当局缴纳放牧费用。[4]巴基斯坦认为放牧得到英国当局的保护和支持并且对信德沿岸的居民有重大利益,因此牧民的私人行为和其他管辖行为一起,不但是确认巴基斯坦主权存在的证据,更是创设该国主权的首要来源。[5]

印度指定的仲裁员质疑鼓励牧民不向对方缴费是否可以成为主权展示的证据。[6]仲裁庭主席首先指出信德这样依赖农业产出的地区,

---

[1] Fisheries Case (The United Kingdom v. Norway), Dissenting OPinion, International Court of Justice Reports, 1951, p. 184.

[2] Fisheries Case (The United Kingdom v. Norway), Dissenting OPinion, International Court of Justice Reports, 1951, p. 157.

[3] Ian Brownlie, *Principles of Public International Law*, 7th editon, Oxford University Press, 2008, p. 138.

[4] Case Corning Indo-Pakistan Western Boundary (Rann of Kutch), United Nations Reports of International Arbitration Awards, 1968, Vol. 17, p. 418 – 430.

[5] Case Corning Indo-Pakistan Western Boundary (Rann of Kutch), United Nations Reports of International Arbitration Awards, 1968, Vol. 17, p. 17 – 18.

[6] Case Corning Indo-Pakistan Western Boundary (Rann of Kutch), United Nations Reports of International Arbitration Awards, 1968, Vol. 17, p. 493.

公共利益和个人利益高度重合，不能像工业社会那样对公私权利做鲜明的区分。具体到达哈拉班尼和查德贝特两地，一百年来多在这里放牧的只有信德人，信德当局对他们的征税行为虽然有限，但是足以证明在当地维持法律和秩序的是信德。卡其当局征收放牧费确实构成政府行为，但是这一行为并不持续，而且招致信德当局的反对。相比之下，信德当局的行为在当地环境中更加满足国际法对主权展示的要求。卡其沼泽由于半海半陆的自然条件不具备定居的环境，因此无法采用稳定可见的方式加以管理。信德居民的放牧行为本身是为了自身经济利益的私人行为，但是通过纳税和政府行为联系在一起，这种类似经营税的税种可以被看作允许牧民使用草场资源的许可费。在仲裁庭看来，这就验证了草场是属于信德当局的假设。[1]

此外，虽然仲裁庭没有评论放牧行为构成主权来源之一的观点，但可以明确的是信德获得的主权并不是由放牧这种私人行为创设的，毕竟这种行为的实施者未受国家授权或确认，也缺乏代替国家实施行为的认识。由此我们也可以得出结论，第三类私人行为的效果在于印证确定存在有效管理行为，从而共同形成主权存在的证据。

三、行为的持续性及和平性

（一）行为的持续性

国际法上的领土取得规则独立于私法上不动产物权取得的重要标志就在于，要求占有的持续性贯穿了所有的领土的取得方式。即便取得先前无人占领的无主地，提出主权主张的国家仍然要经受一系列对历史、实际利用和控制的考察分析，只有在上述层面证明国家占有的持续性，主张国方能取得主权。[2] 对历史性所有权来说，基于广为人知的占有事实而取得的权源本来就建立在长期占有之上，其中对占有所施加的"超越记忆"（Immemorial）定语表明这一权源对时间要素的

---

[1] Case Corning Indo-Pakistan Western Boundary (Rann of Kutch), United Nations Reports of International Arbitration Awards, 1968, Vol. 17, p. 554-563.

[2] D. P. O'Connell, *International Law and Boundary Disputes*, Proceedings of the American Society of International Law at Its Annual Meeting (1921-1969), Vol. 54: 77, p. 78 (1960).

重视。德·维舍将历史性所有权的巩固定义为"经证实的长期利用，……代表着包含关系和利益的集合，这一集合自身能产生将某一片陆地或者海洋归属某一国家的效力"，说明对相关陆地和海洋的长期利用构成权利巩固的起点。西蒙斯认为持续性要素渗透历史性所有权的每一个要件中，不但是沿海国是否提出过历史性水域主张的依据和国家行为有效性的评价标准之一，更是推测相关国家默认态度的重要证据，因为沿海国历史性水域主张和实践存在的时间越长，就越容易推断出国际社会对其主张的默认态度[1]。

  对什么是持续，或者说国际法对持续的要求，国家实践和公法专家曾尝试给出各种定义，包括长期存在的持续利用，已经确立的惯例，持续和不断完善确立的惯例，被国家普遍承认的确定惯例等。[2]国际法委员会认为，所谓持续就是同一主体在相当一段时间内重复同样或类似性质的行为。可见持续的内涵包括时间跨度和常规性，行为的实施首先必须维持一段时间，同时在这段时间内应当保证一定的频率。[3]一段时间内的国家行为如果随之而来的是长时间的不作为，或者实际行使权利的行为只在关键日期之前零星出现，都不能满足持续性的要求。至于多长时间和多高频率可以满足持续性的要求，国际法无法脱离实际案情给出普遍的客观标准，对这两者的确切评价，都与因个案情况而不同的一系列相关因素密切联系。

  时间跨度是一个数量概念，但是对行为持续性的要求难以采用量化的考察方式。国际法委员会认为对取得历史性水域的历史性所有权来说，没有准确的时间长度可以证明国家行为满足权利确实存在的判断要求。[4]这一判断也适用于陆地领土的取得。在特定的争端中裁决机构可能适用双方合意达成的定量时间标准，比如，在"英属圭亚那和委内瑞拉边界仲裁案"中，英美双方达成的仲裁协议规定由争议其

---

[1] Clive R. Symmons, *Historic Waters in the Law of the Sea, A Modern Re-Appraisal*, Martinus Nijhoff, 2008, p. 151, 161.
[2] Historic Bays: Memorandum by the Secretariat of the United Nations, A/CONF. 13/1, 1957, p. 28.
[3] Juridical Regime of Historic Waters, Including Historic Bays, International Law Commission Yearbook, 1962 (2), p. 15.
[4] Juridical Regime of Historic Waters, Including Historic Bays, International Law Commission Yearbook, 1962 (2), p. 15.

中一方控制 50 年以上的土地就视为该国领土。[1]但这仅是个例,并不代表广泛的国际法实践,更不要说成为确定领土归属的国际法规则了。事实上,裁决机构不会自行设立可量化的时间标准,更多的是根据各方主张、证据和案情环境共同判断是否满足持续在时间上的要求。在"喀麦隆和尼日利亚间陆地和海洋边界案"中,尼日利亚主张对乍得湖附近村落的长期占有已经形成所有权的历史性巩固。国际法院认为尼日利亚提供的事实和环境只是在 20 年左右的时间段内,对于权利的巩固来说,这段时间无论如何都太短了。[2]

环境因素对常规性判断同样产生影响。在"帕尔玛斯岛仲裁案"中,胡伯法官认为持续是展示领土主权的原则,但是主权的展示不可能随时出现在领土的每一个位置,满足权利持续要求的行为必然因为相关区域是否适宜居住、是否被无主权争议领土包围、是否可以从公海直接进入等条件而表现出一定的断断续续。[3]因此,尽管 18—19 世纪荷兰主权在帕尔玛斯岛的直接和间接展示并不很多,与持续展示的要求相比还有相当的差距,但是对一个距离遥远且仅有土著人居住的小岛,不能期待国家主权有频繁的展示。[4]

环境对行为常规性影响的极端情况发生在"克利伯顿岛仲裁案"中,1858 年法国军官在巡航中对无人居住,且不存在组织或管理的克利伯顿岛进行了地理测量并代表法国政府宣布占领该岛。除了向法国驻夏威夷总领馆报告了占领时间以及在夏威夷当地报纸公布占领消息,直到 1898 年巡航时发现美国人在岛上采集鸟粪为止,法国并没有对克利伯顿岛实施过任何实质性的管理行为。墨西哥认为法国虽然表达了占领意图,但是没有实际占领的行为。

仲裁员意大利国王艾曼努埃尔三世(Victor-Emmanuel Ⅲ)承认国际法对占领的要求除了占领认识以外,还需要一些实际处理领土的行

---

[1] John Bassett Moore, *A Digest of International Law*, Government Printing Office, 1906, p. 297.
[2] Land and Maritime Boundary between Cameroon and Nigeria (Cameroon v. Nigeria, Equatorial Guinea intervening), International Court of Justice Reports, 2002, p. 352.
[3] Island of Palmas case (Netherlands v. The U.S.A.), United Nations Reports of International Arbitration Awards, 1968, Vol. 2, p. 840.
[4] Island of Palmas case (Netherlands v. The U.S.A.), United Nations Reports of International Arbitration Awards, 1968, Vol. 2, p. 867.

为。案件中法国通过公开方式表达自己的占领态度是毋庸置疑的，至于实际的行为，考虑到克利伯顿岛无人定居的现实，而法国作为第一个占领者又没有受到其他国家的反对，因此法国在1858年宣布占领岛屿时已经完成了主权的实际取得。[1]

影响满足持续性要求的相关因素并非无迹可寻。

首先是争议所处的自然和经济社会条件。争议地区适宜人类居住，交通便利，有重要经济资源，那么取得这类地区主权的行为必须维持一定时间和相当的频率。反之则对行为的时间和频率的要求都会有所降低。值得注意的是在海洋历史性所有权的主张中，对沿海国有重要的经济或其他利益会成为减弱行为持续性要求的因素。"英挪渔业案"中，国际法院就认为在评价挪威划界体系有效性时不能忽略当地特有的经济利益所带来的现实和重要性。[2]

其次是主张权利类型的不同。相对于主张排他性主权来说，主张非排他性权利对行为持续性的要求要低得多。英国曾在"英挪渔业案"诉状中提出持续一个世纪以上的历史性水域主张方能被视为有效，而最后法院认定挪威实践自1869年至1935年间持续实施，尽管没有到达一个世纪，也是一段相当长的时间。[3]而美国和加拿大在第二次联合国海洋法会议上将取得传统捕鱼权的条件定为持续捕鱼十年以上[4]，相比之下满足持续的时间要求降低了许多。

最后是行为的性质和强度以及相关国家的行为。行为的性质和强度不仅是判断是否存在主权展示行为的直接依据，也是判断行为是否持续的辅助标准。由于证据力度的相对性，一国行为是否满足取得权利的持续性要求，很大程度上也取决于对手的行为是否保持一定的时间和频率。

---

[1] Affaire de L'ile de Clippertion, United Nations Reports of International Arbitration Awards, 1931, Vol. 2, p. 1108-1110.
[2] Fisheries Case (The United Kingdom v. Norway), International Court of Justice Reports, 1951, p. 133.
[3] Juridical Regime of Historic Waters, Including Historic Bays, International Law Commission Yearbook, 1962 (2), p. 15.
[4] D. W. Bowett, *The Second United Nations Conference on the Law of the Sea*, International and Comparative Law Quarterly, Vol. 9: 415, p. 424 (1960).

(二) 行为的和平性

对权利展示行为的另一个要求是和平。胡伯法官只是简要解释说和平意味着权利展示过程中与其他国家之间是和平的。[1] 这里的和平可以被视为包含两层含义：一层含义是指在占有的持续过程是不受干扰的。即没有因为其他国家的行为而中断，或者其他国家虽然采取了一定行为但是不产生中断持续占有的法律效果。这一条件的满足需要考察争议的相关国家或者国际社会对主张国行使权利的态度，将在下文集中阐述，此处不再展开。另一层含义代表的就是字面意义上的和平。这首先联系到国际法对非法使用武力的禁止。根据时际法的原则，武力征服在很长一段时间内曾经是有效的领土取得方式。但是国际社会和国际法对使用武力的态度在今天发生了根本性的变化，1931年的"九一八"事变促使国际社会形成不承认以武力方式改变领土状态的"史汀生原则"（Stimson Formula）。1932年国联大会通过决议将"史汀生原则"作为所有成员国的法律义务。[2]

联合国继承了这一规定，《联合国宪章》第2条第4款明确规定："各会员国在其国际关系上不得使用威胁或武力，或以与联合国宗旨不符之任何其他方法，侵害任何会员国或国家之领土完整或政治独立。"在不得对任何国家使用或威胁使用武力已经成为国际法基本原则和强行法的今天，通过武力方式取得原来属于其他国家的领土主权无论经过多长时间的和平持有，依旧不能改变权利取得时的非法性，从而无法授予占领国主权。[3]

对于归属权从未得到明确的领土来说，针对非和平的权利行使方式或者说国家处于战争时期的行为是否纳入有效行为的考虑范围的评判则相对复杂一些。"厄立特里亚—也门仲裁案"中，厄立特里亚提出的一部分管理行为的证据，是由其前身埃塞俄比亚实施的，在1992

---

[1] Island of Palmas Case (Netherlands v. The U.S.A.), United Nations Reports of International Arbitration Awards, 1968, Vol. 2, p. 840.

[2] F. P. Walters, *A History of The League of Nations*, Oxford University Press, 1960, p. 491-492.

[3] 《维也纳条约法公约》第53条和第64条分别规定条约抵触强行法无效以及新的强行法出现后，原有条约与之抵触者无效。这一规则代表了习惯法规则，也适用于习惯法规则的效力判定。

年取得独立之前的将近20年间，厄立特里亚作为埃塞俄比亚的一部分，双方长期处于内战状态。仲裁庭认为作为评价证据的考虑因素，埃塞俄比亚实施的行为并不是"和平"的。[1]在具体证据的分析过程中，仲裁庭认为埃塞俄比亚抓捕和检查船只的行为的最重要目的是镇压厄立特里亚叛乱。仲裁庭认为尽管这些行为和厄立特里亚主张的渔业管理没有直接关系，但是根据埃塞俄比亚在回应也门对埃塞俄比亚逮捕本国渔民时表达的管辖认识来判断，也不乏法律上的重要意义[2]，也就是向争议对方表达了本国的管理意图，即埃塞俄比亚拥有争议地区的管辖权。

和平性要求可能衍生出对权利展示行为的另一个要求，就是行为应当是公开的。行为的和平性包含着权利行使者基于善意采取行动的认识。由于相关国家，尤其是权利直接受影响国家的承认或者默认是历史性所有权存在的另一个要件，因此善意认识在行动中的体现除了和平的行为方式以外，还应包括不在主观和客观上为相关国家认识争议所处的法律状态制造困难，也就是说，展示权利的行为必须是公开的。实践中，不为人知的国家行为虽然并不必然与非和平行为联系在一起，但确实被排除在有效行为的范围之外。"白礁岛案"中，马来西亚向法院提供了该国海军内部文件作为证据，其中所附的地图标明白礁等争议岛屿位于马来西亚的领海内。[3]与马来西亚针锋相对的是，新加坡也提供派遣海军前往争议岛屿附近巡逻的行动命令作为证据。法院认为无论马来西亚的地图还是新加坡的海军命令都是单方面行为且不为对方所知，这些秘密文件直到法律程序开始时才向外界公开。因此，这些文件，连同根据文件实施的巡逻行为，法院都不加以考虑。[4]

---

[1] 仲裁判决在此处的原文意思是除非将内战的行为包含在此处"和平"的术语内，否则厄立特里亚所依赖的埃塞俄比亚的行为便不是和平的。Eritrea-Yemen Arbitration (First Stage), International Legal Materials, Vol. 40: 900, p. 938 (2001).
[2] Eritrea-Yemen Arbitration (First Stage), International Legal Materials, Vol. 40: 900, p. 942 (2001).
[3] Case Concerning Sovereignty over Pedra Branca/Pulau Batu Puteh, Middle Rocks and South Ledge (Malaysia v. Singapore), International Court of Justice Reports, 2008, p. 85 - 86.
[4] Case Concerning Sovereignty over Pedra Branca/Pulau Batu Puteh, Middle Rocks and South Ledge (Malaysia v. Singapore), International Court of Justice Reports, 2008, p. 86.

四、行为的地理范围

(一) 范围的明确性

有效的权利展示行为只有在与主张涉及的地区密切相关时才具备作为证据的关联性。对于行为与地区间的关联性,国际司法实践在一般情况下持严格解释的立场,布鲁姆甚至主张由于通过历史性所有权所获得的权利是侵夺原本属于其他国家或属于国际社会权利的结果,对这类主张的地理范围解释应当是最严格的。[1]

"英挪渔业案"中,徐谟法官对判决中挪威基于历史性所有权取得洛波哈弗特(Lopphavet)海盆的结论表示不能认同。他在个别意见中认为挪威的主张存在一个重大瑕疵,作为管辖证据的捕鱼禁令没能精确表明禁令的适用范围,而对取得如果不存在管辖则为公海的区域来说,精确性是至关重要的[2]。"白礁岛案"中,马来西亚认为本国1969年颁布的领海扩展法案将领海扩展至并超越案件争议所涉及的白礁岛,主张白礁岛和周边水域在当时毫无疑问已经是马来西亚领土,新加坡对此未作抗议。新加坡则认为马来西亚立法中没有以任何方式明确领土、基线和领海边界,因此新加坡无从抗议。法庭支持新加坡的观点,认为马来西亚1969年立法的用语过于宽泛,没有指明法律的适用范围而只是泛泛提及"遍及马来西亚"。法庭进一步认为对立法来说,随立法颁布所出版的大比例地图是其主张精确性的必要来源。[3]

然而在实践中,除非争议涉及的是面积极小的岛屿,其他情况下很难保证国家实际管理的行为遍布争议涉及的全部地区,而对渺无人烟的小岛屿来说,国家的管辖在很多情况下也体现为在岛屿附近的水域巡航执法、打击海盗、管理渔业等活动。这时,司法机构会面临这样一个问题:管辖行为的有效性能够扩展到多大的地理范围。

---

[1] Yehuda Z. Blum, *Historic Titles in International Law*, Martinus Nijhoff, 1965, p. 240.
[2] Fisheries Case (The United Kingdom v. Norway), Seperate Opinion, International Court of Justice Reports, 1951, p. 157.
[3] Case Concerning Sovereignty over Pedra Branca/Pulau Batu Puteh, Middle Rocks and South Ledge (Malaysia v. Singapore), International Court of Justice Reports, 2008, p. 90.

(二) 邻近原则或自然整体原则

与上述范围紧密关联的是"邻近原则",也就是地理上接近某国的土地被视为该国领土的主权取得方式。地理上的接近在殖民时代被用来标注各国未来可能占领的势力范围,因此在19世纪曾被视为取得领土的依据之一。[1]随着实际占有被视为领土主权的最重要标志,这一原则作为主权取得依据在实践中逐步被放弃。

"帕尔玛斯岛仲裁案"中,胡伯法官明确拒绝美国以"邻近原则"作为主权依据,认为这一原则不但与持续有效展示主权的要求相冲突,而且由于缺乏精确性会造成随意的判决结果。但是法官没有完全排除地理上邻近作为衡量国家行为的考虑因素,当岛屿位于自然形成的边界内或者一组岛屿中的非主要岛屿时,单独的主权行为或实施于主岛的行为同样产生主权展示效果。[2]克劳德·H. M. 沃尔多克(C. H. M. Waldock)指出地理上的接近和其他地理考虑一起,构成确定有效占领边界的辅助事实,但是不构成独立的领土权源。[3]菲茨莫里斯认为如果争议地区能够证明和既存的主权属于同一个整体,这种情况可能免除国家实施具体行为的必要或者降低必要行为的程度。[4]詹宁斯补充了"邻近原则"作为确定实际占有范围的考虑因素,其效力取决于另一方能否提供实际占有的证据以及证据的强度。[5]

"厄立特里亚—也门仲裁案"中,也门认为其拥有主权的某些岛屿与争议岛屿共同构成一个自然形成的整体,根据"自然和地理整体原则",也门主张对其中某些岛屿行使的主权行为可以延伸到本案的全

---

[1] Malcolm Shaw, *Title to Territory in Africa*, Clarendon Press, 1986, p. 49-50.
[2] Island of Palmas case (Netherlands v. The U. S. A.), United Nations Reports of International Arbitration Awards, 1928, Vol. 2, p. 855.
[3] C. H. M. Waldock, *Disputed Sovereignties in the Falkland Islands Dependencies*, British Yearbook of International Law, Vol. 25: 311, p. 342 (1948).
[4] Gerald Fitzmaurice, *The Law and Procedure of International Court of Justice*, 1951-1954: Points of Substantive Law. Part II, British Yearbook of International Law, Vol. 32: 21, p. 73-74 (1955-1956).
[5] R. Y. Jennings, *The Acquisition of Territory in International Law*. Manchester University Press, 1963, p. 75.

部争议岛屿。[1]仲裁庭也注意到争议岛屿所形成的群岛穿越相对较窄海区的地理状况,但认为争议岛屿还可以继续分为分别接近厄立特里亚和也门海岸的次级岛屿群。仲裁庭认为"自然和地理整体原则"的应用产生两种可能:一种可能当然是如也门所主张的将对特定岛屿行为所产生的法律效果扩展到全部的争议岛屿。另一种可能则是,靠近各自海岸的岛屿被视为海岸的附属物,属于紧邻的沿海国,除非对岸国家能够提供更清晰更强的权源证据。[2]而由于争议两国独立时间较短,没有机会采取更多的实际管理行为,实际的判决结果很大程度上尊重了"邻近原则"带来的第二种假设,即接近海岸线的岛屿属于邻近的沿海国,最终将靠近也门和厄立特里亚海岸的岛屿主权分别授予两个国家。[3]

总的来说,国家行使权利的行为必须与主张的地域相关联,但是在特殊环境下,如沙漠荒原或者无人小岛,虽然没有直接针对相关地域的行为,也可以根据国家对邻近地区的实际管理假设它们属于同一主权者的管辖。但是,如果争议另一方提供了实际管辖的证据,那么这一假设不再成立,也就是说,邻近原则和自然整体原则都不能对抗建立在有效管理证据基础上提出的竞争主张。

五、地 图

在判断是否存在持续有效的国家管理时,争议双方通常向案件的裁决机构递交支持各自主张的地图作为证据,而裁决机关也将这类图表作为一类特别证据。国际法针对地图的一般规则是,地图本身不产生领土权源,其价值是在涉及领土和边界争议中提供争议地区实际管理情况的信息,它和其他证明争议所处特定环境的证据一起,构成确立或重新解释争议地区所处法律状态的外在证据。[4]当然,如果地图

---

[1] Eritrea-Yemen Arbitration (First Stage), International Legal Materials, Vol. 40: 900, p. 906 (2001).
[2] Eritrea-Yemen Arbitration (First Stage), International Legal Materials, Vol. 40: 900, p. 968-970 (2001).
[3] Eritrea-Yemen Arbitration (First Stage), International Legal Materials, Vol. 40: 900, p. 979-980 (2001).
[4] Frontier Dispute Case (Burkina Faso v. Mali), International Court of Justice Reports, 1986, p. 582.

是领土和边界条约或者国家法律或其他官方文件的组成部分，此时地图能够直接产生法律效果，甚至可以导致"禁止反言"。[1]

地图作为证据的价值大小取决于它所提供信息的可信度。就来源而言，与相关争议无关的中立方地图价值最大。就制作时间和制作方法来说，越是接近争议发生时刻的地图和采用高科技手段制作的地图的证据价值越大。根据制作者和制作目的来评判，官方地图和表明边界或领土归属为目的的地图价值高于私人地图和以商业或其他目的制作的地图。总之，地图在争议中的可依赖性主观上表现为与争议双方利益并无关联性，客观上表现为忠实反映争议地域的实际情况。但是，即便具有极高可信度，地图在争议解决中仍然只是扮演辅助确认国家主权存在证据的角色。仅凭地图本身在一般情况下是不产生任何法律效果的。

在两种情况下，地图自身产生法律效果：第一种情况是地图作为具有法律拘束力的文件的一部分。如果在领土和边界相关条约中附有地图以直观表明条约中文字的含义，此时地图作为缔约方合意的特定表达方式，效力等同于条约。如果在条约生效后，缔约方以地图勘定作业方式落实条约内容的，那么此时地图则根据情况不同，可以被视为当事国嗣后所定关于条约解释或其适用的协定或惯例，成为与条约正文一起构成条约解释的考虑范围。第二种情况是地图构成国家官方文件正文或者附件的一部分。地图表明国家有意实施管辖的地域范围，构成领土取得认识的表达方式。在这两种情况下，地图已经转化为国家行为的直接组成部分，而不是证明争议地点法律情况的间接证据。

无论是作为表明争议情况的外在证据还是意图直接产生有拘束力的法律效果，地图都必须能够"明确定义"争议的情况。"利吉丹岛、西巴丹岛主权案"中，印度尼西亚和马来西亚对荷兰和英国在1891年就荷属婆罗洲和英国保护国之间的边界条约中第4条"边界沿北纬4度10分线继续向东"是否延伸到争议岛屿所处的海域有不同理解[2]。印度尼西亚向法院提供递交给荷兰国会的解释性备忘录中附带的地图，

---

[1] Temple of Preah Vihear Case (Cambodia v. Thailand), International Court of Justice Reports, 1962, p. 36.

[2] Sovereignty over Pulau Ligitan and Pulau Sipadan (Indonesia v. Malaysia), International Court of Justice Reports, 2002, p. 646.

其中存在一条延伸到利吉丹岛和西巴丹岛所在海域的红线。印度尼西亚认为红线代表海上岛屿归属的分界线，并进一步主张由于解释性备忘录已经由外交人员交给英国政府，因此其中所附的地图应当被视为《维也纳条约法公约》第31条第3款（乙）项所指的"嗣后在条约适用方面确定各当事国对条约解释之协定之任何惯例"。法院观察到地图上有4条不同颜色的边界线，只有红色线延伸出海洋一直达到争议岛屿所在的位置，解释性备忘录中没有评论红线延伸的理由，荷兰国会也没有对此进行讨论。[1]而在地图中，位于红线以北的岛屿都被明确标示出来，但是红线以南利吉丹岛和西巴丹岛所在的位置却没有标识。结合双方在缔约过程中的谈判都未明确提及这两个岛屿，法院认为荷兰国会可能根本没有认识到红线以南还存在本案争议的两个小岛，因此也不可能将红线视为岛屿主权的分界线。因此，该地图不能被视为具有《维也纳条约法公约》中当事国对条约解释之协定之任何惯例的作用。[2]

综上所述，除非作为国家间协议或者国家单方面行为的组成部分，地图自身的价值仅限于提供国家行为和主张存在的证据，如果说有效管理是主权的证据，那么地图就是主权证据的证据。也因为地图本身不是国际法认可的领土权源产生方式，因此当地图内容不能明确表达争议情况时，解决办法不是寻找另一份地图，而是直接检查国家展示主权的实际行为。

第三节 相关国家的同意

历史性所有权的另一项要件是相关国家的同意，即相关国家以明示或默示方式肯定权利主张者的行为具有法律效力。实践中，主张权利的各方证据力度相对平衡甚至双方证据都很微弱的情况时有出现，此时，司法机构需要采取一些技术来判断争议国家对事实情况的合意或其他第三国对争议状况的看法。这些技术性手段包括承认、默认和

---

[1] Sovereignty over Pulau Ligitan and Pulau Sipadan (Indonesia v. Malaysia), International Court of Justice Reports, 2002, p. 646.

[2] Sovereignty over Pulau Ligitan and Pulau Sipadan (Indonesia v. Malaysia), International Court of Justice Reports, 2002, p. 650.

禁止反言，其本身不能产生权利，但是可以辅助解释争议的实施和法律情况，在特定的情况下，这些技术手段本身就产生确定主权归属的效果。对于历史性所有权来说，一方面，由于取得对象是原先属于其他国家的领土或者不属于任何国家的公海，因此获得权利相关国家对行使权利行为的认可，在这种情况下变得必不可少。另一方面，随着历史性所有权在领土取得中的适用范围扩展到权属不明的土地，与争议本身并不直接相关国家的态度被纳入考虑范围，成为判断权利是否巩固的重要因素。

一、相关国家

传统国际法眼中的历史性所有权以逆权占有为基础，权利取得的对象或者是其他国家的领土，或者是不能成为主权取得对象的公海。对于前者来说，相关国家是非常明确的，就是土地的原主权国。对后者来说，相关国家在理论上也是清楚的，由于公海被视为人类的共有物，相关国家应该是整个国际社会的成员，也就是说理论上每个国家，都可以被视为历史性水域的相关国家。然而在实践中，要求所有的国家都对沿海国的历史性所有权主张做出反应显然是不现实的，反之多数国家没有对主张做出反应也不能推定它们默认了主张的有效性。进一步说，在对沿海国主张做出反应的国家之间，不同国家的反应对历史性所有权形成的影响也是不一样的。菲茨莫里斯认为来自直接受主张影响国家的同意足以使历史性权利的主张合法化，同样，来自不存在现实或潜在利益国家的反对对实践几乎没有影响。[1] 国际法委员会在考虑单独一个国家的反对是否足以阻却历史性所有权的有效性时曾引用吉德尔的观点，认为单独一个国家的反对不足以阻止惯例的形成，而且更不能在不考虑反对国的性质、地理和其他情况的基础上将全部反对意见置于同等重要的地位。[2]

国际法委员会曾担心接受上述观点会产生"所有国家一律平等，

---

[1] Gerald Fitzmaurice, *The Law and Procedure of International Court of Justice*, 1951 – 1954: *Points of Substantive Law*. Part Ⅱ, British Yearbook of International Law, Vol. 32: 21, p. 31 – 32 (1955 – 1956).

[2] Juridical Regime of Historic Waters, Including Historic Bays, International Law Commission Yearbook, 1962 (2), p. 17.

但有些国家比其他国家更加平等"的效果[1],但是考察历史性水域争议的发生为这种表面的不公平提供了比较现实的解释。由于历史性所有权的争议多数因沿海国周边的国家或在该地区有特殊利益的国家发表反对态度而起,因此司法机构寻找相关国家态度的证据时,其特别重视这些国家已经做出的表态是再自然不过的了。[2]尽管国际法委员会的结论事实上用一个实然角度的解释回答了应然角度的问题,但是答案显而易见,那就是主张国的周边国家和在该地区有特殊利益的国家。

随着国际法实践的发展,历史性所有权的适用范围逐渐扩展到虽不属于无主地,但是主权归属不明的土地。理论上判断这类土地的归属和无主地并无不同,都建立在有效管理证据比较的基础上,因此相关国家之间的态度似乎不是必要条件,更不用说第三方国家的态度,它们对任何一方的承认对另一方而言都是无关之务(Res Inter Alios Acta)。但在实践中,正是因为争议的双方都不曾建立过确定无疑的主权,此时不但争议国家之间就领土情况产生的承认或默认会直接影响主权的归属,第三方国家对"争议领土属于某国"的广泛认知同样是领土取得过程中的重要条件。"领土和海洋争议案"中,尽管国际法院同意哥伦比亚与周边国家达成的条约不影响尼加拉瓜的立场,但也认为第三方国家的实践整体上支持了哥伦比亚的主张。[3]在这里,第三方国家的态度虽然没有产生决定性影响,但是对哥伦比亚的主张起到确认和巩固的作用。事实上,正如詹宁斯所说,无需过分关注理论上的解释,只需要注意到在真实的情况中,承认和事实上的默认几乎总是国际司法机构在处理此类领土争端中首先关注并纳入考虑的因素。[4]因此,至少对适用于取得归属不明的土地的历史性所有权来说,第三方国家的态度是权利的构成要件。

---

[1] Juridical Regime of Historic Waters, Including Historic Bays, International Law Commission Yearbook, 1962 (2), p. 18.
[2] Juridical Regime of Historic Waters, Including Historic Bays, International Law Commission Yearbook, 1962 (2), p. 18.
[3] Territorial and Maritime Dispute (Columbia v. Nicaragua), International Court of Justice Reports, 2012, p. 656.
[4] R. Y. Jennings, *The Acquisition of Territory in International Law*, Manchester University Press, 1963, p. 40

相关国家范围扩展的直接结果是能够产生或确认历史性所有权的反应方式不再局限于默认，明示的承认也可能成为决定历史性所有权存在与否的国家态度。当然，其中最重要的或者说起直接作用的，仍然是直接受历史性所有权主张影响的国家的态度，但是，在考察相关国家的反应之前，需要判断相关国家是否了解权利主张国的主张和行为。

二、认　知

相关国家意识到发生了与其相关的法律情势是它们做出反应的前提条件。布鲁姆认为只有在受新领土主张影响的国家认识到这种情势后，才能期待受影响的国家公开反对新的领土情势。[1] 对历史性水域来说，菲茨莫里斯同样指出仅有反对本身（per se）是否暗示相关国家的同意需要结合所处环境进行判断，特别是有关的实践是否被其他国家所知晓。[2] 因此，我们有必要分析何种情况下可以判断相关国家已经了解了权利主张，反之，在何种情况下相关国家可以以不知情作为缺乏反应的抗辩理由。

（一）告　知

理论上相关国家有两种了解法律情势的途径，一是通过权利主张国的实际告知行为，二通过其他间接途径，其中主要是主张国持续的主权展示行为（将在下文"推断的认知"部分论述）。将本国的权利主张和内容明确告知受相关主张影响的国家，是确定相关国家知晓的最明确方法，以这种方式传递的认知排除可能因行为模糊产生的理解偏差，相关国家可以在了解并理解主张的前提下决定是否做出反应，对实践中判断相关国家作为或不作为的意义帮助最大，但是除非双方或各方之间存在明示的规定，正式的告知行为并不是一项国际法义务。1885 年关于非洲部分殖民地划分的西非会议《柏林总议定书》第 34 条曾规定，此后对非洲领土占领的效力将与是否将占领意图告知其他

---

[1] Yehuda Z. Blum, *Historic Titles in International Law*, Martinus Nijhoff, 1965, p. 130.
[2] Gerald Fitzmaurice, *The Law and Procedure of International Court of Justice*, 1951–1954: *Points of Substantive Law*. Part Ⅱ, British Yearbook of International Law, Vol. 32: 21, p. 33 (1955–1956).

与会国联系在一起[1]，但是议定书中规定的告知义务仅是对缔约国取得非洲殖民地这一特定事项做出的规定。胡伯法官在"帕尔玛斯岛仲裁案"中指出，告知和其他形式的领土取得方式一样，明确的法律规定是其合法性的唯一来源。西非会议上采纳的针对非洲大陆的规则并不当然适用于其他地区。[2]

可见，正式的告知作为法律义务，既没有脱离条约存在过，实践中也从未被适用于非洲以外的其他地区，因此主权主张国告知相关国家取得意图并不是一项习惯法规则。当然，为了了解争议土地的法律情况或者为了获取更多的肯定，国家可以主动将主张告知相关国家。实践中，告知的情况比较少，更多的情况是通过实际行为，推断相关国家已经了解到相关的主张。

(二) 推断的认知

推断知晓的理论基础在于相关国家有理由知晓相应的主张。实践中，相关国家即使没有得到直接的告知，仍可能通过其他途径间接了解与本国有关的权利主张，而理论上，如果国家认为自己是特定土地的主权持有者，那么理应对与本国土地相关主张保持相当的警觉。例如"东格陵兰法律地位案"中，丹麦在与周边一系列国家签订的商贸条约中，都明确将格陵兰岛排除在条约适用范围以外，而挪威本身就是其中一些条约的缔约国。因此法院推断挪威知晓丹麦对格陵兰的主权主张。[3]

国际法并没有规定通过哪些途径获得的认知应当被视为相关国家已经知晓主张的证据，但是主张国的权利展示行为，无疑是最主要的认知获取渠道。布鲁姆提出实践在更多情况下无法证明国家是否真正知晓领土所处的情势，因此国际法选择以基于主张国行为和争议所处环境的情况，作为推测相关国家已经知道主张的证据，称为"推断的

---

[1] John Bassett Moore, *A Digest of International Law*, Government Printing Office, 1906, p. 267–268.
[2] Island of Palmas case (Netherlands v. The U.S.A.), United Nations Reports of International Arbitration Awards, 1968, Vol. 2, p. 868.
[3] Legal Status of East Greenland (Denmark v. Norwegian), Permenent Court of International Justice, Series A./B. 1933, p. 51.

认知"（Constructive Knowledge）。[1] 国际法委员会也认为对于历史性水域来说，考虑相关国家态度的起点事实上是沿海国广为人知的主权行使，而不是其他国家对沿海国行为真实的认知。[2] 那么，不管以何种方式命名推断认知的情况，问题实质上已经转化为对主张国行为和客观环境的条件要求。满足条件则可推定相关国家已经知晓主张，成为判断后续表态的起步点，而不满足条件则可认为相关国家并不了解情况，构成其不作为的抗辩理由。

对权利展示的行为来说，能够产生相关国家认知推断的行为首先应当是公开的。没有公开的行为作为前提，根本无法讨论行为是否产生广为人知的效果。公开性作为判断主权展示行为的有效性因素已经在前文中阐释，此处将考虑的是，对相关国家的认知来说，公开的行为在何种条件下产生认知推测的效果。布鲁姆认为当行为证据在其所处环境中无可置疑地指向领土权利的取得而不存在其他解释的可能时，国际法就将推定受影响国家对这一情势具备"推断的认知"[3]。这段论述可以被视为对认知推断的两阶段工作，即公开的行为足以推断相关国家了解争议的存在以及相关国家对争议的性质和内容理解无误。

和对主权展示行为有效性的判断一样，行为公开性和相关国家认知的关系，同样建立在根据个案案情综合各种因素考虑的基础上。"英挪渔业案"或许为我们判断这些相关因素和参照标准提供了参考。国际法院在案件处理中没有接受英国对挪威直线划界实践并不知晓的主张。法院认为作为北海的沿岸国，这片水域的渔业活动对英国有着重大利益。同时，英国本身就是关注海洋法特别是关注航行自由的海洋国家，没有理由无视挪威1869年关于直线基线划界的法令。相应地，同样位于这一地区的法国在挪威法令颁布后立刻向后者发出解释这一法令的要求。[4] 在该案中，英国特别关注海洋法的国家特征，对北海渔业和海洋自由的特殊利益，以及和挪威共处北海沿岸的地理情况，

---

[1] Yehuda Z. Blum, *Historic Titles in International Law*, Martinus Nijhoff, 1965, p. 130.
[2] Juridical Regime of Historic Waters, Including Historic Bays, International Law Commission Yearbook, 1962 (2), p. 18.
[3] Yehuda Z. Blum, *Historic Titles in International Law*, Martinus Nijhoff, 1965, p. 144 – 145.
[4] Fisheries Case (The United Kingdom v. Norway), International Court of Justice Reports, 1951, p. 139.

构成推断英国知晓挪威实践的相关因素。而对北海利益不及英国，且自身利益更偏向欧洲大陆的法国迅速对挪威实践做出反应则提供了推测的参照系，尽管参照系并不是推断知晓的必要条件。地理位置和直接利益作为相关因素意味着对实践中被视为受历史性所有权主张影响的相关国家来说，主张国公开的权利行使行为就足以产生了解争议存在的推断。

一种观点怀疑这会过分加重相关国家的责任，使它们不得不时刻保持对沿海国行为的关注。[1]国际法委员会则认为如果一个国家对相关海域确实存在利益，那么关注这一海域其他国家的一举一动实在是再自然不过的事情。国家对沿海国行为毫无认识只能说明该国在此没有或只有很少的利益。[2]这一解释适用于陆地领土同样具有说服力，领土主权对国家的义务要求首先体现为保障本国在全部领土内实施排他性权利，当其他国家公开在本国领土行使主权权利时，国家没有任何理由忽视这一行为。同样，对于某一争议领土深感兴趣的国家，也没有理由无视主权竞争国公开的权利行为。因此，相关国家承担对公开行为的注意义务并不过分。

（三）认知的准确性

相关国家可以辩解，尽管行为是公开的，但是不足以产生与主张一致的认识结果，以作为其没有做出反应的合理理由。"利吉丹岛、西巴丹岛主权案"中，印度尼西亚主张附有海上岛屿归属分界线地图的解释性备忘录由荷兰外交人员交给英国驻荷兰大使，并由大使派遣官员携带两份地图复印件送回英国外交部。因此英国政府对地图的不做回应只能解释为对地图上岛屿归属线表示认同。[3]法院则认为解释性备忘录和地图并不是由荷兰政府直接交给英国政府，而是通过后者在海牙的外交官转递的。尽管这名官员注意到了地图的价值，但是并没有向英国政府特别指明其中表示的岛屿分界线。在这种情况下，英国

---

[1] Juridical Regime of Historic Waters, Including Historic Bays, International Law Commission Yearbook, 1962 (2), p. 19.

[2] Juridical Regime of Historic Waters, Including Historic Bays, International Law Commission Yearbook, 1962 (2), p. 19.

[3] Sovereignty over Pulau Ligitan and Pulau Sipadan (Indonesia v. Malaysia), International Court of Justice Reports, 2002, p. 648 - 649.

政府没有对备忘录中的岛屿分界线做出反应不能被认为是默认。[1]

法院对印度尼西亚主张的不认同包括两点依据，首先是行为的主体，即并非在双方政府之间直接完成。其次是负责传递的外交官员没有使英国政府对代表岛屿归属的红线产生正确的认识。法院的逻辑不是说通过外交机构转递的主张不构成告知或能够产生主张认识的行为；而是因为在该案中，岛屿的主权归属本身不是条约谈判内容，备忘录作为条约的附件在文本中也没有提及主权问题，只是在附属的地图中以一条延伸到划界区域以外的直线作为岛屿主权分割的主张。在这种情况下，英国的合理预期是作为条约附件，备忘录内容不会超过谈判所涉及的和条约所规定的内容。如果超过这个预期，则需要荷兰特别指出超出部分的内容以判断这一主张的法律性质。而案件中，低级别的外交官员转递会让英国政府产生备忘录不会超过条约规定的预期，而官员确实没有指出其中红线所代表的岛屿分界线的含义。因此法院推断英国不知道荷兰事实上提出了岛屿主权的要求。而尽管英国驻荷兰的外交官员需要承担未向本国政府指明地图上还有岛屿分界线的责任，但他的过失来自荷兰官员在递交备忘录时就未说明地图上各条边界的含义，因此最主要的责任在于荷兰没有提供充分的机会让英国了解其主张。

事实上，不管是实际还是推断的告知，核心都是对主张的正确认识这一标准。对前者来说，相关国家通过主张国的直接告知获得认识；对后者来说，则通过具体环境下的主张国的行为来判断相关国家的认知。当相关国家已经对争议的法律情况产生正确认识时，受主张影响的国家已经处于需要表达自己态度的时刻，此时的不作为或作为将成为历史性所有权能否成立的关键因素。

三、同意的形式

（一）默认和容忍

对于持有领土主权的国家和持有共有物权利的国际社会成员，国际法并不假设它们对有效占领行为的不做反应就是放弃了自己的权利。

---

[1] Sovereignty over Pulau Ligitan and Pulau Sipadan (Indonesia v. Malaysia), International Court of Justice Reports, 2002, p. 650.

恰恰相反，国际法需要得到相关国家同意的确切证据，才能做出权利已经转移的判断。一般认为，同意的表达形式包括默认和承认。由于历史性所有权并不是国家间转移领土主权的唯一法律依据，因此这两种表达方式也不必然和历史性所有权的产生联系在一起。在历史性所有权的证明过程中，默认即便不是相关国家同意的唯一表现形式，也仍然是最重要的表达方式之一[1]，但是国际法学者对默认的看法并不一致，这种不一致集中体现在定义上。国际法院将默认定义为等同于以单方面行为表达的默示承认（Tacit Consent），这种行为会被其他国家解释为同意。[2]这个笼统定义从文字上看没有排除默认概念本身长期存在的其他可能。

早期的国际法学者将默认视为以行动表达承认的一种方式，承认的效果不是推断的而是直接表达的，他们认为对历史性水域不表态就代表同意的说法是很可疑的，并指出单方面的主权行使，即使没有国家反对，也不能当然产生效力，除非国家以明示或毫无疑问的行动表达了默认。[3]换句话说，消极不作为在任何情况下都不能成为推断同意的起点。

支持消极行为可以视为默认的国际法学者提供了两条思路。一条思路的代表人物伊恩·C. 麦克吉本（I. C. MacGibbon）不但认为国家在面对威胁或危害其权利的情况时的不作为即可被认为是默认，而且认为默认必须是一个消极的概念。[4]布鲁姆拥护这一观点，他提出国际社会中存在这样一个假设，国家不会对威胁自己权利的行为视而不见，那么受影响国家此时的沉默是推断国家对新法律情势默认的基础。非但如此，构成历史性所有权的只能是消极的默认，因为历史性所有权的作用本来就是基于不作为进行的推断，来弥补无法确切获得相关国家的明示承认。积极默认不但在效果上而且在行为方式上都等于承认，那么在已经有国际承认（International Recognition）

---

[1] 对陆地领土的取得来说，约翰逊和布鲁姆都认为历史性所有权是时效取得在国际法领域的体现，因此默认且只有默认才是历史性的法律基础。在取得历史性水域时，相关国家明示和默示的赞同都是国际社会赞同的表达方式。
[2] Delimitation of the Maritime Boundary in the Gulf of Maine Area (Canada v. The U. S. A.), International Court of Justice Reports, 1984, p. 305.
[3] Historic Bays: Memorandum by the Secretariat of the United Nations, A/CONF. 13/1, 1957, p. 34.
[4] I. C. MacGibbon, *The Scope of Acquiescence in International Law*, British Yearbook of International Law, Vol. 31: 143, p. 143 (1954).

作为国际法规则的情况下，默认就没有独立存在的价值了。[1]

另一条思路的代表人物德·维舍认为，证明历史性所有权的巩固不限于所谓的"默认"，足够长时间的不反对就足以证明权利的巩固。在德·维舍的历史性所有权体系内，积极行为的默认依然有其地位，同时长期的消极反应也能产生法律效力。[2]国际法委员会事实上也持这种观点，委员会一方面不同意积极默认的主张，认为这一观点意味着如果没有行为上的同意无论持续多久的有效行为都不能产生法律效力，等于否定时间作为历史性所有权中的历史性要素。另一方面，委员会也担心不作为或者容忍即推断为默认，将过分放宽沿海国取得公海的条件，使历史性水域不再成为海洋法上的例外制度。委员会发现无论如何，各方能取得的共识是相关国家的不作为足够容许历史性所有权的产生。而鉴于"默认"作为术语的模糊性，委员会建议"默认"作为积极默认的术语来使用，而选择"容忍"（Toleration）用来代表消极默认。[3]德·维舍和国际法委员会的共同点是在形式上虚置默认的定义之争，实质上承认单纯的消极不作为可以产生历史性所有权，但不是历史性所有权所需相关国家态度的唯一表达形式。

如果把术语的界定放在一边，可以看到对"默认"的三种观点可以归结为对两个实质性问题的不同回答：第一，长时间不作为是否产生同意的效果。第二，长时间不作为产生的同意效果是不是历史性所有权所需国家态度的唯一表达方式。对第一个问题的回答理论上看起来已有定论。詹宁斯和布朗利都认为国家在有需要并有权利做出抗议的时候，仅仅是忽略抗议就可以产生默认。[4]国际法院在"白礁岛案"的判决可以终结这个问题的讨论。该案中马来西亚持有白礁岛的原始主权，在回答其主权是否移交给新加坡时，法院指出国际法没有对主权转移施加特定形式上的要求，某些环境中拥有主权的国家失于应对

---

[1] Yehuda Z. Blum, *Historic Titles in International Law*, Martinus Nijhoff, 1965, p. 132.
[2] Charles de Visscher, *Théories et Réalités en Droit International Public* 4th edition. Editions A. Pedone, 1970, p. 226.
[3] Juridical Regime of Historic Waters, Including Historic Bays, International Law Commission Yearbook, 1962 (2), p. 16.
[4] R. Y. Jennings, *The Acquisition of Territory in International Law*, Manchester University Press, 1963, p. 36. Aslo see Ian Brownlie, *Principles of Public International Law*, 7th editon, Oxford University Press, 2008, p. 152.

其他国家的主权行为将导致主权转移。特别是其他国家的主权行为要求权利持有者做出回应时，缺乏回应足以构成默认。[1]也就是说，在对相关国家要求最为严格的逆权占有状态下，单纯的消极不作为就足以产生同意的效果。因此，首先应当认定默认可以是消极的行为。

历史性所有权是否只能经由消极不作为产生的观点则牵涉到对承认、默认以及默示承认的定义界定。习惯国际法的要求是取得不符合既存国际法规则的权利，需要得到受影响国家或者国际社会的同意。同时由于国际法尚未发育成熟的现实，行为是否合法的标准是不断变动的。由于国际法缺乏拥有强制管辖权的合法性裁决机构，国家行为是否能在现行的法律规则框架下取得效力必须依靠其他国家的同意。因此，从法律效果的角度来看，探求相关国家态度的目的在于寻求权利受影响国家的单方面承诺。明示的条约或协议、积极的行为和需要做出反应时的消极不作为都产生单方面承诺的效果。一般情况下，同意应当是明示的，但很多情况下国家怠于表明自己的态度。为了保证权利不因其他国家不作为而受到影响，在缺乏明示同意证据时以不作为即同意的假设补足权利取得时相关国家态度的要件。

我们发现此时争议似乎陷入一个概念游戏的怪圈，麦克吉本和布鲁姆的体系中只有消极的不作为被视为默认，而从协议或行为上取得同意都被认为是承认。因此，默认只能是消极的行为，积极的默认就等于明示承认，不但取消了默认的地位，也取消了历史性所有权的地位。布朗利则认为，只有通过条约或者协议表达的同意是承认，而从行为表达的同意是默认，不作为在特定情形下效果等于默认。[2]在"缅因海湾划界案"和"白礁岛案"中，国际法院的态度都是需要反应时的不作为可以等同于（equivalent to）默认。[3]可见国际法院和布朗利立场一致，不作为本身不是默认，只是在特定环境中产生默认的效果。实践中，长时间不作为也总是和默认联系在一起，无论是主张国还是裁决机构，仍然将疏于抗议置于默认测试中检验其是否产生相

---

[1] Case Concerning Sovereignty over Pedra Branca/Pulau Batu Puteh, Middle Rocks and South Ledge (Malaysia v. Singapore), International Court of Justice Reports, 2008, p. 50.

[2] Ian Brownlie, *Principles of Public International Law*, 7th editon, Oxford University Press, 2008, p. 152.

[3] Case Concerning Sovereignty over Pedra Branca/Pulau Batu Puteh, Middle Rocks and South Ledge (Malaysia v. Singapore), International Court of Justice Reports, 2008, p. 51.

关国家单方面效果的目的。[1]

在对第二个问题的三种答案中，共同点在于长时间不作为是权利产生的要素。不同意见在于由行为产生的同意是否产生历史性所有权。事实上，否认这一点的麦克吉本和布鲁姆并不否认不作为是产生领土主权的来源，只是坚持这种来自行为的同意应当被视为承认而不是默认。这一观点在逻辑推演上并无疑问。实践中来自行为的同意构成默认是确定无疑的，但是裁决机构从未明确表态在此基础上的领土主权是否来自历史性所有权，而且，实践中领土和边界争端中确实少有积极默认的先例。因此从实践上无法证明亦无法证伪积极默认产生历史性所有权这个结论。有鉴于此，再加上历史性所有权内涵已经从不符合一般国际法规则的逆权占有扩展到对争议土地的长期占有，与其绕着默认的概念定义兜圈子，不如直接从行为表现将主权确定联系起来，将积极默认和消极默认共同视为历史性所有权的相关国家态度。

（二）承　认

将历史性所有权内涵扩大化的解决思路伴随着另一个问题，即明示的"承认"是不是构成历史性所有权的相关国家态度。理论上各方对这个问题立场一致，以协议或条约方式产生的领土主权，其效力基于国家间形式上的合意，不需要国家实际管辖的行为，因此与历史性所有权无关，但是实践似乎并非全然如此。对历史性水域来说，唯一的法律基础就是历史性所有权。而国际承认是取得海洋法上历史性所有权的决定性因素，其表现形式既包括明示的承认也包括没有抗议。[2] 也就是说，相关国家以条约或口头形式明示承认沿海国的主权主张一样可以作为海洋历史性所有权的效力来源。

而对于取得归属权不明的土地来说，第三方国家通过条约和协议表达的承认和直接争议国的默认同样起到明确争议土地法律地位的作用。詹宁斯认为尽管第三方国家的承认在没有实际占有的情况下不能

---

[1] Land and Maritime Boundary between Cameroon and Nigeria (Cameroon v. Nigeria, Equatorial Guinea intervening), International Court of Justice Reports, 2002, p. 349 – 355.

[2] Historic Bays: Memorandum by the Secretariat of the United Nations, A/CONF. 13/1, 1957, p. 34 – 35.

创造权利，但确实协助和加速了巩固的进程。[1]当然，第三方国家的承认可以作为主张国有效占领的间接证据，但不能对抗直接相关国的态度表达。[2]

因此，这样一个结论也许比较贴合实际情况：相关国家同意的具体形式包括明示的条约或协议、积极的行为和需要做出反应时的消极不作为。领土取得中，原先持有主权的国家通过行为表达的同意或对主张国主权展示行为不做反应，直接决定历史性所有权的存在与否。如果争议土地权属不明，则相关国家通过行为表达的同意或者不作为以及第三方国家的明示同意可以成为明确争议土地法律状态的证据，用以判断主张国的权利是否已经巩固。对历史性水域来说，相关国家通过协议或行为表达的同意，或者不作为都被视为国际承认的表现形式，构成历史性所有权产生的要件。

四、抗　议

在产生历史性所有权的相关国家态度中，通过长时间不作为产生的同意效果是基于国家不应该对不利本国权利行为置之不顾的假设，那么当国家以抗议的实际行为表明其反对态度时，前述的假设将不复存在，从而进一步通过两种作用影响历史性所有权的产生。一方面，推翻不作为等于同意的假设，直接阻止历史性所有权的取得。另一方面，则作为否定主张国主权展示的有效性的间接证据。对于主权的原持有国来说，抗议终止了同意的假设，此时主权的原持有国即便没有有效管理的行为，也能继续维持本国的合法主权。[3]而对归属不明的争议领土来说，竞争主张国的抗议不但阻却推测默认的产生，还进一步暗示对方的主权展示并非不受干扰，从而影响占领是否有效的判断，

---

[1] R. Y. Jennings, *The Acquisition of Territory in International Law*, Manchester University Press, 1963, p. 40-41.

[2] Territorial and Maritime Dispute between Nicaragua and Honduras in the Caribbean Sea (Nicaragua v. Honduras), International Court of Justice Reports, 2007, p. 726.

[3] "喀麦隆和尼日利亚之间的陆地与海洋边界案"中，喀麦隆主张自己持有条约赋予的领土主权，因此不需要表现出实际主权展示，尼日利亚所主张的管理行为实际上是对喀麦隆主权的侵犯。国际法院注意到喀麦隆持有条约赋予的主权，因此认为判断案件的要点在于有没有证据表明该国默认将主权转移给尼日利亚。Land and Maritime Boundary between Cameroon and Nigeria (Cameroon v. Nigeria, Equatorial Guinea intervening), International Court of Justice Reports, 2002, p. 353.

这一点对历史性水域主张也是适用的。[1] 当然，要达到产生上述效果的目的，国际法对抗议施加了一定的条件限制，这些条件可以被简单归纳为对谁来抗议、如何抗议以及何时抗议三个问题的回答。

(一) 抗议的主体

有效的抗议应当来自处于如果不作为则被视为同意的那部分相关国家，换句话说，第三方国家的承认对历史性所有权的巩固有辅助作用，但是它们的抗议对权利的取得与否不产生影响。在陆地领土的争议中，有权利提出抗议就是持竞争主张的一方，一般只有一个国家。而正如上文分析相关国家时所述，历史性水域的相关国家往往不止一个，问题是如果只有其中一部分国家甚至一个国家抗议沿海国的主张，此时抗议能否阻却历史性所有权的产生？如果不能，那么，抗议国家能否取得类似习惯法形成过程中持续反对者的权利？

麦克吉本将抗议对本国权利的影响分为两类处理，当其他国家的同意使历史性所有权实践业已成为法律秩序的一部分时，单独一个国家的反复抗议，如果没有启动其他争端解决机制，不但不影响权利的效力，自身也将失去反对的权利。[2] 如果一国在主张国实践开始阶段就采取所有可能措施表明反对的态度，情况则比较复杂。"英挪渔业案"中英方质疑挪威的观点暗示在只有一个国家抗议的情况下，如果新的主张被接受为对其他所有国家都有效，那么不管抗议国反对了多长时间，采取了包括外交和法律层面的解决措施，都要受新主张拘束的观点。麦克吉本认为这种情况积极反对的国家因其他国家的不作为而失去本国权利缺乏合理性，无论是从逻辑还是公义的角度来看，适当的结论都应该是明确证明持反对态度的国家，不因其他国家的接受而失去本国的权利。[3]

对于部分或者单一的抗议能否阻却历史性所有权的产生，应该看到实践中即使得到世界公认的历史性海湾，也极少能取得所有相关国

---

[1] I. C. MacGibbon, *Some Observation on the Part of Protest in International Law*, British Yearbook of International Law, Vol. 30: 293, p. 319 (1953).

[2] I. C. MacGibbon, *Some Observation on the Part of Protest in International Law*, British Yearbook of International Law, Vol. 30: 293, p. 318 (1953).

[3] I. C. MacGibbon, *Some Observation on the Part of Protest in International Law*, British Yearbook of International Law, Vol. 30: 293, p. 318 (1953).

的一致同意。因此在多数相关国家肯定的情况下，少数或个别国家的不赞成并不妨碍历史性所有权的产生；但是抗议国家数量对权利产生的影响并非建立在数学统计的基础上，国际法没有赋予每个国家的抗议以同等效力，特定环境中一国的抗议效力高于另一国，甚至可能高于多国同意之和。[1]例如布鲁姆就认为海洋大国的抗拒足以阻却一个得到多数国家肯定的实践而取得国际法上的效力。[2]因此，少量或个别国家的抗议对历史性所有权的影响还需要根据客观环境和各国所抗议的方式和内容做出综合判断。

(二) 抗议的内容和方式

国际法对有效的抗议方式和内容并没有特别的规定。就内容而言，抗议的有效性和效力取决于抗议内容是否准确代表了现实，至少应表明抗议国坚信被抗议的行为已经危害到本国的权利。[3]"喀麦隆和尼日利亚间的陆地与海洋边界案"中，喀麦隆在抗议照会中陈述，喀麦隆政府再次确认被尼日利亚占领的土地是喀麦隆领土，并强烈抗议尼日利亚国民和军队对喀麦隆领土的非法占领。此外，要求尼日利亚政府召回正占领喀麦隆土地的尼日利亚人并放弃一切试图占领的行为。[4]因此，询问性质的政府间通信一般不能被视为表达对主权归属的不同意见。另外，抗议书一般会陈述抗议的理由并声明本国权利不受被抗议国行为的影响[5]，这样做可以让抗议国在争端解决过程中占据有利地位，但并不是有效抗议的必然要求。至于抗议的表达方式，通过政府间外交渠道传递的抗议是国家实践中最常见的做法，这种抗议既可以是书面的，在确保内容准确性的基础上也可以采取口头传递方式。[6]

---

[1] Historic Bays: Memorandum by the Secretariat of the United Nations, A/CONF. 13/1, 1957, p. 18.
[2] Yehuda Z. Blum, *Historic Titles in International Law*, Martinus Nijhoff, 1965, p. 170.
[3] I. C. MacGibbon, *Some Observation on the Part of Protest in International Law*, British Yearbook of International Law, Vol. 30: 293, p. 297 (1953).
[4] Memoire de la Republique du Cameroun, International Court of Justice Reports, 2002, p. 591.
[5] I. C. MacGibbon, *Some Observation on the Part of Protest in International Law*, British Yearbook of International Law, Vol. 30: 293, p. 297 (1953).
[6] D. H. N. Johnson, *Acquisitive Prescription in International Law*, British Yearbook of International Law, Vol. 27: 332, p. 341 (1950).

由于抗议的目的不在于单纯表达不同意见，而是通过意见表达阻止历史性所有权的产生以保存本国权利，后者显然对抗议的方式提出了更高要求。首先，抗议应当持续和不断重复。单独一次抗议后非但不能阻却对方权利的产生，甚至不足以表达本国的反对态度。一次抗议后的长时间沉默更容易让国际社会认为抗议缺乏法律上的依据，或者抗议国对其权利并不十分在意。其次，伴随提出纠纷解决意识的抗议相对于单纯的抗议更有效力。私法中对抗时效取得的唯一途径就是提起诉讼，由于国际法长期缺乏具有强制管辖权的司法机构和领土主权对国家的极端重要性，在领土和边界争议中拟制这一私法规定曾长期被认为是不现实的。[1] 随着国际法规则体系的完善和国际组织的不断建立，约翰逊主张如果事件属于联合国安理会或国际法院适合处理的范围，那么抗议国无论出于任何原因仍持续抗议，只要没有把争议提交这些相关国际机构即可构成默认。[2] 这个观点就字面而言显得过于绝对，目前国际社会仍不足以提供像国内法一样的法律实施环境，但从观点的实质看，抗议的根本目的不是发出不同的声音，而是在争议的实际解决中维护本国权利。因此抗议至少应该伴随着采取措施和平解决争端的意思表示，但是不应局限于特定的形式。

（三）抗议的时间

抗议的时机同样是影响抗议有效性的因素，一般规则是有效的抗议应当在历史性权利形成的过程中提出。在对方权利已经巩固之后方才提出不同意见当然不能影响权利归属的判定。"陆地、岛屿和海洋边界案"中，证据表明萨尔瓦多于1916年开始在案件争议的岛屿行使主权，而洪都拉斯直到1991年才第一次提出抗议。国际法院认为，洪都拉斯是在萨尔瓦多已经长期行使主权以后才提出抗议，可视为洪都拉斯对对方有效管理的行为已经表明了它的默示同意，因此抗议对推定默认的影响来得太晚了。[3]

---

[1] The Chamizal Arbitration between the United States and Mexico (The United State v. Mexico), American Journal of International Law, Vol. 5：778, p. 807 (1911).

[2] D. H. N. Johnson, *Acquisitive Prescription in International Law*, British Yearbook of International Law, Vol. 27：332, p. 341 (1950).

[3] Land, Island and Maritime Frontier Dispute (El Salvador v. Honduras Nicaragua intervening), International Court of Justice Reports, 1992, p. 577.

相对应的是过早提出抗议的法律效果,也就是预期抗议(Anticipatory Protest)的意义。一般性的规则意味着在被抗议国家还没有实施被抗议行为前,相关国家没有提出抗议的义务,其沉默不会被赋予法律意义。但在实践中普遍存在这样一种情况,当一国了解到另一国家正在制定可能危及本国权利的国内法,或者另外的国家间正在缔结与本国主张相关的条约时,该国家应在立法尚未实施、条约未生效之前就提出抗议。例如当沿海国纷纷扩展本国领海宽度时,坚守传统领海宽度观念国家的抗议很多时候都早于沿海国扩展领海立法的实施时间。[1]预期到其他国家未来的行为可能影响到本国权利时,事先提出抗议是国家的权利。实践中这样做可以明确争议的存在,从而在立法或条约缔结中考虑抗议国的主张,甚至直接启动争议解决的程序,但预期抗议本身没有特殊的法律价值,其有效性的判断和产生的法律效果与在历史性所有权的巩固过程中提出的抗议没有区别。

第四节 小 结

本章的初步结论包括:

1. 由于国家实践的延续性和国际法规则的变化,需要依靠时际法调整判断历史性权利时所适用的具体规则。

2. 在具体争议中,需要考察关键日期以确定争议所处的法律情况和证据在时间上的相关性。

3. 无论作为原告还是被告,都由主张本国享有历史性所有权的一方承担证明责任。

4. 占有是产生历史性所有权的起点,相关国家的同意是历史性权利得到巩固的必要条件,两者缺一不可。

5. 在现代国际法中,通过主权展示行为表达的有效管理代表了对土地的占有。

6. 实施本国立法的行为是展示有效管理的最好方式。由于确信在本国管辖区域内而发生的私人行为可以成为有效管理存在的佐证。

7. 管理行为必须公开、和平并在一定时间段内反复实施。

---

[1] Yehuda Z. Blum, *Historic Titles in International Law*, Martinus Nijhoff, 1965, p. 159.

8. 与主张国之间存在现实利益关系的国家明确了解到权利主张是推断其不作为产生同意效果的前提。

9. 在取得历史性水域和取得原属他国的领土中，原权利持有国一定时间的不作为表明它们的同意态度。

10. 所有权的历史性巩固用于取得权属不明土地时，提出竞争主张一方的明示同意或通过行动表达的默认也是同意的表现形式。

11. 第三方国家不是同意的相关国家，其明示承认是有效管理的证据。

12. 相关国家在历史性所有权巩固之前公开、明确表达反对意见可以阻止历史性权利的产生。

第四章 领土取得中的历史性所有权

上一章节的讨论在司法实践的基础上解决了历史性所有权的构成问题，使其成为可以用于争议解决的法律规范和操作规程。但对于领土取得来说，历史性所有权的主张即便成立，也不意味着其主张国家一定能够取得领土主权，而是面临与其他领土取得方式在证据强度和权源优先性上的比较。因此，我们仍然需要将这一权利放置到具体的案件环境中，在假定其自身已经成立的前提下考察它在争议解决中的作用和发挥作用的方式，才能理解历史性所有权在领土取得的国际法规则体系中所扮演的角色。

除此之外，本章还需要解决另一个问题，就是现行的领土取得规则如何评价另一种历史性所有权，也就是接受现代国际法规则前国家与领土间形成的特定关系。判断这类特定关系有效性是否适用历史性所有权的全部规则，是否需要补充其他条件，如果证明特定关系的存在将对领土主权的最终归属产生怎样的影响等，都需要借由本章的研究给予进一步的论述。

第一节 历史上的长期占有

一、法律基础

在具体的争议中，历史性所有权往往被主张国赋予广泛的权利内容："敏基埃岛和艾科俄斯岛案"中法国主张的原始权利来自诺曼底公爵是法王封臣的事实[1]；"印度和巴基斯坦之间西部边界案"（"卡

---

[1] The Minquiers and Ecrehos Case (France v. The United Kingdom), International Court of Justice Reports, 1953, p. 56.

其沼泽案")中，巴基斯坦认为信德跨越边界攻击卡其代表了"历史的趋势"（Currency of History），是巴基斯坦历史性所有权的构成要件。[1]"陆地、岛屿和海洋边界案"中，萨尔瓦多主张由于争议岛屿在殖民时期的行政和宗教管辖权都属于当时西班牙殖民地下属的萨尔瓦多省，因此以该省为主体的萨尔瓦多继承了这些岛屿享有历史性所有权。[2] 在"西撒哈拉法律地位咨询案"中，摩洛哥主张西撒哈拉的游牧部落和摩洛哥苏丹间存在形同于地方与中央关系的民族、文化和宗教的纽带。考虑到伊斯兰国家的特殊结构，这一纽带应被视为摩洛哥对西撒哈拉的长期占有。[3]

然而，无论基于历史上的长期占有所形成的权利被代之以何种称谓，都必须符合历史性所有权的要件构成，也就是说特定的国家主张，必须接受主权者的有效管理和相关国家认同的检验，只有同时具备两者的主张，才能被视为是历史性所有权。当然，不具备历史性所有权要件的历史事实并非就对领土取得丝毫不产生影响，它们仍然构成主权归属中的历史性考虑因素。[4]

需要特别注意的是，正如第二章所描述的，国际社会曾存在与现行国际法规则截然不同的领土观念和取得规则，因此在检验历史上的长期占有是否形成历史性所有权时，需要根据时际法对有效管理和相关国家态度做出符合当时特定环境的调整。

（一）权利持有者已具备主权者的特征

长期占有所产生的历史性所有权，权利的持有者必须在占有发生时已经是独立的国际法主体。国家在当前国际法体系中作为唯一可以持有领土的权利主体是没有疑问的，问题在于在人类历史多样化的演进中，曾形成过形形色色的政治实体，它们都与所生活的土地产生了一定联系，但是否因此就享有国际法上认可的领土权利，则首先要考

---

[1] Case Concerning the Indo-Pakistan Western Boundary (Rann of Kutch), United Nations Reports of International Arbitration Awards, 1968, Vol. 17, p. 437.
[2] Land, Island and Maritime Frontier Dispute (El Salvador v. Honduras Nicaragua intervening), International Court of Justice Reports, 1992, p. 351.
[3] Western Sahara Advisory Opinion, International Court of Justice Reports, 1975, p. 44.
[4] Eritrea-Yemen Arbitration (First Stage), International Legal Materials, Vol. 40: 900, p. 921 (2001).

察这些组织实体的政治属性。

在欧洲国家登陆其他大陆后,首先面对的问题是如何区分当地不同于欧洲国家组织形式的实体在国际法上的地位,以便确定与不同性质实体进行交往的规则。当时的国际法以是否具有政治组织为标准将这些实体分为"文明"、"半文明"和"部落"三类,在领土关系中,前两者享有领土主权,后者所居住的土地是无主地[1],不享有领土主权。因此,作为领土主权的来源,基于历史事实所产生权利的持有者应该是主权者。

"陆地、岛屿和海洋边界案"的争议双方在"特别协定"中规定了争议适用的法律规则应当考虑包括法律、历史、人文或其他任何由诉讼双方提出并根据国际法可以承认的证据和主张。[2]萨尔瓦多因此认为既然条约规定考虑历史证据,那么法院有义务适用包括历史性所有权在内的领土取得规则。[3]丰塞卡海湾中的岛屿从1522年开始陆续被西班牙占领,担任该案件审理的国际法院分庭认为当时西班牙在中美洲的殖民地是一体的,萨尔瓦多在当时并非独立的国际法主体,不能单独主张国际法上的原始权利或者历史性所有权。如果说存在对争议岛屿的历史性所有权,那也只属于西班牙。[4]可见国际法院明确指出历史性所有者、持有者应当是主权者,也就是案中的西班牙,而不是当时仅作为西班牙下属行政区的洪都拉斯和萨尔瓦多。但本案涉及的是殖民当局及其内部组织间的权力关系,这一法理能否适用于独立实体需要进一步证明。

在"西撒哈拉法律地位咨询案"中,联大请求国际法院对西撒哈拉在被西班牙殖民前和摩洛哥王国以及毛里塔尼亚团体间的法律纽带(Legal Tie)是什么提供咨询意见。[5]国际法院虽然没有明确提出决议中法律纽带的性质,事实上联大询问的就是西撒哈拉和这两个政治实

---

[1] Malcolm Shaw, *Title to Territory in Africa*, Clarendon Press, 1986, p. 31 - 32.
[2] Land, Island and Maritime Frontier Dispute (El Salvador v. Honduras Nicaragua intervening), International Court of Justice Reports, 1992, p. 557 - 558.
[3] Land, Island and Maritime Frontier Dispute (El Salvador v. Honduras Nicaragua intervening), International Court of Justice Reports, 1992, p. 558.
[4] Land, Island and Maritime Frontier Dispute (El Salvador v. Honduras Nicaragua intervening), International Court of Justice Reports, 1992, p. 565.
[5] Question of Spanish Sahara, United Nations General Assembly Resolution 3293 (XXXI), A/RES/3292 (XXXI), A/PV. 2318, 1973.

体间是否存在领土关系。摩洛哥主张"法律纽带"就是依据当时独立的摩洛哥王国因为历史上对西撒哈拉的占有所产生的领土主权。[1]而相对应的另一方毛里塔尼亚，当西班牙在西撒哈拉的殖民开始时，毛里塔尼亚团体还不是一个拥有主权的政治实体。[2] 因此，毛里塔尼亚在争议中没有主张历史上曾经和西撒哈拉地区产生过领土主权性质的法律联系，放弃了西撒哈拉地区在独立后应当直接并入该国的要求，也就是放弃了通过历史性所有权主张领土主权。

"厄立特里亚—也门仲裁案"中，非主权的政治实体能否持有领土权源的问题再次浮现，仲裁庭曾质疑古代也门是否属于一个享有主权的独立实体。只是因为在考察古代也门的地理范围时确定即便古代也门属于主权实体，其主权范围也不涉及红海中的岛屿，才搁置了对古代也门是否可以成为主权实体的进一步讨论。[3]

相反的例子发生在"白礁岛案"，"白礁岛案"的争议点之一是在1840年代这个关键日期中，马来西亚的前身柔佛苏丹国是否持有白礁岛的主权。而建立于1511年的柔佛苏丹国在当时已经被公认是拥有新加坡海峡两岸土地控制权的主权者，这一点是法院判断白礁岛在1840年代主权属于柔佛的起点。[4]

正反两面的司法实践共同说明了一个问题，就是主张因长期占有而取得历史性所有权的一方，在历史上的占有发生时必须已经成为有权主张领土的主权者。

（二）历史上的占有也要以有效管理为基础

领土主权是主权者与领土间的关系，因此现行的国际法规则要求以行为方式取得领土的基础必须是国家对土地行使排他性的有效管理。德·维舍认为国家行为确定领土的目的仅仅在于维护国际秩序的稳定，既没有反映领土形成的历史过程，也无法展示出有关民族纽带和国家整体的人类精神。而只有人类和民族保留重要地位的领土概念才能反

---

[1] Western Sahara Advisory Opinion, International Court of Justice Reports, 1975, p. 42 - 43.
[2] Western Sahara Advisory Opinion, International Court of Justice Reports, 1975, p. 57.
[3] Eritrea-Yemen Arbitration (First Stage), International Legal Materials, Vol. 40: 900, p. 919 (2001).
[4] Case Concerning Sovereignty over Pedra Branca/Pulau Batu Puteh, Middle Rocks and South Ledge (Malaysia v. Singapore), International Court of Justice Reports, 2008, p. 33.

映国际关系中有关领土的真实情况。[1] 实践中,确实一部分国家在历史上并没有领土主权的概念,也没有确定的边界和国土,或者曾经认可过不同于现代国际法的领土取得规则。那么,这是否意味着根据时际法,在考虑基于历史上存在的占有时,可以适用不同于有效管理的规则?

"西撒哈拉法律地位咨询案"中,摩洛哥主张与西撒哈拉土地间的"法律纽带"就是领土主权的一部分,依据是根据伊斯兰国家的特殊结构,居住在西撒哈拉的游牧部落和摩洛哥苏丹间存在民族、文化和宗教关系就是地方与中央关系。[2] 法院则认为,国家的特殊结构只是允许行使主权的行为以特殊方式表达出来,不能排除有效行使主权证据的要求,宗教纽带和政治效忠关系不能取代对土地有效管理的要求。[3]

"厄立特里亚—也门仲裁案"中,红海两岸居民由于长期自由捕鱼而形成的社会、经济和文化形态契合伊斯兰法的概念,而在后者的法律体系中从来没有存在过"领土主权"的概念。[4] 仲裁庭虽然认可这一情况应当被视为影响裁决的历史性考虑因素,但是判断也门的历史性所有权主张时,采用的标准依然为是否形成对争议岛屿的有效管理,只是在确定岛屿主权的前提下,建立传统渔业机制将双方渔民基于伊斯兰法律的权利转化为现代国际法体系的权利内容。[5]

裁决机构在上述案件中的对经济、社会、宗教、人文等方面的关系不能产生领土主权的具体结论并非没有受到批评。阿蒙(Ammoun)副院长在他的个别意见中认为咨询意见限缩了西撒哈拉整体和摩洛哥苏丹间的政治联系,这种效忠关系可以被视为摩洛哥当局的主权行为。[6] 也有学者提出批评说,对照国际法院在"敏基埃岛和艾科俄斯岛案"和"西撒哈拉法律地位咨询案"的做法,仲裁庭没有更进一步

---

[1] Charles de Visscher, *Théories et Réalités en Droit International Public* 4th edition, Editions A. Pedone, 1970, p. 222.
[2] Western Sahara Advisory Opinion, International Court of Justice Reports, 1975, p. 44.
[3] Western Sahara Advisory Opinion, International Court of Justice Reports, 1975, p. 48.
[4] Eritrea-Yemen Arbitration (First Stage), International Legal Materials, Vol. 40: 900, p. 920-921 (2001).
[5] Eritrea-Yemen Arbitration (First Stage), International Legal Materials, Vol. 40: 900, p. 979 (2001).
[6] Western Sahara Advisory Opinion, International Court of Justice Reports, 1975, p. 83-84.

处理也门所主张的古老权利和争议岛屿主权可能产生的关联。[1]国际法院在"白礁岛案"中承认领土主权既意味着对土地的控制，也意味着对人的管理[2]，但是人文纽带更大程度上应该理解为考虑主权者与土地关系时的补充或者调整因素，而非取代因素。

可见，即便是在对历史的考察中，主权者实施的带有权利展示性质的行为依然是判断历史性所有权存在的起步因素，而且权利的展示必须满足持续和平的有效管理要件。"卡其沼泽案"中，仲裁员将信德和卡其从成为独立的政治实体后到英国进入该地区前这段时期沼泽地区的历史归纳为三个方面：(1) 在两到三个世纪间，双方持续发生从各个方向穿越沼泽的武装冲突。(2) 信德统治者曾经在沼泽南部边缘部署过游击队并持续一段时间，而卡其同样在沼泽北部部署过军事哨所和防御堡垒。(3) 信德人穿越沼泽攻击卡其更为频繁。[3]

巴基斯坦认为信德跨越边界攻击卡其代表了"历史的趋势"，是巴基斯坦历史性所有权的构成要件，暗示在没有英国介入的情形下，信德将通过持续攻击取得卡其地区的主权。[4]仲裁员虽然承认以侵略为始而以侵略者获得主权告终的情况在理论上和实践中确实长期存在，但是坚持仅靠侵略行为是无法产生领土权源的。[5]仲裁员叙述了历史上记载的信德在攻击卡其过程中曾屠杀多达8万人的事实，由此反问"什么样的历史性所有权可以建立在由战争引发的如此罪行之上"[6]，答案显然是没有建立在非和平基础上的历史性所有权。

因此，体现在实践中的规则仍然是基于历史事实产生的权利，意味着权利行使方式的多样化，但必须满足有效管理的根本要求，即和

---

[1] Nuno Sérgio Marques Antunes, *The Eritrea-Yemen Arbitration: First Stage-the Law of Title to Territory Re-averred*, International and Comparative Law Quarterly, Vol. 48: 299, p. 299 (1999).
[2] Case Concerning Sovereignty over Pedra Branca/Pulau Batu Puteh, Middle Rocks and South Ledge (Malaysia v. Singapore), International Court of Justice Reports, 2008, p. 40.
[3] Case Concerning the Indo-Pakistan Western Boundary (Rann of Kutch), United Nations Reports of International Arbitration Awards, 1968, Vol. 17, p. 436.
[4] Case Concerning the Indo-Pakistan Western Boundary (Rann of Kutch), United Nations Reports of International Arbitration Awards, 1968, Vol. 17, p. 437.
[5] Case Concerning the Indo-Pakistan Western Boundary (Rann of Kutch), United Nations Reports of International Arbitration Awards, 1968, Vol. 17, p. 437.
[6] Case Concerning the Indo-Pakistan Western Boundary (Rann of Kutch), United Nations Reports of International Arbitration Awards, 1968, Vol. 17, p. 437.

平持续展示权利。而对于其他形式的纽带，在特定条件下它们是判断领土归属权的参考因素，但是本身不能产生领土权源。

（三）相关国家态度是确认争议地法律状态的证据

争议一方提出基于历史事实的权利主张，目的在于证明本国相对于竞争主张国更早占有争议土地，也意味着历史上的占有和争议的关键日期之间有相当的时间距离。时间的距离往往意味着直接对土地实施管理的证据在数量和准确性上都会有所不足。这种情况下为了明确土地在特定历史阶段的法律状态，往往需要借助间接证据，其中包括其他国家对领土占有状态的态度。"西撒哈拉法律地位咨询案"中，针对摩洛哥引述的一系列有关沉船救援和有关摩洛哥领土范围的条约和外交信件，据此主张对西撒哈拉的领土主权已得到了国际承认[1]，法院承认摩洛哥所主张的相关国家态度确实存在，但是认为这些针对特定事项的表态只是确认了苏丹确实对生活在当地的一些部落具有政治权威或个人影响力，并不能认为其中暗示其他国家对摩洛哥在西撒哈拉主权的承认。[2]

而在"白礁岛案"中，马来西亚没有提供柔佛苏丹国曾在历史上占有白礁岛的直接证据。因此，法院考察了格劳秀斯在17世纪的著作以及荷兰和英国当时在东南亚殖民机构的文件，寻找是否存在柔佛苏丹国对白礁岛享有主权的国际认识。[3] 由于英国和荷兰分别是分裂后柔佛苏丹国的宗主国，因此这两国在东南亚的殖民机构向本国的汇报被法院赋予重要的证据意义。根据文献证据，结合当时白礁岛的地理位置和其他历史环境，法院肯定柔佛苏丹国从建立之时起就是一个主权国家，直到1824年因为继承问题分裂为止，该国控制了包括新加坡海峡中全部岛屿在内的广大陆地和海洋区域，其中也包括白礁岛所在的区域。[4]

可见，在缺乏进行有效管理的直接证据时，相关国家对占有状态的认可可以使主张国对土地的占有状态成为众所周知的事实，从而使

---

[1] Western Sahara Advisory Opinion, International Court of Justice Reports, 1975, p. 49.
[2] Western Sahara Advisory Opinion, International Court of Justice Reports, 1975, p. 53.
[3] Case Concerning Sovereignty over Pedra Branca/Pulau Batu Puteh, Middle Rocks and South Ledge (Malaysia v. Singapore), International Court of Justice Reports, 2008, p. 34.
[4] Case Concerning Sovereignty over Pedra Branca/Pulau Batu Puteh, Middle Rocks and South Ledge (Malaysia v. Singapore), International Court of Justice Reports, 2008, p. 35.

历史事实成为有权得到国际法保护的权利。

(四)争议土地在特定历史时期的法律状态不能存在争议

当争议双方都提出基于历史占有的主张时,裁决机关的处理方式并不是比较证据的相对强度,而是考察证据能否表明争议的法律状态,否则将不处理双方与此相关的权利主张。"敏基埃岛和艾科俄斯岛案"中,英国主张以有效控制方式建立起对争议岛屿的古老权源(Ancient Title),证据就是主权的持续展示。[1] 事实上,根据证据的比较,英国的"古老权源"显然比法国根据封建权利主张的"初始权源"在强度上更优越,但是法院认为所有证据都不能表明岛屿的主权归属,因此决定考察距离争议发生时更近的直接占有行为。[2] 同样在"卡其沼泽案"中,即便是支持印度立场的仲裁员也承认信德穿越沼泽远比卡其频繁[3],但仲裁庭主席认为信德和卡其双方在英国殖民者出现前相互争夺沼泽的军事行动只能表明当时沼泽地带的归属处于不断变动中,无法确立其稳定的归属。[4]

相反的例子是"白礁岛案",马来西亚并未能提供柔佛直接针对白礁岛展示权利的证据,但是通过格劳秀斯的著作和英、荷两国的政府文件,法院认为未分裂前的柔佛苏丹国享有白礁岛的初始权源。除了上述证据外,法院的判断还依托两项客观环境:首先,白礁岛位于两条重要的国际航道之间,是众所周知的航行障碍,不可能不被当地人留意;由于白礁岛所在区域属于柔佛苏丹国,那么推断位于该区域中且已经被发现的白礁岛同样属于该国是合理的。[5] 其次,在整个柔佛苏丹国时期,没有其他国家对新加坡海峡中的岛屿提出主张,也就

---

[1] The Minquiers and Ecrehos Case (France v. The United Kingdom), International Court of Justice Reports, 1953, p. 50 - 51.

[2] The Minquiers and Ecrehos Case (France v. The United Kingdom), International Court of Justice Reports, 1953, p. 57.

[3] Case Concerning the Indo-Pakistan Western Boundary (Rann of Kutch), United Nations Reports of International Arbitration Awards, 1968, Vol. 17, p. 436.

[4] Case Concerning the Indo-Pakistan Western Boundary (Rann of Kutch), United Nations Reports of International Arbitration Awards, 1968, Vol. 17, p. 532 - 533.

[5] Case Concerning Sovereignty over Pedra Branca/Pulau Batu Puteh, Middle Rocks and South Ledge (Malaysia v. Singapore), International Court of Justice Reports, 2008, p. 35.

是不存在与柔佛苏丹国相竞争的主权主张。[1]如果说第一项客观环境证据可以解释为法院推测柔佛占有白礁岛符合逻辑，那么第二项环境证据则直接表明法院判断权利是否存在时强调的是特定土地在当时的归属没有争议。

表面上，对历史上的占有施加必须不存在争议的要求，似乎不符合领土取得中考察证据相对强度的规则。但是如果将对历史的考察还原到整个争议解决的进程中去，就能观察到这一要求的合理性。实践中，争议双方通常会提供不止一个法律基础用来支持各自的主张，而且就同一争议，不同的法律基础必须构成完整的权利链条。因此，裁决机构考察历史上的占有状态，根本作用在于明确争议土地法律地位的起点。虽然领土取得的规则已经演变为重视与争议接近时间的主权展示，但是争议土地是否已经存在特定的历史权利将直接影响到对主权展示证据强度和有效性标准的调整。由此，一方面仅靠基于历史事实的权利本身并不决定主权归属，因此证据内容严格符合国际法上历史性所有权的要件并不必要。另一方面这一权利的存在与否将直接影响整条主权权利链的有效性评价，因此历史事实必须在清楚表明争议土地法律状态的情况下才能纳入考虑范围。

整体来看，基于历史上占有所产生的历史性所有权也是领土主权的取得方式，因此要件上仍必须满足一般国际法提出的要求，要遵循主权者通过与特定土地间的联系而产生领土取得权利的一般法理。不同点则是因为时际法的要求，证据的限制以及权利在整个主权权利链中所处的特殊位置，因而在证据的种类以及评价上有自己独特的标准。

二、对主权归属的影响

考察历史上的长期占有所产生的权利的目的是确定争议土地法律地位的起点。假设权利确实存在，这种权利的属性是什么，以及对主张国和提出竞争主张国来说，这种权利对主权的最终归属可能产生怎样的影响，将是本节需要解决的问题。

---

[1] Case Concerning Sovereignty over Pedra Branca/Pulau Batu Puteh, Middle Rocks and South Ledge (Malaysia v. Singapore), International Court of Justice Reports, 2008, p. 35.

(一) 权利的性质

"白礁岛案"中,国际法院认为白礁岛在1824年时属于柔佛苏丹国,更明确指出这种权利的性质就是完全的主权。[1]可见,历史上的占有所产生的权利可以是完整的领土主权。但是通往主权似乎并不是这类历史性所有权的唯一路径,在"敏基埃岛和艾科俄斯岛案"和"卡其沼泽案"中,国际法院和仲裁庭都指出各自案件中的有关历史性所有权的主张如果得到认可,它的作用在于创造有关主权的假设(Presumption of Sovereignty)。[2] 主权的性质在国际法上有明确的答案,那么所谓主权假设的性质以及它的法律效果是什么?

司法实践对这个问题没有明确的答案,但是借助"发现"作为主权来源的演变,我们可以探索基于主权假设在国际法体系中的位置。"帕尔玛斯岛仲裁案"中,美国主张继承了西班牙在16世纪通过"发现"取得的领土主权,胡伯法官认为即便承认根据16世纪的领土取得规则"发现"产生一定的权利,判断这一权利对争议结果的影响仍要依照国家行为符合国际法发展要求的时际法规则。根据争议实际发生时的国际法规则,"发现"产生"原初权源",其效果在于给予主张权利的国家一段合理的时间完成对土地的有效占领。[3]同样,在"敏基埃岛和艾科俄斯岛案"中,法院指出根据时际法,即便认可法国拥有封建权源,除非在历史发展过程中被另外一种有效的权源所取代,否则封建权源将随着时间的流逝而消失,对争议解决不产生任何效力。[4] 在某种程度上可以说,单纯的"发现"和"封建权源"一样,都不再被认为是领土主权来源的历史事实,也就是说,不再被认为是领土权源的历史事实所产生的权利,其性质就是原初权利,其所产生的主权假

---

[1] Case Concerning Sovereignty over Pedra Branca/Pulau Batu Puteh, Middle Rocks and South Ledge (Malaysia v. Singapore), International Court of Justice Reports, 2008, p. 41.
[2] The Minquiers and Ecrehos Case (France v. The United Kingdom), International Court of Justice Reports, 1953, p. 57. Also see Case Concerning the Indo-Pakistan Western Boundary (Rann of Kutch), United Nations Reports of International Arbitration Awards, 1968, Vol. 17, p. 436.
[3] Island of Palmas Case (Netherlands v. The U.S.A.), United Nations Reports of International Arbitration Awards, 1928, Vol. 2, p. 846.
[4] The Minquiers and Ecrehos Case (France v. The United Kingdom), International Court of Justice Reports, 1953, p. 56.

设就是主张国将在合理期限内通过有效权源完成占领。

相比之下,对历史上通过不同主权行使方式产生的权利来说,这种权利的法律基础和通过主权展示产生的权源并没有区别,只存在有效管理表现方式的不同。因此基于历史上的占有所产生的权利是符合现代国际法对领土取得的基本规定的,也就是说权利并不因为时际法而自动消失,那么它所产生的权利在效力上至少是高于原初权利的。如果没有相互竞争主张的出现,那么持有这一权利的国家将会通过行使主权不断巩固对土地的有效管理,而这一状态也会逐步得到相关国家的认可,由此产生对历史性所有权的巩固从而获取完整的主权。因此,对于基于有效管理的历史事实产生的主权假设,就是通过权利的不断巩固最终产生主权。

由此可见,对于基于历史上的占有所产生的权利,既可能形成主权,也可能成为所有权的历史性巩固的起点。随之而来的问题是,如果基于历史上的占有所产生的权利,面临相互竞争的领土权源,或者被另一种权源所取代,那么这类权利对主权的最终归属又将产生怎样的影响。

(二) 权利的存续

基于历史上的占有所产生的权利,如果产生取得完全主权的效果,那么意味着已经完成从领土权源到领土主权的巩固过程,这时问题已经变成如何在存在竞争权源的情况下判断主权的存续。杰赛普曾批评时际法的引入将让国家不得不时刻关注权源规则的变化以防止主权失效,詹宁斯和菲茨莫里斯则认为这种担心没有必要,因为完全的主权一旦确立,国家只需要少量的权利展示行为便能维持。"喀麦隆和尼日利亚间陆地和海洋边界案"中,喀麦隆作为持有主权的一方,在乍得湖沿岸村庄只实施了不规律的少量管理行为,相比之下,尼日利亚平民和政府在这些争议村庄中的活动似乎更符合持续展示权利的要求。即便如此,由于喀麦隆持有这些争议村庄的主权而且在尼日利亚提出主权主张后立刻提出抗议,少量的管理行为和明确表达的反对态度一起维持了喀麦隆的主权。[1]同样,在"白礁岛案"中,通过众所周知

---

[1] Land and Maritime Boundary between Cameroon and Nigeria (Cameroon v. Nigeria, Equatorial Guinea intervening), International Court of Justice Reports, 2002, p. 352.

的历史事实取得岛屿主权的柔佛苏丹国在此后一个世纪中甚至没有登上过白礁岛,但是直到1953年柔佛苏丹国表示不主张白礁岛所有权,法院才确认柔佛苏丹国曾经拥有的主权因为这一明确的主权放弃态度而不复存在[1]。因此,可以进一步得出结论,拥有完全主权的国家,其权利便持续存在,除非通过作为或者不作为表明放弃主权的态度。即便竞争国家对特定土地已经实施了有效管理的行为,只要主权国在合理期限内表达反对的态度,这一态度本身仍能使主权得到延续。

对于仍未达到完全主权的主权假设,由于这种假设产生自历史上的有效管理,此时面对竞争主张时的权利存续问题,事实上就是证据强度的相对比较。一直延续的主权假设因为产生时间更早而可能取得相对强度上的优胜,而已经中断的主权假设则因为没有满足有效管理的持续性要求而变成相对较弱的证据。

由此,对基于历史上的占有所产生权利在面临竞争主张时的不同存续情况可以总结为:第一,如果已经取得完全主权,那么没有放弃主权的意思表示,即可维持权利。第二,如果权利的有效性一直延续到争议发生时或争议发生时被有效的其他领土权源所替换,那么权利产生时间更早的权源将成为效力较强的权源。第三,反之,如果权利被其他国家的领土权源所取代,那么历史性所有权由于权利链的中断而仅能作为有关领土取得的较弱证据。

(三) 归还理论

实践中还可能出现一种情况,基于历史事实所产生的主权或者主权假设,因为殖民或战争的原因被另一国家的主权所取代,那么被取代的主权或者主权假设是否保留了在取代它的主权消失后而恢复之前土地所处法律状态的权利,也就是说国家是否有权在介入因素消失后要求"归还"原先存在权利的领土。

要求"归还"的主张在国际法实践并不鲜见。"卡其沼泽案"中,巴基斯坦主张英国对信德的殖民不能剥夺信德穆斯林团体享有的剩余主权,因此独立后的巴基斯坦作为剩余主权的继承者,有权主张卡其

---

[1] Case Concerning Sovereignty over Pedra Branca/Pulau Batu Puteh, Middle Rocks and South Ledge (Malaysia v. Singapore), International Court of Justice Reports, 2008, p. 81.

沼泽的主权[1]。"西撒哈拉法律地位咨询案"中，国际法院设定的议题是西撒哈拉地区和摩洛哥之间法律纽带的性质，但是个别法官在声明中直截了当地指出案件的实质争议在于：西班牙殖民前摩洛哥对西撒哈拉的领土权源是否足以支持让西撒哈拉地区重新并入摩洛哥的主张。[2]"厄立特里亚—也门仲裁案"中，也门根据历史性所有权，主张红海中的争议岛屿在奥斯曼帝国解体后，应当归还给也门。[3]

归还原则是国家继承中可能出现的情况。布朗利认为在殖民地独立过程中，第三方国家都认可的历史延续性可能产生归还，这种情况下继承国家可以恢复由于殖民势力介入而失去的政治或法律身份。[4]对于归还原则是否也适用于领土取得，"厄立特里亚—也门仲裁案"的仲裁庭认为至少在该案的环境中，也门无法说服仲裁庭采纳归还是国际法的一部分。[5]但同时可以看到实践中，法院往往回避讨论归还原则本身是否适用的问题，而是通过考察与之相关的事实，得出即使适用归还原则也不影响领土归属的结论。

第一类情形是权源被取代后不存在剩余主权。"卡其沼泽案"中英国对信德和卡其的殖民管理方式是不同的，信德作为英国直接管辖的领土，卡其则享有完全的主权。因此仲裁庭认为在印度不断明确沼泽地带边界的过程中，管辖信德的英国缺乏反应虽然是对维护自身在信德的利益存在失职，但由于英国是信德的主权者，因此英国的默认也就意味着信德对卡其潜在权利的放弃。[6]同样在"厄立特里亚—也门仲裁案"中，仲裁庭认为奥斯曼帝国在征服古代也门后建立的权利是完全主权，古代也门即使享有历史性所有权，也不可能在此时保留

---

[1] Case Concerning the Indo-Pakistan Western Boundary (Rann of Kutch), United Nations Reports of International Arbitration Awards, 1968, Vol. 17, p. 23.
[2] Western Sahara Advisory Opinion, International Court of Justice Reports, 1975, p. 70 – 71.
[3] Eritrea-Yemen Arbitration (First Stage), International Legal Materials, Vol. 40: 900, p. 902 – 903 (2001).
[4] Ian Brownlie, *Principles of Public International Law*, 7th editon, Oxford University Press, 2008, p. 668.
[5] 由于本案中仲裁庭被请求适用相关的国际法规则，因此将法院的表态理解为归还不是适用于该案的国际法的一部分较为合理。Eritrea-Yemen Arbitration (First Stage), International Legal Materials, Vol. 40: 900, p. 923 (2001).
[6] Case Concerning the Indo-Pakistan Western Boundary (Rann of Kutch), United Nations Reports of International Arbitration Awards, 1968, Vol. 17, p. 553.

剩余的权利。[1]由于没有剩余权利导致权利链条中断，因此也门也就丧失了要求归还争议地的依据。需要注意的是，在这两个案件中，信德和也门不但因为另一权源的介入失去了对争议土地的权利，而且本身的主权地位也没能得到保留。

第二类情形是介入的权源消失后对原先领土有法定的安排。"厄立特里亚—也门仲裁案"中也门无法主张归还的另一个原因在于《洛桑条约》第16条规定了原属奥斯曼帝国的红海岛屿在西方势力离开红海之前保持主权未定的状态。作为非缔约国，也门尽管法律上不受条约的拘束，但由于也门在《洛桑条约》缔结后的很长时间内都不是享有主权的独立国家，在现实中无法改变争议岛屿主权未定的现状。[2]

可以说，当国际法实践面对上述两种情况时，归还原则将无法适用。但是反过来是否也能假设这样一种可能：在原权利国本身的主权持续存在的情况下，其一部分具有主权或者主权假设的土地被另一国家取得，那么在这部分介入因素消失后，原权利国是否有权收回失去的领土。这种假设在司法实践中未有先例，但在国家实践中并非没有存在的一席之地。缔结于1919年的《凡尔赛和约》规定阿尔萨斯和洛林于1918年11月11日停战时归还法国。事实是在停战时法国实际已经占有了阿尔萨斯和洛林，并实施了有效管理，从而满足了取得主权的条件。事后条约对归还的安排，某种程度上只是确认法国恢复主权的事实，而不是创设主权。既然条约只是起到确认的作用，那么法国对阿尔萨斯和洛林的主权显然不是来自新的有效管理，而是恢复了普法战争前对这两片区域的主权。因此法国在一战后重新取得阿尔萨斯和洛林主权的法律依据可以被解释为：由于作为独立国家的法国本身仍然存在，而德国对阿尔萨斯和洛林主权的介入因素消失，因此这两块土地被归还给法国。《凡尔赛和约》则作为第三方国家的普遍同意，肯定了这一权利来源的合法性。

由此，得出如下结论可能并非毫无合理性，即归还就其本身来说很可能不是领土取得的相关规则，但在实践中存在这样一种可能性，

---

[1] Eritrea-Yemen Arbitration (First Stage), International Legal Materials, Vol. 40: 900, p. 923 (2001).

[2] Eritrea-Yemen Arbitration (First Stage), International Legal Materials, Vol. 40: 900, p. 923 (2001).

在原权利国本身的主权持续存在的情况下，一部分具有主权或者主权假设的土地被另一国家取得，那么在这部分介入因素消失后，如果对争议土地的归属没有特定的安排，或者安排不明确的，原先的权利持有国有权主张归还。如果上述理论成立，那么将对中方对于钓鱼岛的主权主张产生重要的积极影响。

第二节　所有权的历史性巩固

所有权的历史性巩固在领土取得中的地位缺乏明确的定位。"喀麦隆和尼日利亚间陆地和海洋边界案"中，法院认为喀麦隆所主张的历史性巩固，本身存在高度的争议，不能取代现行的任何一种领土取得方式。[1]但是，法院没有说明现行的领土取得方式指的是什么，但是可以排除基于法律的权源和基于国家行为的权源这种对权源的分类，所有权的历史性巩固只是基于国家行为产生的其中一类领土取得方式，不可能挑战它的两个上位概念。因此，法院所指尚不能被取代的应该是已经被长期认可的五种传统领土取得方式，尤其是和巩固同样基于有效管理的先占和时效。

法院的这一表态并没有取消巩固的生存空间。第一，先占和时效有明确的适用对象，但两者没有覆盖通过行为取得领土的全部方式。第二，拟制私法概念的时效是否适用于取得已经存在确定主权的土地仍然存在争议。事实上，所有权的历史性巩固，这一概念的提出和围绕它的理论争议，本身就是为了解决上述两个问题。本节将尝试从现有的实践入手，通过寻找这两个问题的答案，确定所有权的历史性巩固是否具有相对于其他领土取得方式的独立地位，如果具备独立地位，那么它对现有的领土取得方式产生的影响究竟是补充性的，还是取代了其中某一特定的领土取得方式。

---

[1] Land and Maritime Boundary between Cameroon and Nigeria (Cameroon v. Nigeria, Equatorial Guinea intervening), International Court of Justice Reports, 2002, p. 352.

一、取得主权不明但不属于无主地的土地

(一) 时效不是取得主权不明土地的方式

主权争议的对象是归属不明但不属于无主地的土地,是实践中时常出现的情况,处于无主地和完全主权间的"灰色地带"。英国和法国在将敏基埃岛和艾科俄斯岛争议递交给国际法院时,在特别协定中注明双方都不认为争议岛屿处于无主地的状态。[1]在"陆地、岛屿和海洋边界案"中,针对萨尔瓦多请求法院适用"先占"规则时,分庭认为丰塞卡海湾中的岛屿都曾属于西班牙,不是无主地,而是殖民地独立过程中没有得到明确分配的土地。[2]问题在于,私法中不存在物权不明情况,因此拟制于私法的领土取得传统方式显然没有为这一类土地的取得预设下明确的规则。

约翰逊用自古以来的长期占有形容这类土地的权源,然后进一步将这一领土取得方式归入取得时效的范畴。[3]这一归纳方法并不能准确描述主权不明土地的权源。一方面取得时效的适用范围是否包括主权不明的土地在今天仍具有争议,虽然詹宁斯等人都认为国际法中存在统一的时效概念,取得原属他国的领土和取得主权不明土地都是基于取得时效,两者之间没有质的区别。[4]但是在实践中,到目前为止,没有国家提出以取得时效作为他们对主权不明土地的法律基础,可见这种将这类土地的权源归为时效至少在实践层面缺少支持。

更重要的是,国际法领域中,历史上的长期占有同样拟制于私法,但是一个根本的区别在于私法中物权取得规则从来都是一致的,而国际法的领土取得却是几经演变。对于前现代国家占有土地导致对主权最终归属的影响,国际法既不是断然拒绝也不是全部采纳,而是借助

---

[1] The Minquiers and Ecrehos Case (France v. The United Kingdom), International Court of Justice Reports, 1953, p. 52.

[2] Land, Island and Maritime Frontier Dispute (El Salvador v. Honduras Nicaragua intervening), International Court of Justice Reports, 1992, p. 565.

[3] D. H. N. Johnson, *Consolidation as a Root of Title in International Law*, Cambridge Law Journal, Vol. 3 (2): 215, p. 223 (1956).

[4] R. Y. Jennings, *The Acquisition of Territory in International Law*, Manchester University Press, 1963, p. 22.

历史上的长期占有强调历史上是否存在清楚的占有状态。这种占有要求历史上的直接和间接证据能够清楚表明争议地区的法律状态。而在取得主权不明的土地则是要根据现行有效的领土取得规范决定争议土地的最终归属，虽然也考虑历史上的长期占有所产生的权利，但是更侧重接近关键日期时实施的有效管理和相关国家态度。

实践中，国家也将历史上的长期占有和接近关键日期的国家行为作为独立的主权依据，"卡其沼泽案"中巴基斯坦提出历史上信德和卡其曾在沼泽中线形成历史性边界，但同时巴基斯坦在独立后的有效管理也是取得北部卡其沼泽的依据。[1]萨尔瓦多在"陆地、岛屿和海洋边界案"中也提出类似主张，将历史性所有权和得到洪都拉斯默认的有效管理分别视为对丰塞卡海湾中岛屿主权的法律依据。[2]

可见，主权不明土地的权源不是基于历史事实所产生的长期占有，更不是时效。

（二）巩固是主权不明土地的取得方式

事实上，取得不明土地主权更接近于一种逐渐强化的过程。在最初阶段，国家对争议土地的主权展示无论从管理方式的性质或者管理行为的数量上都比较弱，这时土地与国家之间的联系也相对疏离。随着时间的延伸，国家将会越来越切实地管理和开发这片土地，主权展示的行为也因此而越来越频繁。同时，在国家间交往的过程中，越来越多的国家会意识到这片土地和在土地上实施管理的国家之间的关系，从而通过各种形式肯定这片土地就是主张国的一部分。

一方面，国家管理和国际承认的不断积累最终产生质变，在国家和土地以及生存其上的人民之间形成一种特定的相互依存和利益关系，完成领土主权的最终取得。虽然在司法实践中，裁决机关根据可以量化的证据性质和数量来决定主权归属，但不是因为证据本身可以产生主权，而是证据所代表的国家与土地间的利益关系产生了领土主权。可以说这是国家与土地之间关系不断强化的过程，而"巩固"无疑是

---

[1] Case Concerning the Indo-Pakistan Western Boundary (Rann of Kutch), United Nations Reports of International Arbitration Awards, 1968, Vol. 17, p. 23.

[2] Land, Island and Maritime Frontier Dispute (El Salvador v. Honduras Nicaragua intervening), International Court of Justice Reports, 1992, p. 558.

描述这种进程的最好术语。

另一方面，法律意义上的巩固需要满足特定的条件，也就是前一章所界定的有效管理和相关国家的态度，因此理论上并不是所有主权不明土地的取得都可以归属于所有权的历史性巩固。单纯的有效管理，并没有配合相关国家的同意态度，也可能取得主权不明的土地，但不能认为是基于所有权的巩固。而单纯依赖有效管理提出主权主张的实践并不常见，因为国家能够持续而不受干扰地展示主权本身就暗示了相关国家的同意态度，而随着控制的时间越来越长，土地与国家间的联系总会在国际关系中有所体现。

实践中更多出现的反而是另一种情况。目前的领土和边界争议主要发生在人类无法定居或者无法建立社会组织的地区，例如远离海岸的岛屿和杳无人迹的沙漠，这些地区由于自然地理环境的限制，一方面难以建立常规的管理方式，另一方面由于缺乏经济和其他价值也没有常规管理的必要性。因此，如同"卡其沼泽案"中争议国家的表现，双方都仅实施了极为有限的管理而且证据的类型和数量相当平衡[1]，此时，单纯依赖有效管理所反映的国家和土地间关系不足以产生排他性主权的联系，还需要考察国际社会对主权归属情况的认识来巩固通过管理建立起来的权利关系。正是因为包含了相关国家态度的要件，使得所有权的历史性巩固被认为特别适用于解决岛屿和游牧地区的主权争议。[2]

因此，所有权的历史性巩固既包含了取得主权不明土地需要的法律要件，又能够确切描述国家实际取得主权的过程，尤其是对相关国家态度的侧重符合当前国际法实践的需求，因此可以认为是对这类土地权源的恰当称谓。

二、取代原持有国的领土主权

权利的历史性巩固和时效在概念的构成上都包括有效管理和相关国家的同意，如果时效本身被认为是取代原持有国领土主权的合法方

---

[1] Case Concerning the Indo-Pakistan Western Boundary (Rann of Kutch), United Nations Reports of International Arbitration Awards, 1968, Vol. 17, p. 563.

[2] Eritrea-Yemen Arbitration (First Stage), International Legal Materials, Vol. 40: 900, p. 920 (2001).

式，那么是否意味着两者间的区别仅仅体现在术语的变化上？

(一) 巩固是时效的术语替换

布鲁姆主张国际法上存在时效取得的事实，但是为了避免这一术语的国内法含义造成国际法上的误解而采用历史性所有权作为替换。事实上，在 2008 年的"白礁岛案"中，新加坡曾试图将时效作为白礁岛主权的来源之一。西玛（Simma）法官和亚伯拉罕（Abraham）法官在他们的联合反对意见中也明确指出对取得时效的讨论不足是他们反对判决的理由之一。[1] 德·维舍在提出所有权的历史性巩固时，认为这一取得方式与时效的区别在于巩固也适用于主权不明的土地，暗示了在他看来，巩固用于取得其他国家主权即在"逆权占有"的状态下，与时效没有区别。[2]

詹宁斯则认为两者之间存在实质性的细微差别，时效是基于和平有效地占有，只不过这种占有的状态在争议中不能不证自明，而是需要相关的证据，特别是第三方国家的态度。而在所有权的历史性巩固中，其他国家的同意不仅是证明占有证据，更是确定占有的决定性因素。[3] 在詹宁斯看来，时效和巩固尽管在实践中似乎难以区分，两者的实质区别在于概念要件之间的关系，时效中相关国家的同意是存在有效管理的证据，而巩固中的相关国家的同意则是独立的要件因素。如果确实如此，那么进一步的推论应该是时效和巩固虽然具备同样的构成要件，但是法律基础不同。通过时效取得其他国家领土的法律基础在于和平持续的占有，而通过巩固取得主权的核心要素则在于相关国家的同意。

在研究基于历史上的占有所产生的权利时已经得出结论：即对于已经确立了完善主权的地区，无论主权的权源来自何种法律基础，只有主权持有者的放弃，才能成为权利转移的前提，而不论提出竞争主张一方是否实施了有效的管理。在"喀麦隆和尼日利亚间陆地和海洋

---

[1] Case Concerning Sovereignty over Pedra Branca/Pulau Batu Puteh, Middle Rocks and South Ledge (Malaysia v. Singapore), International Court of Justice Reports, 2008, p. 112.
[2] Charles de Visscher, *Théories et Réalités en Droit International Public*, 4th edition, Editions A. Pedone, 1970, p. 222.
[3] R. Y. Jennings, *The Acquisition of Territory in International Law*, Manchester University Press, 1963, p. 25.

边界案"中，尽管法院认为尼日利亚在乍得湖附近村落行使管理的时间，不足以建立所有权的历史性巩固，但是真正维护喀麦隆主权的是法院无法从喀麦隆的行为中得到该国默认边界状态改变的态度。

根据只有主权持有者的放弃才能产生主权转移的规则，詹宁斯对时效的认识显然是错误的。而事实上，詹宁斯本人在讨论承认和默认与领土取得的关系时也指出，在"逆权占有"的状态下，除了要建立实际的占有外，还必须取得原主权者的默认。[1] 而之前对时效以占有为基础的看法，更多的是因为詹宁斯认为时效同样适用于取得主权不明的土地，为了统一两种不同形式时效的法律基础而得出这一结论。但是，一方面，正如上一节总结的，基于时效主张主权不明土地的主权并未得到实践支持；另一方面，时效和巩固，前者侧重占有后者侧重同意的区分也很难应用在领土归属的实际判断中。

因此，可以认为在取得主权原属其他国家的土地时，巩固和时效没有区别。

（二）放弃主权不等于所有权的历史性巩固

原主权国放弃领土主权的态度不意味着权利的历史性巩固必然发生。单纯的主权放弃可以产生各种结果，例如《洛桑条约》中规定的红海中的岛屿在奥斯曼帝国放弃主权后处于主权未定的状态。[2] 此外，对有利另一方主张的主权放弃需要持严格解释的立场。因此，在"卡其沼泽案"中，仲裁庭主席承认英属印度殖民地政府主张沼泽北部边缘确实存在一条一致和连续的边界。信德当局对这一主张不作回应，可以被解释为默认或者接受这些主张，产生放弃沼泽领土潜在权利的结果。但是由于印度当局也无法提供除主张以外的有效管理证据，因此信德的放弃不意味着接受卡其一方的领土主张。[3] 仲裁庭继续考察第三个问题的答案，实际上就是判断双方是否在巩固的基础上取得主权不明的沼泽未划界部分土地。

---

[1] R. Y. Jennings, *The Acquisition of Territory in International Law*, Manchester University Press, 1963, p. 39.

[2] Eritrea-Yemen Arbitration (First Stage), International Legal Materials, Vol. 40: 900, p. 923 (2001).

[3] Case Concerning the Indo-Pakistan Western Boundary (Rann of Kutch), United Nations Reports of International Arbitration Awards, 1968, Vol. 17, p. 553.

"白礁岛案"的裁决过程也反映了放弃不等于转移的法理,针对1953年柔佛苏丹国不主张白礁岛所有权的回信,法院对其法律效果的判断十分谨慎,结论被严格限制在柔佛苏丹国和新加坡当局的主观态度上,即柔佛苏丹国不认为自己拥有主权而新加坡当局也不认为柔佛苏丹国拥有主权。这时,柔佛苏丹国放弃主权的态度已经明朗,但是新加坡当局的行为尚停留在管理灯塔和询问岛屿主权的阶段,没有当然认为主权由此转移,事实上在马来西亚和新加坡之间,白礁岛的主权处于未定状态。[1]进一步来看,法院考察了双方1953年后的行为证据,也没有因为柔佛苏丹国的主权放弃而排除了柔佛苏丹国继承者马来西亚主张主权的可能性,仍然是通过比较双方有效管理和相互对对方行为的态度决定白礁岛的最终归属。

可见,所有权的历史性巩固在取代其他国家领土时,原持有国家的同意要么是有效管理的结果,要么与有效管理同步。总之,有效管理先于相关国家同意所取得的领土主权,领土的取得方式才能被认为是所有权的历史性巩固。

三、作为法律权源的解释工具

早在"帕尔玛斯岛仲裁案"中,胡伯法官设想了这样一种可能,邻国之间已经根据条约划分了各自主权范围,那么在条约范围内国家可以极少行使主权亦能排除对方进入本国领土,但如果条约规定的边界模糊导致是否存在普遍主权的疑问,此时国家权利的展示将成为决定领土主权适当和自然的标准。[2]但是胡伯法官没有说明这种情况下,国家权利的展示与领土主权的关系是什么。"缅因海湾划界案"中,国际法院详细区分了包括条约和法定占有在内的法律上的权源和有效管理之间的关系,其中指出当法律权源不能确切表明领土范围时,有效管理是解释实践的必要条件。[3]这就解释了当存在有效法律权源情

---

[1] 法院的结论是此时主权属于英国,因为柔佛苏丹国和新加坡一样,其主权者都是英国。Case Concerning Sovereignty over Pedra Branca/Pulau Batu Puteh, Middle Rocks and South Ledge (Malaysia v. Singapore), International Court of Justice Reports, 2008, p. 82.
[2] Island of Palmas Case (Netherlands v. The U.S.A.), United Nations Reports of International Arbitration Awards, 1968, Vol. 2, p. 840.
[3] Delimitation of the Maritime Boundary in the Gulf of Maine Area (Canada v. U.S.A.), International Court of Justice Reports, 1984, p. 587.

况下，国家职能展示的作用，即澄清了法律权源试图表达的内容。

这一原则同样适用于解释巩固与法律权源间的关系。"陆地、岛屿和海洋边界案"中，国际法院认为"法定占有"是该案唯一适用的规则。但由于殖民时期管理行为不足以表明争议岛屿在独立时确切的行政归属，分庭决定考虑新独立国家在独立后短时期内与岛屿有关的行为，甚至是临近争议关键日期的有效管理，特别是可能构成默认的行为，以帮助理解1821年时岛屿的归属情况。[1]分庭特别强调考察有效管理和默认的目的不是界定创造领土主权的独立权源，而是在殖民行政管辖模糊的地区，明确"法定占有"原则下岛屿的分配情况。[2]

此时，所有权的历史性巩固构成争议通过各自行为表达的默认协议，作为法定权源的解释工具，巩固的角色可以比照《维也纳条约法公约》第31条第3款"嗣后在条约适用方面确定各当事国对条约解释之协定之任何惯例，作为与条约上下文一并考虑的内容"[3]。也因为国家行为不直接产生权利，而是用于解释权利的具体内涵，也就是说，巩固和地图及其他书面证据一样，在同一位阶起到说明法定权源如何规定争议土地法律地位的作用，因此，巩固虽然代表国家的直接行为，但是不再享有作为直接证据的优先地位。

因此，在已经存在有效法律权源的情况下，所有权的历史性巩固本身不能独立产生权利，而是与其他类别的证据一起，说明法律权源对争议土地归属情况的规定。

第三节　小　结

本章的初步结论包括：

1. 历史上因占有所形成的权利是主权者通过与特定土地产生关联而享有的领土权利，这种权利必须来自符合时际法要求的有效管理形式。

2. 由于直接行使权利的证据随着时间延长而不断模糊，以及国际

---

[1] Land, Island and Maritime Frontier Dispute (El Salvador v. Honduras Nicaragua intervening), International Court of Justice Reports, 1992, p. 562.
[2] Land, Island and Maritime Frontier Dispute (El Salvador v. Honduras Nicaragua intervening), International Court of Justice Reports, 1992, p. 564.
[3] Vienna Convention on the Law of Treaties, United Nations Treaty Series, 1969, Vol. 1155.

司法要件对能够产生权利的历史事实提出明确反映争议法律状态的要求，占有状态得到广泛认可，是权利存在的独立要件。

3. 基于历史事实产生的权利，既可能形成完全的主权，也可能成为权利巩固的起点，但无论如何，其法律效力要强于原初权利，维持原有管理方式和强度不中断即可保持权利。

4. 历史上的长期占有所形成的权利，如果被另一主权所取代或出现了较强的竞争权源，则可能导致领土主权权利链中断，失去法律效力或成为较弱的权源。

5. 很难说领土取得中是否存在与"归还"相关的国际法规则，但是应该承认实践中存在主权或主权假设的原持有国在介入因素消失后主张归还的可能。

6. 所有权的历史性巩固是国家取得主权不明土地的补充方式。

7. 当存在完全主权时，除非主权原持有国表示放弃，否则主权不会失去；除非竞争主张国已经实施有效管理，否则放弃主权不意味着移交给竞争主张国。

8. 在取得原属他国的领土时，所有权的历史性巩固法律效力上等同于时效。

9. 当法律权源是争议土地的唯一主权来源时，所有权的历史性巩固是法律权源的解释工具。

第五章 海洋法上的历史性所有权

在历史性所有权的演进中我们已经看到，海洋法领域的实践不但为历史性所有权提供丰富的证据，促进了对历史性所有权一般理论的认识，更帮助历史性所有权在国际法规则体系中占据稳固的一席之地。1958年《领海和毗连区公约》以及1982年《海洋法公约》都将与历史性所有权相关的条款列为海洋法的条约规定。尊重历史性所有权也被认为是一项习惯国际法规则。国际法院在"大陆架划界案"中指出，历史性所有权应该得到尊重，并以长久以来的惯例方式加以保护。[1]另外，作为海洋法上历史性所有权载体的历史性水域，在海洋法整体制度中处于特殊位置，即海洋法肯定历史性水域的有效性，但是其有效性的基础却并不来自海洋法本身，而是来自一般国际法，更确切地说，是历史性所有权的存在与否。[2]与此同时，国际法院还特别指出，并不存在单独的历史性水域或历史性海湾制度，只存在基于每一个被承认为历史性水域的特别制度。[3]如果说历史性水域法律制度推动了历史性所有权一般性理论的发展，那么此时，对特定历史性水域的判定将依赖于海洋这一具体语境中历史性所有权的应用。因此，本章的研究将围绕历史性所有权理论如何应用于历史性水域实践这一问题展开研究。

海洋的自然环境和国际法一般原则都会对历史性所有权基本要件的适用产生深刻的影响。对于"有效管理"要件来说，海洋法中历史

---

[1] Continental Shelf Case (Tunisia v. Libyan Arab Jamahiriya), International Court of Justice Reports, 1982, p. 73.
[2] Fisheries Case (The United Kingdom v. Norway), International Court of Justice Reports, 1951, p. 130.
[3] Continental Shelf Case (Tunisia v. Libyan Arab Jamahiriya), International Court of Justice Reports, 1982, p. 74.

性所有权的判定不存在相互竞争的权源，这就是说衡量是否对特定水域实施有效管理的，不是权源间的比较，而是一个包括海洋自然环境和特定利益在内的综合性标准。此外，随着专属经济区和大陆架制度在条约和习惯法层面的确立，海洋形成公海、沿海国享有主权权利和管辖权的水域以及沿海国享有完全主权的水域三个层面。根据主权行使行为与主张相称的原则，只有与取得历史性水域直接相关的行为才能被视为是满足"有效管理"要件的要求。而对于"相关国家的同意"而言，尽管历史性水域的法律基础平行于海洋法，但是仍然受到"公海自由"这一基本原则的制约。因此，沿海国的历史性水域主张本质上是一种逆权占有，而这一权利的原持有者理论上是整个国际社会，这两点将是考虑相关国家态度对历史性水域影响时需要牢记的因素。

在上述先决因素影响下，历史性所有权概念将如何适用于历史性水域的取得；在适用过程中，涉及哪些影响因素，以及海洋法的相关法律制度的产生和发展又对现今的历史性水域取得产生怎样的影响，这些将是本章具体处理的问题。对这些问题的分析将建立在国际司法实践和公法家学说的基础上，此外，历史性水域主张国的国内法实践和单方面主张也将作为国家实践的证据，和前两者一起构成本章的材料来源。

第一节　历史性水域的法律基础

一、权利来源

通过有效管理体现的占有关系和相关国家的同意作为历史性水域的权源，得到国际法实践和公法家学说的一致支持，但是我们仍然需要进一步回答作为历史性水域权源的是哪一类具体的历史性所有权，是历史上的长期占有还是所有权的历史性巩固，如果是后者，那么代表的是对归属不明物的直接占有，还是对他主物的逆权占有？和对陆地领土的取得一样，关于这些问题的不同回答虽然不影响对构成要件各自有效性的判断，但是将决定要件在形成权源时的相互关系，从而将是否存在历史性水域的答案导向不同的方向。

历史上的长期占有，或者说自古以来形成的惯例曾被认为是历史性水域的权利来源[1]，即便如此，这一权利来源的意思与领土取得中历史上的占有也不一致。对历史性水域主张来说，实际的占有状态必须延续到关键日期，占有状态的中断并不会使之前的有效管理产生初始权利的效果，而是将其法律效果归于消灭。从这个角度来说，历史性水域的权源应当是权利的历史性巩固而不是自古以来的占有。

对直接占有和逆权占有来说，在海洋法语境中判断两者作为历史性水域权源的标准，与其说是原先权利持有者的不同，不如说是与既存的国际法规则的关系不同。在"北大西洋渔业仲裁案"中，仲裁庭指出在缺乏一般国际法规则的情况下，沿海国基于已经确立的惯例可以提出历史性海湾的主张。[2] 可见，当时由于尚不存在有关海湾封口线宽度的海洋法规则，沿海国根据习惯法的领土取得规则提出占有并不违背国际法，此时历史性水域的取得属于对海洋的直接占有。随着海洋习惯法规则的逐步出现和编纂，直接占有与逆权占有间的争论在"英挪渔业案"中全面爆发，英国认为挪威对直线基线法的主张是一种不符合一般国际法的实践，这一主张有效性的来源只能是基于长期执行并获得其他国家的默许或不反对。[3] 挪威则提出另一种理解，挪威大使声明挪威政府并不依赖历史证明主张一般法律所不允许的例外权利，其引用历史，并与其他相关因素一起，证明挪威适用一般国际法的方法是合理的。[4] 法院认为挪威的实践并不违反"基线不得偏离海岸一般走向"的国际法规则，但法院并未就此认定挪威的实践对英国具有当然的约束力，而是从行为中推断英国默认了挪威的实践。[5]

从这一实用主义的案件处理手法中很难看出国际法院对历史性水域权源的看法，因为，无论是以直接占有还是逆权占有的角度作为出

---

[1] Historic Bays: Memorandum by the Secretariat of the United Nations, A/CONF. 13/1, 1957, p. 28 – 29.

[2] The North Atlantic Coast Fisheries Case (Great Britain v. United States), United Nations Reports of International Arbitration Awards, 1910, Vol. 11, p. 197.

[3] Fisheries Case (The United Kingdom v. Norway), International Court of Justice Reports, 1951, p. 130.

[4] Fisheries Case (The United Kingdom v. Norway), International Court of Justice Reports, 1951, p. 133.

[5] Fisheries Case (The United Kingdom v. Norway), International Court of Justice Reports, 1951, p. 139.

发点,都可以对英国因为默认而接受挪威实践的拘束效力作出合理的解读。一种解释是挪威的实践符合习惯法的要求,理论上效力及于英国,但是英国仍有以持续反对方式拒绝接受拘束的机会,英国未能及时表示反对,失去持续反对者身份。另一种解释则是挪威实践不违反国际法但是并不拘束英国,英国由于长期不作为形成默认从而接受挪威实践的有效性。

1957年联合国秘书处准备的"历史性海湾"备忘录收录了国家实践和学者意见,其中多数看法认为,作为历史性海湾法律基础的历史性所有权是对一般国际法规则的减损[1],但仍有少部分学者认为历史性所有权可以建立在符合一般国际法规则的前提之上。[2]在随后的"包括历史性海湾在内的历史性水域法律制度研究"中,国际法委员会并未正面回答历史性水域的取得是基于直接占有还是逆权占有的问题,但是委员会对历史性水域制度是否构成海洋法的例外制度的回答提供了解决这一问题的思路。国际法委员会认为只有在特定领域已经存在一般性规则的情况下,才会存在不符合一般规则限制但仍享有国际法上有效性的历史性水域,即是否存在与历史性水域主张针锋相对的国际法规则是判断历史性所有权权源性质的依据。[3]根据这一思路,我们可以进一步分析现行海洋法体系内的历史性水域的权利来源。

如果说在国际法委员会对历史性水域问题展开研究时,有关领海宽度或者海湾封口线等的一系列海洋法规则尚未成形,在沿海国主权和海洋自由之间存在需要通过一般国际法规则进行填补的灰色空间。那么当前《海洋法公约》已经生效并且其中多数规则被认为反映了习惯国际法的情况下,事实上产生了以公约规则替换一般国际法对海洋进行确权管理的结果。例如,以《海洋法公约》的群岛国制度部分取代了基于一般国际法的群岛历史性水域。此时,主张《海洋法公约》规定沿海国主权范围以外水域的所有权只能建立在逆权占有的基础上,也就是说,由于公海权利原先持有者的同意,沿海国得以维持占有原

---

[1] Historic Bays: Memorandum by the Secretariat of the United Nations, A/CONF.13/1, 1957, p.16-21.
[2] Historic Bays: Memorandum by the Secretariat of the United Nations, A/CONF.13/1, 1957, p.19.
[3] Juridical Regime of Historic Waters, Including Historic Bays, International Law Commission Yearbook, 1962 (2), p.10.

属公海水域的事实并将其上升获得国际法尊重和保护的权利。虽然主张国占有历史性水域的历史往往可以追溯到相关国际法规则确定之前，某些历史性水域被宣布占有的时间甚至早于公海自由这一习惯法规则形成的时间[1]，但是由于时际法的存在，即使在公海自由成为习惯国际法之前占有的水域，其现实有效性也要接受相关国家态度的检验。如果这一占有没有被国际社会所认可，那么沿海国单凭占有的事实并不能产生法律上的排他性所有权。

历史性水域的权源属于逆权占有的界定是否同时意味着历史性水域也应该被视为海洋法的例外性规则？尽管实践中历史性所有权要件的考察要求并不因为历史性水域是否具有例外性而有所变化，但是在公海自由原则下取得海洋是否构成国际法的例外制度，这一问题至少在学术意义上是不可回避的[2]。

布鲁姆认为历史性所有权的一般性质就是减损一般情况下适用的国际法规则，因此取得海洋的历史性所有权也具有例外性。[3]多数直接针对历史性水域发表的学者意见也认定这一水域的存在是海洋法规则的例外。[4]国际法委员会认为当能够证明存在一般习惯法规则时，那么与其相对应的历史性所有权主张可以被视为例外。[5]

值得注意的是，委员会为这一结论设置了前提，即历史性水域只能成为习惯法规则的例外，理由是两者都以国家实践为基础，因此具有可比性。[6]遵循同样的法律基础方能产生可比性的思路，国际法院在"大陆架划界案"中指出突尼斯主张的历史性所有权和大陆架权利分属两套不同的法律制度，前者来源于取得的行为而后者来自作为陆地延伸的事实，两片区域有时会部分或整体地重合。而突尼斯主张通

---

[1] Land, Island and Maritime Frontier Dispute (El Salvador v. Honduras Nicaragua intervening), International Court of Justice Reports, 1992, p. 589.
[2] M. W. Clark Jr., *Historical Bays and Waters, A Regime of Recent Beginning and Continued Usage*, Oceana Publication, 1994, p. 69.
[3] Yehuda Z. Blum, *Historic Titles in International Law*, Martinus Nijhoff, 1965, p. 261.
[4] Clive R. Symmons, *Historic Waters in the Law of the Sea, A Modern Re-Appraisal*, Martinus Nijhoff, 2008, p. 49 - 50.
[5] Juridical Regime of Historic Waters, Including Historic Bays, International Law Commission Yearbook, 1962 (2), p. 10.
[6] Juridical Regime of Historic Waters, Including Historic Bays, International Law Commission Yearbook, 1962 (2), p. 10.

过长期利用和管辖取得权利的区域在大陆架制度下本身就是不需要行使权利而存在的"水下突尼斯",因此突尼斯所主张的历史性所有权对大陆架划界的制度不产生法律效果。[1]

由此可以说,在特定条件下,历史性水域确实是海洋法的例外制度,而特定条件是指在与特定的历史性水域相关的法律制度中已经存在普遍适用的习惯法规则。例如,存在 24 海里海湾封口线的习惯法规则,则相应存在不考虑海湾封口线宽度的历史性海湾规则作为例外。而对于直线基线划界法来说,《海洋法公约》已经将适用直线基线的地理条件和经济利益编纂为国际法规则,那么直线基线划界就不能被认为是领海基线的例外规则。

可见,对历史性水域的权源是基于直接占有还是逆权占有是一个历史命题,在当前的海洋法体系内讨论历史性水域问题,其法律基础应当被界定为是逆权占有性质的所有权的历史性巩固。这一逆权占有的状态相对于特定的国际法规则来说是一种例外,但就规则本身而言,历史性所有权与海洋法分属独立的规则体系,不存在可比性,也不存在适用的优先性。

二、历史性所有权的发现方式

(一)司法裁决

国际司法裁决,虽然不是发现历史性水域的最主要方式,但称得上是争议最少的历史性水域发现方式。国际司法实践中直接判定历史性水域是否存在的判例并不多见,包括决定丰塞卡海湾法律地位的一系列裁决和解决挪威直线基线划界实践合法性的"英挪渔业案"。在争端解决过程中,司法机构依然根据有效管理和相关国家同意两个要件判断历史性水域主张的成立与否,但由于得到司法效力的背书,被国际司法认可的历史性水域往往被附加上了终局性和普遍性的额外特点。

一方面,国际司法机构的肯定裁决意味着历史性水域的主张已经完成了巩固,取得固定的国际法地位,即便相关的国际法一般规则在

---

[1] Continental Shelf Case (Tunisia v. Libyan Arab Jamahiriya), International Court of Justice Reports, 1982, p. 74.

此后发生变化，为了维护国际法和国际社会秩序的稳定，其法律地位也不会因时际法的改变而有所改变。另一方面，尽管与历史性水域相关的争议发生在两个或多个特定国家之间，裁决效力不拘束除案件参与者以外的其他国家，但是国际司法可以被理解为代表了国际社会对特定历史性水域主张的态度，从而使争议涉及的历史性水域取得针对所有国家的有效性。

此外，国际司法机构的裁决还反映了历史性水域的发展实践，从而被编纂形成相关的习惯法规则，成为此后历史性水域成立与否的参照标准。例如《领海及毗连区公约》第12条第1款和《海洋法公约》第15条所规定的海岸相邻或相向国家间，如存在历史性所有权时则不适用领海中间线划界的规则，就是反映了"格里斯巴达纳仲裁案"中历史性所有权对领海划界规则的影响。而在里程碑式的"英挪渔业案"后，判决中有关采取直线基线时可考虑长期惯例证明特殊经济利益的内容，迅速体现在紧随其后制定的《领海及毗连区公约》第4条中，并在《海洋法公约》第7条中得到进一步继承和确认，转化为海洋法的一般性适用规则。

当然，依靠国际司法确定历史性水域的地位也存在一定的不足。由于国际社会权力机构分散，国际司法也同样反映出非科层制的结构特色，会出现互不隶属的国际司法机构重复裁决同一历史性水域法律地位的情况。在"陆地、岛屿和海洋边界案"中，国际法院在考虑是否对丰塞卡海湾进行划界之前，重新考察了中美洲法院在"萨尔瓦多诉尼加拉瓜案"中获得的海湾属于三国共有的历史性海湾这一结论。尽管国际法院认为前案中历史性海湾的结论并无不妥，但是仍然根据历史性所有权的要件再次考察了丰塞卡海湾的情况。[1]也就是说国际法院在实质意义上认同了中美洲法院的判决，而不是因为前案是生效判决而接受该案的判决结果。[2]

国际司法权力机构松散产生的另一个问题是难以建立管辖权，如何说服乃至强制当事国将争议提交国际司法机构裁决是国际法面临的

---

[1] Land, Island and Maritime Frontier Dispute (El Salvador v. Honduras Nicaragua intervening), International Court of Justice Reports, 1992, p. 601-602.

[2] 这一结论与前文终局性结论并不矛盾，也不意味着国际司法对丰塞卡海湾法律地位的判定违背了一事不再理。争议各方对此前中美洲法院裁定的海湾具有封闭的历史性海湾地位没有异议，争议在于是否划界。

先天性难题,这一问题同样反映在历史性水域争议的解决中。《海洋法公约》第 298 条将历史性海湾和所有权的争端作为强制争端解决程序的任择性例外[1],等于将争端解决的管辖权交给成员国自行选择。而由于历史性水域是国家完全主权的组成部分,国家接受国际司法的动机将在更多非法律因素的影响下表现得更为勉强,因此国际司法并不是一种高效的权源发现方式。

除了国际司法裁决外,一国的国内司法裁决也是发现历史性水域的重要途径,事实上,国内司法实践是历史性水域理论的最早起源。这类国内法裁决和作为有效管理证据的司法行为不同,后者通过在沿海国历史性水域主张的区域范围内行使司法权力的方式,证明对相关区域的有效管理,而前者则直接在司法裁决过程中根据历史性所有权的要件作出是否存在历史性水域的直接判断。

大部分国内司法裁决不是直接以决定历史性水域为目的,更多的是在确定法院决定中立、确立管辖权或者其他目标的过程中对争议涉及区域的法律地位作出判断。例如在"直美电缆有限公司诉美国英美电报公司案"中,英国枢密院面对的问题是纽芬兰授予英美电报公司专营权的地理范围,在考虑专营权授权范围是否囊括整个康塞普申海湾时,枢密院指出英国政府长时间控制海湾,而英国的主张被其他国家长期默认,使得海湾被纳入英国排他性的管辖范围[2],这等于间接宣布了康塞普申海湾的历史性水域地位。

也有一些国内司法是以直接决定历史性水域为目的。以美国为例,由于联邦制的国家架构,美国在国内法体系中存在联邦和州之间的历史性水域,从 1947 年的"合众国诉加利福尼亚案"开始,联邦最高法院在一系列判决中建立起美国领海范围内的水下资源属于联邦的规则。作为回应,国会在 1953 年通过《水下陆地法案》,将内水及海岸线向海部分 3 英里的水下资源授予沿海各州,但是法案中没有给出内水和

---

[1] United Nations Conventions on the Law of the Sea, United Nations Treaty Series, 1982, Vol. 1833.
[2] Historic Bays: Memorandum by the Secretariat of the United Nations. A/CONF. 13/1, 1957, p. 4 – 5.

海岸线的定义。[1]在1967年的"合众国诉加利福尼亚州案"中,最高法院决定采用《领海和毗连区公约》中对内水的定义,也随之接受了公约规定的领海基线体系,包括海湾封口线和历史性海湾的概念。[2]在上述现实和法律背景下,联邦最高法院处理包括"合众国诉路易斯安那州案"、"合众国诉阿拉斯加案"以及"合众国诉缅因案"等一系列历史性水域案件,其中最有代表性的是"合众国诉路易斯安那州"系列案中的"亚拉巴马州和密西西比州边界案"。[3]案件中,亚拉巴马州和密西西比州认为,整个密西西比河口是历史性海湾,因而应采用河口封口线作为该地区的海岸线,而联邦政府则主张密西西比河口是普通海岸,应使用的是低潮线。[4]法院采纳特别报告员支持两个沿海州立场的报告,认为美国在1803—1971年期间对密西西比河口实施了有效管理并且得到其他国家的承认[5]。

尽管国内司法机构在裁决历史性水域过程中,同样采用是否符合历史性所有权的构成要件作为依据,它的判决结果并不当然产生被国际法所认可的历史性水域地位。不过,法院对存在历史性水域的肯定性结论和争端解决过程中,对有效管理和相关国家态度的考察,并非全无国际法意义。首先,法院的判决表明沿海国最晚至判决作出时提出了历史性水域主张,并产生公开宣示的效果,使本国实践为国际社会所知。[6]其次,法院在裁决过程中有效管理和相关国家态度的考察虽然不直接产生国际法的效果,但是为明确历史性水域的法律地位提供了证据。过往的实践证明,已经被国内司法认定的历史性水域,往

---

[1] Kathleen L. Walz, *The United States Supreme Court & Article VII of the 1958 Convention on the Territorial Sea & Contiguous Zone*, University of San Francisco Law Review, Vol. 11: 1, p. 4–6 (1976–1977).

[2] Louisiana Boundary Case, 394 U. S. 11, 1969, p. 3.

[3] 每个案件代表联邦政府和这一区域各州的一系列案件,例如"合众国诉路易斯安那州案"就代表了联邦政府和墨西哥湾沿岸各州间因水下资源分配产生的案件。而"亚拉巴马州和密西西比州边界案"是联邦最高法院第一次支持州的历史性所有权主张。James Michael Zimmerman, *The Doctrine of Historic Bays: Applying an Anachronism in Alabama and Mississippi Boundary Case*, San Diego Law Review, Vol. 23: 763, p. 778 (1986).

[4] Alabama and Mississippi Boundary Case, 470 U. S. 93, 1985, p. 1076–1077.

[5] Alabama and Mississippi Boundary Case, 470 U. S. 93, 1985, p. 1080–1084.

[6] Clive R. Symmons, *Historic Waters in the Law of the Sea*, *A Modern Re-Appraisal*, Martinus Nijhoff, 2008, p. 124.

往最后也获得了国际法的认可。

无论是在国际法还是国内法环境中,司法检验总是能为权源的存在与否提供最为确切的答案。需要牢记的是,无论如何,赋予历史性水域法律地位的,只能是该水域符合历史性所有权存在的要件,司法过程是历史性所有权发现的方式,而不是权利的实质来源。因此,在确定历史性水域的过程中,需要对通过国家的单方面主张发现的权源保持同样的关注,而由于国家实践的多样性和不确定性,从其中确定历史性所有权的存在需要面对更多的问题。

(二)单方面历史性水域主张

总体来说,检验单方面历史性水域主张是否成立根本上基于前文论证的历史性所有权的构成要件。同时,海洋管理的特点、海洋法的体系以及历史性水域逆权占有的特征都将对"有效管理"和"相关国家的同意"在海洋法框架内的表现产生特定的影响。

"有效管理"要件的实现应当遵循"管理行为与主张相称"的原则。国际法委员会曾指出海洋法上历史性所有权的范围原则上不超于主张国主权实际实施的范围[1]。这一看法的含义除涉及前文已经讨论的地理范围限制以外,由于海洋法存在多层级海域管理的现实,因而不同的管理行为影响不同水域的法律地位。在陆地领土的取得过程中,包括民刑事司法管辖、行政管理和经济社会管理在内的行为都可以被视为国家对其主张的土地实施有效管理的证据。而对历史性水域的取得来说,主张国的管理行为并不当然被视为主张所有权的证据,主权行使的意图将因主张的特征而变动[2]。小田(Oda)法官反对丰塞卡海湾获得历史性水域地位的理由之一就是,尽管沿海三国提供了对海湾进行巡逻管理的证据,但是这一职能早就得到国际法的普遍接受,成为沿海国家在毗连区的权利之一[3]。因此,作为取得内水和领海法律地位的历史性水域,对水域的管理行为必须与沿海国主张应享有的排他性权利相一致,具体表现为排他性的资源占有和管理以及对其他

---

[1] Juridical Regime of Historic Waters, Including Historic Bays, International Law Commission Yearbook, 1962(2), p. 13.

[2] L. J. Bouchez, *The Regime of Bays in International Law*, Sythoff, 1964, p. 249.

[3] Land, Island and Maritime Frontier Dispute (El Salvador v. Honduras Nicaragua intervening), International Court of Justice Reports, 1992, p. 757.

国家船只的航行管理。

对主张领海性质的历史性水域来说，由于无害通行权的存在，沿海国的有效管理最主要体现为对渔业和底土自然资源的占有，以及排除或者管理其他国家在此区域内从事相关作业的权利。在科技发展使得沿海国可能抽取底土和海水中蕴藏的自然资源之前，渔业活动是沿海国在领海的最重要经济活动。但是渔业管理行为的法律意义需要区别于长期捕鱼产生的权利，也就是传统捕鱼权利。"厄立特里亚—也门仲裁案"的仲裁庭认可争议双方渔民由于在共同宗教信仰下，因长期捕鱼所形成的渔业资源共有机制，提出在主权分配后双方渔民仍然享有自由进出传统渔业活动水域、自由使用岛屿从事与传统渔业相关活动的权利。而取得岛屿主权以及相应领海权利一方，有义务采取措施保证双方渔民继续享有传统渔业活动带来的利益。[1]这类利益保障方式，作为传统捕鱼权的一种表现形式，本质上是一种沿海国权利扩张后的利益补偿机制，这一权利尽管来自国家之间的安排，但是权利的创设者和享受者都不是国家，权利本身也没有主权行使和排他性的特征，因而并不能成为主张所有权的依据。

此外，随着海洋法的发展，特别是毗连区、大陆架和专属经济区的出现并成为习惯法规则，对自然资源的排他性占有和管理的依据不再是国家主权的行为，而是国际法赋予的权利。国际海洋法提供沿海国对领海范围以外自然资源的主权权利和管辖权，这不仅意味着沿海国不再只能依赖历史性水域主张作为获得更大范围权利的依据，因而不再有强烈的提出历史性水域主张的动机[2]，反之对历史性水域主张来说，也意味着在检验沿海国有效管理的行为时，还需要进一步考察是否来自海洋法相关制度的授权。

而对于主张具有内水性质的历史性水域来说，对航行的管理才是沿海国有效管理的最重要证据。国际法委员会曾引述吉德尔的观点，排除其他国家船只或使其他国家船只接受沿海国对超过正常航行需要

---

[1] Eritrea-Yemen Arbitration (Second Stage), International Legal Materials, Vol 40: 979, 979 - 1001 (2001).

[2] Clive R. Symmons, *Historic Waters in the Law of the Sea, A Modern Re-Appraisal*, Martinus Nijhoff, 2008, p. 272 - 273.

的管理，为沿海国取得历史性水域的意图提供了令人信服的证据。[1]实践中，沿海国在提出历史性水域主张后往往宣布对水域航行进行管理，例如苏联宣布彼得大帝湾为内水的法令在规定海湾部分领海基线后，明确要求其他国家船只或飞行器在基线范围内的航行和飞越须接受苏联有关机构的授权。[2]利比亚在宣布锡拉湾为本国历史性海湾时也主张外国私人和国家船舶在未得到利比亚允许并符合利比亚相关航行规定的情况下不得进入海湾。[3]

和对自然资源的管理行为一样，对航行的管理同样需要确定管理权利不是来自国际法的授权，也就是沿海国在特定区域因正常航行需要而依据国际法采取的管理措施不会产生取得所有权的效果。1970年，加拿大颁布《北极水域污染预防法案》，其中规定100海里的污染控制区，在此区域内加拿大有权控制外国船舶的航行。有加拿大学者认为这一立法以及随后的实施有助于加拿大对西北航道提出历史性水域主张。[4]但是，具有习惯法编纂性质的《海洋法公约》第234条已授权沿海国实施防止和控制船只在该国专属经济区内的冰封区域海洋造成污染的行为[5]，因此，加拿大的立法和实施行为很难在未来成为主张西北航道为该国历史性水域的证据。

对"相关国家的同意"要件来说，既然确定历史性水域的权源来自对逆权占有的巩固，这意味着相关国家的同意对历史性水域取得的影响，不仅在于证明沿海国已经通过有效管理完成对其主张水域的占有，更在于表达了国际社会对主张国占有的认可态度。在这一过程中，相关国家对主张的正确认识以及国家同意或抗议态度的表达都适用前文已经得出的结论。但是实践中，历史性水域的争议通常发生在具体的争议方之间，而历史性水域一旦获得认定，将成为一个具有普遍拘

---

[1] Juridical Regime of Historic Waters, Including Historic Bays, International Law Commission Yearbook, 1962 (2), p. 14.
[2] M. W. Clark Jr., *Historical Bays and Waters, A Regime of Recent Beginning and Continued Usage*, Oceana Publication, 1994, p. 160.
[3] Yehuda Z. Blum, *The Gulf of Sidra Incident*. American Journal of International Law, Vol. 80: 668, p. 668-669 (1986).
[4] M. W. Clark Jr., *Historical Bays and Waters, A Regime of Recent Beginning and Continued Usage*, Oceana Publication, 1994, p. 160.
[5] United Nations Conventions on the Law of the Sea, United Nations Treaty Series, 1982, Vol. 1833.

束力的法律现实。因此，对于单方面主张的历史性水域来说，实践产生的问题就是如何协调特定的同意方和普遍法律效力的关系。

在对历史性所有权要件的一般性研究中已经发现，实践中常常由利益相关国和邻国代表国际社会对历史性水域主张做出反应。[1]但是前文的研究局限在如何判定单个国家的态度上，如果相关国家对历史性水域主张持有不一致的态度，将对水域法律地位的确定产生怎样的影响以及相关国家是否因为自己的表态而当然接受拘束则仍需要在实践环境中作进一步的区分和讨论。

在"包括历史性海湾在内的历史性水域法律制度"研究中，国际法委员接受国际法院在"英挪渔业案"中的提法，认为国际社会的普遍认同是历史性所有权中的相关国家态度的判断标准[2]，后来的学者进一步将普遍认同定量为取得大多数相关国家的同意。[3]可见，无论如何，一国或者极少数国家的同意，在更多相关国家反对的情况下无法产生普遍性的历史性水域。这一结果并不因同意采取的形式而有所区别。1982年越南和柬埔寨签署协议，以特殊地理条件、对两国经济和国防的重要性为理由，将包围两国在内的泰国湾和北部湾的直线基线连接起来，从而在邻近两国陆地边界的地区创设出一片具有内水性质的"共同历史性水域"[4]。从相关国家态度的角度可以把越南和柬埔寨之间的双边协定看作两国对各自历史性水域主张的认可，尽管两国间的主张和相互同意采取条约的形式，但是主张历史性水域的条约对于其他国家来说，无疑施加了接受航行管理乃至禁止驶入的义务，因此根据施加义务的条约不拘束第三方的国际法规则，双方的协议不影响其他国家做出反应的权利。[5]当然，在协议的两国之间，由于条约的拘束，即使不存在普遍意义的历史性权利，双方仍应以条约的规定行事，只是其法律基础不再是主权而是国际法授予的沿海国管理权利。

---

[1] Juridical Regime of Historic Waters, Including Historic Bays, International Law Commission Yearbook, 1962 (2), p. 13.

[2] Juridical Regime of Historic Waters, Including Historic Bays, International Law Commission Yearbook, 1962 (2), p. 18.

[3] Clive R. Symmons, *Historic Waters in the Law of the Sea, A Modern Re-Appraisal*, Martinus Nijhoff, 2008, p. 219 - 220.

[4] Jonathan I. Charney, Lewis M. Alexander, *International Maritime Boundaries*, Martinus Nijhoff, 2004, p. 2359.

[5] L. J. Bouchez, *The Regime of Bays in International Law*, Sythoff, 1964, p. 259.

另一种相反的情况是，相当数量的国家对历史性水域主张持积极或默认的赞同态度，而个别国家则保持反对的态度。一般情况下，个别相关国家的反对态度不足以否定已经被更多国家接受的历史性水域主张，同时在"英挪渔业案"中我们也观察到具备国际法上有效性的挪威实践也是因为英国的默认方才对该国产生拘束，那么如果一国从沿海国最初提出主张时就持续表达反对态度，将对本国权利产生怎样的影响？

多数意见认为被视为内水或者领海的历史性水域范围内将不再存在其他国家的剩余权利，因此阻止历史性水域对本国产生影响的唯一途径就是在历史性所有权尚在形成的过程中积极表达反对意见以防止权利的生成。[1]但是和条约的保留一样，国际法并不存在基于多数成员同意而剥夺个别成员权利的规则。由于反对态度的根本目的在于在任何情况下维持本国的权利不受侵害，而历史性水域制度，作为基于国家实践的习惯法，逻辑上也不应排斥对习惯法上的持续反对者规则的适用。因此至少在理论上存在这样的可能，一国长期实施的实践和对历史性水域主张的持续反对态度，可以产生针对历史性水域的历史性所有权，即在承认存在具有普遍有效性的历史性水域的基础上，保留持续反对国家的特定权利，例如在内水范围内的历史性航行权。

第二节 相关因素的影响

历史性水域的取得并不是单纯基于抽象的有效管理和相关国家的同意，而是这两个要件所形成的权源在特定的环境下产生将水域和主张国主权相联系的法律状态。一方面，国际法规则和实践都重视特定的自然和社会环境与历史性水域的紧密关联。《海洋法公约》规定实在而重要的经济利益是确定特定直线基线的考虑因素。[2]"英挪渔业案"中，国际法院也将挪威沿岸的特殊地形和渔业构成挪威西北沿岸

---

[1] M. W. Clark Jr., *Historical Bays and Waters, A Regime of Recent Beginning and Continued Usage*, Oceana Publication, 1994, p. 155.

[2] United Nations Conventions on the Law of the Sea, United Nations Treaty Series, 1982, Vol. 1833.

居民必要的生活来源，视为评价挪威划界方法有效性必须要考虑的因素。[1]可见，权利所处具体环境中的特定因素直接影响到对历史性水域的判断。

另一方面，有关历史性水域的相关因素与影响陆地领土取得的相关环境，两者在内容和作用上都不完全一致。就内容而言，国防和经济利益不能成为影响对陆地领土有效管理要求的理由；就作用来说，环境因素的存在在陆地取得中体现为影响有效管理的认定，而在取得历史性水域的实践中，相关因素不但和权源一起，成为沿海国单方面主张历史性水域的理由，也共同影响着司法机构对是否存在历史性水域的判断。[2]

本节将逐个讨论实践中涉及历史性水域的相关因素，并对相关因素与权源的关系，以及在历史性水域取得中产生的影响和作用作出简要的评价。

一、自然因素

（一）地理构造和特殊地形

作为海洋法律制度，历史性水域的取得有时却受到与它相关的陆地情况的影响，包括水域是否被陆地包围的地理构造以及与水域相关的陆地地形特征。

历史性水域，特别是历史性海湾的地理构造是决定水域是否可以被沿海国取得的重要考虑因素。海湾的定义本身来自对水域自然地理的描述，《海洋法公约》第 10 条第 2 款将海湾定义为凹入程度和曲口宽度构成一定比例，使其有被陆地环抱的明显特征的水域，而对于不具有这一特征的水曲，除非面积等于或大于横越曲口所划的直线作为直径的半圆形的面积，否则不应视为海湾。[3]虽然随后的第 6 款排除

---

[1] Fisheries Case (The United Kingdom v. Norway), International Court of Justice Reports, 1951, p. 127.

[2] L. J. Bouchez, *The Regime of Bays in International Law*, Sythoff, 1964, p. 293.

[3] Historic Bays: Memorandum by the Secretariat of the United Nations, A/CONF. 13/1, 1957, p. 1 – 39. Also see Juridical Regime of Historic Waters, Including Historic Bays, International Law Commission Yearbook, 1962 (2), p. 2.

了这一条款对历史性海湾的效力，但并不意味着免除了海湾的地理构造对历史性所有权的影响。

从《海洋法公约》的体系看，对海湾的定义被置于内水部分的条款内，因此公约所指的海湾应进一步被解释为其中水体可视为内水的海湾。事实上，公约对海湾的界定确实不是海湾在自然意义上的定义，即便对"陆地环抱的海湾"采取最自由的解释，仍有大量现实中被称为海湾的水体不能满足这一定义。[1]历史上，陆地环抱海湾的地理现实就是沿海国可以根据"岬角理论"封闭海湾湾口的理论基础，而由此产生的所谓法律上的海湾和历史性海湾的区别，仅在于国际法上是否存在与海湾封口线宽度有关的习惯法规则。因此可以说，至少在实践中，地理情况符合公约定义描述的海湾，如果只是限于海湾封口线宽度而无法成为法律上的海湾，那么它本身相对于不符合公约对海湾定义的水域而言，更适合成为沿海国家取得的对象。

但是反过来说，不符合海湾定义的水体将因为其地理状态而增加取得的难度，这一结论是否成立？理论上，水域未被陆地环抱意味着与公海联系的强化，增加了沿海国对海湾进行有效管理的难度，而相关国家也更可能因为本国的航运利益对沿海国的主张表达反对态度。不过至少在实践中，不符合公约对海湾的定义没有成为相关国家反对的直接理由。[2]

除了构造形态以外，水域的地形条件也是影响历史性水域取得的陆地条件之一，在实践中这一自然条件往往与它所形成的利益关系结合在一起成为考虑因素。中美洲法院在"萨尔瓦多诉尼加拉瓜案"中指出，丰塞卡海湾中遍布大小不一的火山岛，岛屿的分布形成了4条深水航道使丰塞卡海湾成为天然良港，另外，海湾湾口的山地地形和湾内散布的岛屿可以为海湾提供重要的保护。[3]法院认为这些事实和海湾长期被占用的历史共同表明丰塞卡海湾是沿海三国排他所有的历史性海湾。[4]在"英挪渔业案"中，挪威的北部沿岸分布的石垒

---

[1] Mitchell P. Strohl, *International Law of Bays*, Martinus Nijhoff, 1963, p. 56.

[2] Mitchell P. Strohl, *International Law of Bays*, Martinus Nijhoff, 1963, p. 350–356.

[3] The Republic of El Salvador v. The Republic of Nicaragua, The American Journal of International Law, Vol. 11 (3), p. 675–676 (1917).

[4] The Republic of El Salvador v. The Republic of Nicaragua, The American Journal of International Law, Vol. 11 (3), p. 681 (1917).

(skjaegaard)所代表的特殊地形构成法院考虑该国实践有效性的标准。国际法院主张由于这些特殊地形，挪威的大陆和海岸没有明确的界线，石壁的外沿便是挪威的海岸线。而石壁的山地地形特征结合挪威的高纬度也意味着沿海地区农业产出的贫瘠和不稳定，从而渔业构成海岸居民的必要生活来源。[1]

可见，历史性水域所处环境的地理构造和地形特征以各自的方式影响着历史性水域的取得，如果说水域周围陆地的构造影响了是否适于取得的初步假设，那么水域所处的地形往往暗示着沿海国在此具有应当成为历史性水域考虑因素的特殊利益关系。

（二）大面积水域

在讨论水域面积作为影响历史性水域的因素之前，首先需要解决的问题是多大体量的水域可以称得上是大面积水域。和不存在统一的历史性水域制度一样，这个问题也没有可以量化的标准答案，而是应当根据个案的实际情况作出判断。当然对于已经达到一定体量的水域，在任何情况下都可以被认为属于大面积水域，例如对海湾来说，封口线明显超过24海里，或者水域面积远远高过以24海里海湾封口线为直径的根据同心圆法计算所得面积的水域，可以被视为大面积水域，而对于岛屿国家主张的历史性水域来说，水域与陆地面积比明显超过群岛国制度规定的范围，可以被视为大面积水域。

由于历史性水域的水体法律地位是具有主权性质的内水或领海，将大面积水域作为取得对象，显然违背现代海洋法尽可能多地保留"公海自由"的初衷。国际法实践中公认的历史性水域极少出现属于大面积水域的情况。[2]而在近期的国际法实践中，沿海国出于本国利益的需要，似乎并不介意对大面积水域提出主权主张。1940年，委内瑞拉在对法国的照会中提出面积为7700平方海里的委内瑞拉湾（Gulf of Venezuela）为该国历史性水域。[3]1973年，刚取得政权4年的卡扎

---

[1] Fisheries Case (The United Kingdom v. Norway), International Court of Justice Reports, 1951, p. 133.

[2] Historic Bays: Memorandum by the Secretariat of the United Nations, A/CONF.13/1, 1957, p. 6.

[3] Óscar Vila Masot, *The Gulf of Venezuela: A Case Study of Historic Waters*, Editorial Arte, 1991, p. 163.

菲政府改变前政府的领海主张，提出面积约为 22000 平方海里的锡德拉湾为该国内水。[1] 1982 年越南和柬埔寨主张的"共同历史性水域"则将超过 5000 平方海里的水域纳入两国的排他性主权。[2]

从法律上说，历史性所有权并不排除取得大面积水域。杰赛普认为时效主张可以针对大面积的水域，衡量主张有效性的应当是定义而不是水域的面积，大面积历史性水域在国际法实践和惯例中并不违法。[3]《海洋法公约》规定历史性海湾不适用关于海湾的一般规定，那么意味着历史性海湾在封口线长度和测量方式上都不受 24 海里和同心圆法的约束，也就是说国际法在规则层面不禁止对大面积水域提出历史性所有权的主张。

然而在实践中，一方面主张大面积历史性水域意味着需要在更大的地理范围内行使本国管辖权，而在另一方面则可能因为主张面积的扩大影响到更多国家的利益从而招致反对意见，加大了权源证明的难度。利比亚对锡德拉湾的主张几乎被所有地中海沿岸邻国所反对，美国在 1974 年声明反对后，1981 年在海湾内更是以军事行动的方式表明拒绝接受利比亚的主张。[4] 而越南和柬埔寨的共同历史性水域也因为对主张区域缺乏有效管理且从未得到相关国家同意而遭到泰国和美国的抗议，其有效性仍需要接受进一步的检验。[5]

加拿大的哈德逊湾可能是唯一得到国际公认的大面积历史性水域。[6] 这个最宽处到 600 海里，深入陆地达到 1000 海里的巨大海湾能

---

[1] Yehuda Z. Blum, *The Gulf of Sidra Incident*. American Journal of International Law, Vol. 80: 668, p. 668 (1986).

[2] Jonathan I. Charney, Lewis M. Alexander, *International Maritime Boundaries*, Martinus Nijhoff, 2004, p. 2359.

[3] Philip C. Jessup, *The Law of Territorial Waters and Maritime Jurisdiction*, G. A. Jennings Co., Inc., 1927, p. 382.

[4] Yehuda Z. Blum, *The Gulf of Sidra Inciden*, American Journal of International Law, Vol. 80: 668, p. 668 - 669 (1986).

[5] Jonathan I. Charney, Lewis M. Alexander, *International Maritime Boundaries*, Martinus Nijhoff, 2004, p. 2359.

[6] Historic Bays: Memorandum by the Secretariat of the United Nations, A/CONF. 13/1, 1957, p. 6. Also see Mitchell P. Strohl, *International Law of Bays*, Martinus Nijhoff, 1963, p. 233.

够得到国际社会的承认有其独特的原因。[1]首先，加拿大占有海湾的历史可以追溯到1670年英国政府将整个海湾流域的陆地和水域授予哈德逊湾公司，此后直至1906年加拿大正式立法宣布哈德逊湾为该国领水期间，加拿大当局实施了包括破冰、巡查、航行救助等一系列管理行为。[2]其次，由于哈德逊湾位于高纬度地区，海湾中仅能实施季节性捕鲸作业，其他国家很难因为海湾所有权与加拿大产生利益冲突，因此没有国家对加拿大的主张提出正式的反对意见。最后，哈德逊湾虽然面积巨大，但是仅通过一条宽度约为38海里的哈德逊海峡与大西洋连接[3]，从地理构造角度非常适于成为沿海国的取得对象。而海湾常年冰封，水域深入加拿大腹地且只有一条通道连通大洋，也意味着哈德逊湾在对加拿大国家安全有重大影响的同时，对国际航运影响甚微。[4]综合上述种种原因才促成哈德逊湾成为公认的大面积历史性水域。

二、利益因素

历史性水域对沿海国家的重大利益即便不在表面上构成沿海国提出主权的理由，也肯定是国家主张管辖的动机所在。而相关国家的同意或反对背后潜藏的含义，也是沿海国的主权主张是否对本国利益产生影响。正如小克拉克所说，水域被取得不会对邻国利益产生不利影响或者水域的不取得不会对沿海国产生不利影响都会影响到对法律上要件的判断。[5]从这个角度来看，历史性水域的发展中以"重大利益"来描述这种利益显得只顾及主张国与水域间的关系，不够全面，真正的利益因素分析应当是历史性水域对主张国利益的正面影响和对国际社会利益的负面影响进行比较与权衡。

---

[1] Historic Bays: Memorandum by the Secretariat of the United Nations, A/CONF. 13/1, 1957, p. 6.
[2] Mitchell P. Strohl, *International Law of Bays*, Martinus Nijhoff, 1963, p. 237 - 239.
[3] Mitchell P. Strohl, *International Law of Bays*, Martinus Nijhoff, 1963, p. 234.
[4] Mitchell P. Strohl, *International Law of Bays*, Martinus Nijhoff, 1963, p. 234.
[5] M. W. Clark Jr., *Historical Bays and Waters*, *A Regime of Recent Beginning and Continued Usage*, Oceana Publication, 1994, p. 155.

(一) 经济利益

水域中的自然资源与本国经济利益和国民生活密切相关是沿海国提出历史性水域主张的重要依据，也是司法裁决中影响历史性所有权判定的重要因素。"英挪渔业案"中，挪威北部沿海自然条件恶劣，当地渔民的生计基本依赖石垒附近的渔业资源，而一旦允许装备先进的英国渔船在此捕鱼将对当地居民基本生活造成毁灭性影响。因此法院在评价挪威实践的每一个要素时，都必须考虑挪威渔民在经济上对这片水域的依赖[1]，并因此放宽了对挪威行为审查的要求。特别是在洛波哈弗特海盆能否成为历史性水域的争论中，根据时际法，一纸颁发于17世纪且范围不明的授权书很难满足争议发生时确认主权主张的法律要求。[2]法院的支持态度主要基于保护当地渔民捕鱼作业的考虑。

以历史性所有权为法律依据扩展管辖范围是沿海国家在沿海国主权/公海自由两分法机制下，为获取经济利益而常用的手段。但是海洋法新制度的出现和科学技术的发展，正在不断削弱沿海国家以经济利益为目的提出历史性水域主张的必要性和可行性。

首先，随着领海宽度的扩大以及专属经济区和大陆架制度的出现，海洋法授予沿海国家的排他性经济利益，远远超过这些国家根据历史性所有权所能得到的利益。因此，沿海国单纯因经济目的提出历史性水域主张缺乏必要性。

其次，在国际司法实践中，经济条件是在不断改变的，难以准确将其与授予法律权利联系起来。"大陆架划界案"中，突尼斯主张划界不能影响突尼斯以拉斯阿贾迪尔镇为起点，朝向东北45°角平分线向海延伸与50米等深线相交处和突尼斯领海基线之间的历史性所有权[3]，理由之一就是该地区的传统渔业资源对突尼斯有重要价值。国际法院则认为经济因素对一国来说是财富还是灾难，随时间和情景而定。任何一个目前的贫穷国家都可能因为一种重要资源的发现而一跃

---

[1] Fisheries Case (The United Kingdom v. Norway), International Court of Justice Reports, 1951, p. 127.

[2] Fisheries Case (The United Kingdom v. Norway), International Court of Justice Reports, 1951, p. 184.

[3] Continental Shelf Case (Tunisia v. Libyan Arab Jamahiriya), International Court of Justice Reports, 1982, p. 32.

成为富国。[1]因此，突尼斯的主张未被接受。

最后，保护与经济因素相关的传统权利不是只有通过建立历史性水域一条途径。"厄立特里亚—也门仲裁案"中，根据第一阶段岛屿主权分别归于两国的现实，不影响该地区传统渔业机制继续存在的裁决[2]，厄立特里亚请求仲裁庭建立共同资源区，并在除此以外的水域确定一条"历史性中间线"[3]，这事实上是提出根据历史性所有权改变领海划界的中间线规则取得额外的历史性水域。仲裁庭认为传统渔业机制在来源和作用上的特殊性使得权利的保护和行使，不依赖特定的国际海洋边界，因此也就不需要以保护传统渔业机制为目的建立共同资源区。[4]至于调整中间线的主张，仲裁庭认为只有当划界对渔业活动产生的影响足以对当地渔民生计造成灾难性后果时，才应考虑根据历史性渔业实践调整中间线，而厄立特里亚提供的证据未能说服仲裁庭相信有调整中间线的需要。[5]

因此，从实践中可以发现，经济因素仍然是各国主张历史性水域的重要动机，但单独依靠经济因素而提出主张，很难对历史性水域的取得产生实质影响。

（二）战略利益与政策取向

沿海国家提出历史性所有权主张的水域往往因为其地缘位置而具有重要的战略意义，这种意义最主要体现在保卫国家安全和本国的特殊利益上。司法实践很早就关注到战略利益和历史性水域主张之间的关系，在"北大西洋渔业仲裁案"中，仲裁庭已指出对历史性海湾来说，如果沿海国对其提出的主张能得到特殊环境的证明即可归于沿海

---

[1] Continental Shelf Case (Tunisia v. Libyan Arab Jamahiriya), International Court of Justice Reports, 1982, p. 77.
[2] Eritrea-Yemen Arbitration (First Stage), International Legal Materials, Vol. 40: 900, p. 979 (2001).
[3] Eritrea-Yemen Arbitration (Second Stage), International Legal Materials, Vol. 40: 979, p. 994 (2001).
[4] Eritrea-Yemen Arbitration (Second Stage), International Legal Materials, Vol. 40: 979, p. 1002 (2001).
[5] Eritrea-Yemen Arbitration (Second Stage), International Legal Materials, Vol. 40: 979, p. 995 (2001).

国主权所有，而特殊环境中最重要的就是国防需要。[1]在丰塞卡海湾的法律争议中，中美洲法院对战略利益所包含的内容进行了全面的分析，法院除了认为海湾由于其地形地貌，可以成为用于驻泊军舰的深水良港外，还指出就地理位置而言，丰塞卡海湾位于南北美洲地缘的交会点，同时洪都拉斯正计划修建贯通该国的铁路，建成后丰塞卡海湾将成为沟通太平洋和大西洋交通线的重要节点。[2]因此，丰塞卡海湾对沿海国重要的政治价值和得到主要大国承认的长期占有，两者的结合共同表明丰塞卡海湾的历史性海湾属性。

国家实践普遍将保护安全作为主张历史性水域的理由，其中，美国的历史性海湾主张集中体现了通过历史性所有权保护国家利益的观点。吉德尔认为美国对特拉华湾和切萨皮克湾的态度，验证了国家安全利益是建立沿海国主权与历史性海湾之间真实联系的必然要求。[3]军事理论家马汉（Alfred Thayer Mahan）曾在著作中对特拉华湾和切萨皮克湾被封锁的情形提出警告，在第二次独立战争中，英军就是从切萨皮克湾长驱直入占领了华盛顿。[4]目前，位于切萨皮克湾入口处的诺福克拥有美国本土最大的海军基地。其他的历史性海湾也多位于重要的核心城市附近，长岛海湾（Long Island Sound）是纽约向东通向大西洋的门户，而属于加利福尼亚州的蒙特雷湾（Monterey Bay）和圣莫妮卡湾（Santa Monica Bay）则直接拱卫着美国在西海岸的两大经济中心——旧金山和洛杉矶。

沿海国对战略利益的看法，除了与现实的国家安全和地缘利益相关联，还常常与该国的政策取向密切相关，这一点在利益遍及全球的大国实践中体现得尤为明显。美国作为深受海权思想影响并以贸易立国的国家，海洋自由对其有着重要的利益。[5]从联邦政府对待历史性

---

[1] The Republic of El Salvador v. The Republic of Nicaragua, The American Journal of International Law, Vol. 11 (3), p. 700 (1917).
[2] The Republic of El Salvador v. The Republic of Nicaragua, The American Journal of International Law, Vol. 11 (3), p. 704 (1917).
[3] Yehuda Z. Blum, *Historic Titles in International Law*, Martinus Nijhoff, 1965, p. 95.
[4] [美] A. T. 马汉：《海权对历史的影响》，安常荣、成忠勤译，解放军出版社2011年版，第47页。
[5] 马汉认为，海权的三个根本环节是产品、海运和殖民地。因此，海权论的指导思想不是取得海洋，而是占据港口和海峡，控制海上交通线。[美] A. T. 马汉：《海权对历史的影响》，安常荣、成忠勤译，解放军出版社2011年版，第34—38页。

海湾的态度也可以发现，在海军力量足以排除外来入侵后，美国对海洋的兴趣就不再是将公海的一部分纳入本国的领土范围。

一个典型的例子是美国联邦政府对阿拉斯加附近亚历山大群岛（Alexander Archipelagic）的态度的转变。在1903年的"阿拉斯加边界仲裁案"中，美国政府主张该群岛与阿拉斯加间的水域是美国内水，而在2005年的"阿拉斯加诉合众国案"中，联邦政府则持完全相反的态度。[1]部分解释在于联邦政府权力扩展的需要，从国家战略的角度则可以认为，1903年时的美国刚从俄罗斯手中获得阿拉斯加领土，其时的美国海上力量还不足以排除其他国家从海上干预美国的风险，而这一风险在2005年时已经不复存在了。

与美国相反，苏联是一个陆权国家，这一态度使得苏联对海洋权利的主张也带有强烈的陆地思维，那就是将尽可能多的水域纳入本国的管辖。[2]这一政策取向对苏联海洋法观念最典型的影响体现在苏联主张在内水和公海之间还存在"封闭海"（Closed Sea）的法律制度，即在具有封闭特征的海峡、封闭海和半闭海中，有权基于地理、历史和军事战略的理由采取不同于国际法规则的管理措施。[3]

就历史性水域来说，对彼得大帝湾的内水主张是苏联政策取向最显著的体现，1957年苏联宣布彼得大帝湾为内水，但并未宣布海湾为历史性海湾。事实上，由于苏联教科书在"英挪渔业案"后采取更为宽泛的内水定义，对海湾的封口线不做宽度限制[4]，说明在苏联看来，封闭彼得大帝湾本身就不是违反国际法的逆权占有。因此苏联在面对绝大多数相关国家的抗议时[5]——即使在面对日本提出历史性所有权是苏联取得彼得大帝湾的法律基础，苏联仍然不认为其他国家的同意是这一权源的必要条件。[6]1966年出版的《苏联海军国际法手

---

[1] Clive R. Symmons, *Historic Waters in the Law of the Sea*, *A Modern Re-Appraisal*, Martinus Nijhoff, 2008, p. 115.

[2] Oseph J. Darby, *Soviet Doctrine of the Closed Sea*, San Diego Law Review, Vol. 23: 685, p. 689 (1986).

[3] Oseph J. Darby, *Soviet Doctrine of the Closed Sea*, San Diego Law Review, Vol. 23: 685, p. 690 (1986).

[4] M. W. Clark Jr., *Historical Bays and Waters*, *A Regime of Recent Beginning and Continued Usage*, Oceana Publication, 1994, p. 166.

[5] Mitchell P. Strohl, *International Law of Bays*, Martinus Nijhoff, 1963, p. 351 - 355.

[6] Mitchell P. Strohl, *International Law of Bays*, Martinus Nijhoff, 1963, p. 352.

册》验证了这一观点，书中指出历史性水域的特征包括特殊经济价值、特殊战略价值、历史传统和特殊地理条件，满足任意其中一条即可被视为苏联的历史性水域。[1]

（三）对航行自由的影响

如果说沿海国对经济和战略利益的诉求有助于历史性水域主张获得更广泛的认同，那么历史性水域对航行自由产生的不利影响将削弱相关国家支持或默认这一主张的可能性。阿拉巴马赔偿委员会第二法庭在"阿勒格尼安号案"中指出，切萨皮克海湾入口完整的岬角构造和水体深入美国陆地并被美国国土包围，沿岸州在殖民地时期就对海湾中水域提出主权主张且这些主张从未被质疑，而这些特征又决定了海湾不可能成为国际航行通道，因此切萨皮克湾应当被视为美国内水。米切尔·P. 斯特罗尔（Mitchell P. Strohl）认为切萨皮克湾的司法解释意味着在影响历史性海湾的因素中，最重要的就是在海湾建立起排他主权是否对其他国家国民造成不利影响。[2]

航行自由对历史性水域取得的影响，集中体现在围绕加拿大对北极群岛水域主张的争议上。西北航道是一条从格陵兰岛到阿拉斯加北岸的航道，这是大西洋和太平洋之间最短的航道，而航道的主体部分就从加拿大的北极群岛之间穿过。[3]虽然人们早在19世纪中叶就发现了这条航道，但由于航道常年处于冰封状态而无法对其加以利用。随着温室效应带来的气候变化，西北航道中的冰雪消融，航道的航运价值逐步显现，不久后西北航道将具有运行商业航线的价值。[4]

加拿大对北极群岛和群岛大陆架拥有无可争议的主权和主权权利，但一直没有明确群岛间水域的法律地位。[5]1970年，加拿大宣布领海宽度从3海里拓展到12海里，这意味着整个西北航道已经在加拿大领

---

[1] M. W. Clark Jr. , *Historical Bays and Waters*, *A Regime of Recent Beginning and Continued Usage*, Oceana Publication, 1994, p. 198.

[2] Mitchell P. Strohl, *International Law of Bays*, Martinus Nijhoff, 1963, p. 278.

[3] Donat Pharand, *The Arctic Waters and the Northwest Passage: A Final Revisit*, Ocean Development and International Law, Vol. 38: 3, p. 3 (2007).

[4] Donat Pharand, *The Arctic Waters and the Northwest Passage: A Final Revisit*, Ocean Development and International Law, Vol. 38: 3, p. 4 (2007).

[5] Mark Killas, *The Legality of Canada's Claims to the Waters of its Arctic Archipelago*, Ottawa Law Review, Vol. 19 (1): 95, p. 95 (1987).

海范围内。[1]1973年,加拿大宣布北极群岛水域为加拿大内水。[2] 1985年,美国海岸警卫队"北极海"号破冰船在未取得加拿大同意的情况下对西北航道进行为期12天的考察航行,加拿大随后发表一系列声明,确认包括西北航道在内的北极群岛水域是加拿大内水,并在当年9月10日签署法令以直线基线系统封闭北极群岛水域。[3]加拿大外交部长在一份声明中将北极群岛水域称为加拿大的"历史性内水",理由是加拿大的北极主权包括陆地、冰面和它们向海面的延伸,是不可分割的,加拿大因纽特人对冰面的利用就像占有和使用陆地一样。加拿大政府的立场之一就是维护加拿大对岛屿、冰面和水域不可分割的主权。

美国以西北航道是用于国际航行的海峡为理由反对加拿大的主张。海岸警卫队在评论加拿大的内水主张时指出,美国政府的一贯立场是西北航道符合习惯国际法对用于国际航行的海峡的定义,因此应当根据国际法上的过境通行制度保护海峡中的航行和飞越自由。[4]加拿大政府和学者则坚持西北航道是加拿大的内水航道,多纳特·法朗德(Donat Pharand)检索了自1907年西北航道开通以来的全部航行记录,总结认为除了美国的两次航行以外,从未有其他国家船只在未经过加拿大的同意和接受加拿大管理的情况下进入水道,因此西北航道是严格意义上的加拿大内水,其他国家船只在此不享有无害通行的权利。[5]

围绕西北航道的争议以1988年美加《北极合作协议》的签署暂时告一段落,加拿大授予美国破冰船在西北航道内的通行权,美国则承诺破冰船的航行将遵守加拿大有关航行和污染防治的法律,但不承认

---

[1] Mark Killas: *The Legality of Canada's Claims to the Waters of its Arctic Archipelago*, Ottawa Law Review, Vol. 19 (1): 95, p. 97 (1987).

[2] Mark Killas: *The Legality of Canada's Claims to the Waters of its Arctic Archipelago*, Ottawa Law Review, Vol. 19 (1): 95, p. 100 (1987).

[3] Mark Killas: *The Legality of Canada's Claims to the Waters of its Arctic Archipelago*, Ottawa Law Review, Vol. 19 (1): 95, p. 101 (1987).

[4] M. W. Clark Jr., *Historical Bays and Waters*, A Regime of Recent Beginning and Continued Usage, Oceana Publication, 1994, p. 211.

[5] Donat Pharand, *The Arctic Waters and the Northwest Passage: A Final Revisit*, Ocean Development and International Law, Vol. 38: 3, p. 59 (2007).

接受管理会产生任何承认加拿大主权的法律效果。[1]尽管这一结果具有强烈的实用主义色彩,难以提供国家实践的明确证据,但是通过围绕西北航道的历史性水域争议可以看到,对航行自由的现实和潜在影响与历史性水域的取得与否产生直接的关联。事实上,观察有关海峡和群岛国制度的习惯法编纂过程就能发现,《海洋法公约》迫切将历史性海峡和群岛水域编纂为受相关通行权限制的海洋法律制度,却能保留历史性海湾适用一般国际法的重要原因之一就在于海湾由于其封闭性,沿海国取得主权对航行自由的影响远小于区域内贯穿海上交通线的群岛和海峡。

三、影响因素不能独立成为取得历史性水域的理由

早期国家实践和司法实践并没有明确的权源意识,而是将相关因素与权源一起视为取得历史性水域的理由。中美洲法院认定丰塞卡海湾为历史性海湾的依据不但包括和平和持续的长期占有,以及国际社会对占有的普遍默认,还包括特殊的地理构造形成的对沿海国家经济、农业、商业和国防利益的保护。[2]在海牙国际法编纂会议上,英国、加拿大和比利时认为主张历史性海湾的国际惯例需建立在特殊地理环境基础上。挪威、希腊和葡萄牙等国则主张应当综合历史、地理和经济因素,特别是渔业考量作为判断的依据。[3]由于第一次联合国海洋法会议未能就历史性海湾得出一致意见,相关因素和权源关系的问题和其他争议一起交由国际法委员会进行研究。

国际法委员会总结了预备文件中收集的国家实践和公法家学说,认为关于相关因素和权源关系的核心问题不在于权源是否需要得到诸如自然条件和特殊利益关系的支持,而是这些特殊的环境因素能不能在主张国缺乏法律要件时,提供取得历史性水域的合法性基础。[4]也

---

[1] M. W. Clark Jr., *Historical Bays and Waters*, *A Regime of Recent Beginning and Continued Usage*, Oceana Publication, 1994, p. 231.

[2] The Republic of El Salvador v. The Republic of Nicaragua, The American Journal of International Law, Vol. 11 (3), p. 700 – 704 (1917).

[3] Historic Bays: Memorandum by the Secretariat of the United Nations, A/CONF. 13/1, 1957, p. 20 – 21.

[4] Juridical Regime of Historic Waters, Including Historic Bays, International Law Commission Yearbook, 1962 (2), p. 20.

就是说，在缺乏法律基础的情况下，沿海国能不能由于特殊的自然和利益关系取得历史性水域。

国际法委员会认为特殊的自然和利益关系可以取得历史性水域的观点表面上具有一定的合理性，因为对刚刚取得独立的国家来说，客观原因使他们无法主张历史上对水域的占有。但委员会同时认为这种对新独立国家切身利益的保护并不一定只能通过历史性水域实现，而是将水域对沿海国的重大利益作为独立的法律基础，建立国际法上的重大利益海湾或重大利益水域。[1]

由于历史因素的存在，历史性水域制度不可避免地不利于新独立国家的主张，国际法对此并非毫无认识。[2]解决之道首先应当是对海洋历史性所有权的主张采取"一事一议"的客观标准。其次则是建设更为公平的海洋法制度以满足新独立国家合理的权利要求。专属经济区和大陆架制度赋予沿海国排他性的经济权利，而国际海底区域等倾斜性制度更是帮助发展中国家在海洋开发中取得应有的利益。对发展中国家来说，相比于提出单方面所有权主张，积极参与海洋国际法制度建设是维护自己利益更好的途径。

另外，对重大利益是否成为取得公海的基础，国际法存在巨大的争议，主流的观点对此持否定的态度。[3]退一步说，即便重大利益能够产生取得水域的结果，正如国际法委员会所指出的，这种并非基于历史性所有权的取得也不能被称为历史性水域。虽然苏联学者曾提出可以基于其他非历史性所有权而取得历史性水域的观点，但此时历史性水域被等同于海洋法一般规则以外的内水和领海[4]，因此可以看作是对术语的扩大误用。可见，相关因素即便可以取得水域的主权，其法律基础也不是历史性所有权。

总的来说，当前的海洋法制度、国际法实践和公法家学说都不支

---

[1] Juridical Regime of Historic Waters, Including Historic Bays, International Law Commission Yearbook, 1962 (2), p. 20.

[2] M. W. Clark Jr., *Historical Bays and Waters, A Regime of Recent Beginning and Continued Usage*, Oceana Publication, 1994, p. 105.

[3] D. P. O'Connell, edited by I. A. Shearer, *The International Law of the Sea*, Clarendon Press, 1982, p. 20 – 21.

[4] M. W. Clark Jr., *Historical Bays and Waters, A Regime of Recent Beginning and Continued Usage*, Oceana Publication, 1994, p. 80.

持单凭自然和利益关系的相关因素将公海的一部分纳入沿海国主权,至少这种纳入的结果不能被称为历史性水域。

第三节 小 结

本章的初步结论包括:

1. 目前,沿海国取得历史性水域的法律基础是逆权占有型的历史性所有权。

2. 获得国际司法程序肯定的历史性水域一般代表了国际社会的认同,具有普遍效力。

3. 沿海国国内法认定的历史性水域代表了国家的主张意图和一定程度上的司法管辖,但有效性仍需要相关国家的认可。

4. 如果国内司法中检验了包括有效管理和相关国家同意在内的要件,那么司法判决体现了习惯法规则的应用结果。

5. 沿海国单方面提出历史性水域主张时,有效管理的行为须与取得排他性主权的意图相一致。

6. 多数相关国家的同意足以满足历史性水域的产生要求,个别或极少数国家从了解沿海国主张之日起的持续反对,将为它们保留在历史性水域内的通航或捕鱼权利。

7. 除历史性所有权的两个要件外,历史性水域的取得一般还考虑水域的自然和相关国家利益等因素。相关因素与两个要件是平行关系。

8. 相关因素中的重大利益不能脱离历史性所有权的要件成为主张历史性水域的法律基础。

结　论

　　通过上述基于实践的研究，笔者尝试澄清有关历史性所有权概念并得出应用的初步结论。就历史性所有权的概念而言，虽然以所有权为名，但权利实现的结果指向是获取主权。同时，历史性所有权也不是领土主权权源，而是一种权源的取得方式。

　　历史性所有权包括两部分构成要件，即有效管理和相关国家的同意。通过有效管理实现的占有是产生历史性所有权的起点，相关国家的同意是历史性所有权得到巩固的必要条件，两者缺一不可。由于国家实践的延续性和国际法规则的变化，需要依靠时际法调整判断权利所适用的具体规则。但是无论如何，公开、和平、持续地实施本国立法的行为是展示有效管理的最好方式。至于相关国家的同意态度，历史性所有权经历了从只接受消极同意到也接受积极同意的变化。在逆权占有的情况下，为了区别于国际承认，原权利持有国一定时间内的不作为构成相关国家的同意，但是在直接占有权属不明的土地的情况下，提出竞争主张一方的明示承认或通过行动表达的默认也是同意的表现形式。

　　历史性所有权既适用于取得陆地领土，也适用于取得海洋中的历史性水域，既适用于直接占有，也可以用于逆权占有。同样的构成要件，在适用于不同情况时表现出不同的关系。在取得历史性水域或其他国家的领土，由于权利转移自原先的权利持有者，因此获得持有者以容忍方式表达的同意是具有决定性的。在适用于直接占有归属不明的土地时，竞争主张国的同意态度则可以直接使历史性所有权获得巩固，同时，其他第三方国家对主张国占有土地状态的认可则从侧面证明了主张国的有效管理是公开以及和平的。对于历史上的长期占有，由于年代久远，直接管理的证据数量较少或者难以准确说明争议领土的法律地位，因此相关国家在此时的记录代表了国际社会对占有状态的认识，具有举足轻重的地位。实践中，对于归属有争议的土地来说，如果不存在相关国家的态度，则可以仅根据有效管理证据的强弱判定归属，但这种情况下主权的取得方式就不再是历史性所有权。

由此，我们可以说，在陆地领土的取得中，直接占有型的历史性所有权是补充性的领土取得方式。这一补充性体现在两个方面，首先，它补充了占有无主地和占有他国土地之间的理论缝隙，形成先占无主地，通过所有权的历史性巩固取得归属不明土地，以及通过逆权占有的历史性所有权取得原属他国土地这样一套完整的领土取得体系。其次，对于取得归属不明的土地来说，所有权的巩固仅在存在相关国家态度的前提下成为领土取得方式，也是补充性的，主张国可以不通过主张历史性所有权取得这类土地的主权。而对于原属他国的领土来说，相关国家的同意是主权转移的必备要件。

所有权的历史性巩固，一旦获得认定，所产生的法律效果就是取得领土主权，相比之下，根据历史上的占有所形成的权利却未必能取得争议发生时的主权。历史上的占有即便在关键日期获得了当时的主权，主张国也依然要保证权利在此后不曾中断，才能在争议发生时保留主权。当然，这种情况下，历史性所有权所产生的权利即便被取代，也不意味着全部失去效力，原先权利的持有国仍然可以通过条约的安排保留未来要求返还土地的权利。

和取得陆地领土的历史性所有权相比，作为历史性水域法律基础的权利在类型上要简单得多，不过这并不意味着沿海国的历史性水域主张会更容易获得国际社会的认可。现实情况恰恰相反，沿海国单方面提出历史性水域主张时，有效管理的行为须与取得排他性主权的意图相一致。由于当前海洋法已经赋予了沿海国大量的管辖权利，事实上能够产生主权取得效果的只有对航行的排他性管理。在实施有效管理的同时，沿海国还必须获取多数相关国家的同意以满足历史性水域的产生要求。虽然个别或极少数国家的持续反对不影响权利的取得，但是持续反对将保留它们在历史性水域内的另一种历史性的通航或捕鱼权利。除了满足两个要件外，历史性水域的取得一般还要考虑水域的自然和利益因素，一般来说，对沿海国意义巨大而对国际通航作用不大的水域更容易成为沿海国成功获取主权的对象。但是无论如何，对沿海国的重大利益不能脱离历史性所有权成为历史性水域的法律基础。

参考文献

一、中文文献

（一）著 作

王铁崖：《中外旧约章汇编》，生活·读书·新知三联书店1957年版。

中华人民共和国外交部：《中华人民共和国对外关系文件集》，世界知识出版社1958年版。

傅铸：《关于我国领海的问题》，世界知识出版社1959年版。

张博泉、苏金源、董玉英：《东北历代疆域史》，吉林人民出版社1981年版。

王铁崖：《国际法引论》，北京大学出版社1998年版。

梁治平：《法辩：中国法的过去、现在与未来》，中国政法大学出版社2002年版。

高鸿钧：《伊斯兰法：传统与现代化》（修订版），清华大学出版社2004年版。

高健军：《中国与国际海洋法——纪念〈联合国海洋法公约〉生效10周年》，海洋出版社2004年版。

彭建英：《中国古代羁縻政策的演变》，中国社会科学出版社2004年版。

郑海麟：《钓鱼岛列屿之历史与法理研究》（增订本），中华书局2007年版。

林学忠：《从万国公法到公法外交——晚晴国际法的传入、诠释与应用》，上海古籍出版社2008年版。

赵宏：《环渤海经济圈产业发展研究》，中国经济出版社 2008 年版。

段洁龙：《中国国际法实践与案例》，法律出版社 2011 年版。

国家海洋局海洋发展战略研究所课题组：《中国海洋发展报告（2011）》，海洋出版社 2011 年版。

徐国栋：《优士丁尼法学阶梯评注》，北京大学出版社 2011 年版。

国务院新闻办公室：《钓鱼岛是中国的固有领土（白皮书）》，人民出版社 2012 年版。

自然资源部海洋发展战略研究所课题组：《中国海洋发展报告（2020）》，海洋出版社 2020 年版。

［德］K. 茨威格特、H. 克茨：《比较法总论》，潘汉典、米健、高鸿钧等译，法律出版社 2003 年版。

［意］朱塞佩·格罗索：《罗马法史》，黄风译，中国政法大学出版社 2009 年版。

［美］阿瑟·努斯鲍姆：《简明国际法史》，张小平译，法律出版社 2011 年版。

［美］A. T. 马汉：《海权对历史的影响》，安常荣、成忠勤译，解放军出版社 2006 年版。

（二）论　文

李浩培：《论条约法上的时际法》，载《武汉大学学报（社会科学版）》1983 年第 6 期。

赵理海：《从国际法看我国对南海诸岛无可争辩的主权》，载《北京大学学报（哲学社会科学版）》1992 年第 3 期。

杨强：《论明清渤海区域的经济发展》，载《中国社会经济史研究》2004 第 16 期第 1 卷，第 97－109 页。

孙喆、王江：《对 1689—1727 年中俄外交关系的考察》，载《中国边疆史地研究》2006 年 1 期，第 9－16 页。

二、外文文献

(一) 条约,决议和其他文件

Reservation Exclusively for Peaceful Purposes of the Sea-Bed and the Ocean Floor, and the Subsoil Thereof, Underlying the High Seas Beyond the Limits of Present National Jurisdiction and Use of their Resources in the Interests of Mankind, and Convening of A Conference on the Law of the Sea, United Nations General Assembly Resolution 2750 (XXV), A/PV. 1933, 1970.

Articles Concerning the Law of the Sea, Reports to General Assembly, International Law Commission Yearbook, 1956 (2), p. 1 – 103.

Historic Bays: Memorandum by the Secretariat of the United Nations, A/CONF. 13/1, 1957, p. 1 – 39.

Comments by Governments on the Draft Articles Concerning the Law of the Sea Adopted by the International Law Commission at Its Eighth Secession, A/CONF. 13/5 and Add. 1 – 4, 1958.

Geneva Convention on Territorial Sea and Contiguous Zone, United Nations Treaty Series, 1958, Vol. 516.

Statement of Activities of the Conference during Its First and Second Sessions Prepared by the Rapporteur-General: Mr. Kenneth O. Rattray, Annexes Ⅱ, Appendix Ⅰ. A/CONF. 62/L. 8/REV. 1, 1958.

Regime of Historic Water, Resolution Adopted on the Report of the First Committee, United Nations Conference on the Law of the Sea Official Records, 1958 (2): 157.

Study of the Juridical Regime of Historic Waters, including Historic Bays, United Nations General Assembly Resolution 1143 (XIV), A/CONF. 13L. 56, 1958.

Study of the Juridical Regime of Historic Waters, including Historic Bays, United Nations General Assembly 1453 (XIV), A/PV. 847, 1959.

Juridical Regime of Historic Waters, Including Historic Bays, International Law Commission Yearbook, 1962 (2), p. 1 – 27.

Vienna Convention on the Law of Treaties, United Nations Treaty Series, 1969, Vol. 1155.

Question of Spanish Sahara, United Nations General Assembly Resolution 3293 (XXIX), A/RES/3292 (XXIX). A/PV. 2318, 1973.

United Nations Conventions on the Law of the Sea, United NationsTreaty Series, 1982, Vol. 1833.

Untied States Department of State Bureau of Ocean and International Environmental and Scientific Affairs, Limits in the Sea No. 36, National Claims to the Maritime Jurisdiction, 8th Revision, 2000.

(二) 案 例

The Grisbadarna Case (Norway v. Sweden), United Nations Reports of International Arbitration Awards, 1909, Vol. 11, p. 155 – 166.

The North Atlantic Coast Fisheries Case (Great Britain v. United States), United Nations Reports of International Arbitration Awards, 1910, Vol. 11, p. 167 – 226.

The Chamizal Arbitration between the United States and Mexico (The United State v. Mexico), American Journal of International Law, Vol. 5: 778, p. 778 – 833 (1911).

The Republic of El Salvador v. The Republic of Nicaragua, The American Journal of International Law, Vol. 11 (3): 674, p. 674 – 730 (1917).

Island of Palmas Case (Netherlands v. The U. S. A.), United Nations Reports of International Arbitration Awards, 1928, Vol. 2, p. 829 – 871.

Affaire de L'ile de Clippertion, United Nations Reports of International Arbitration Awards, 1931, Vol. 2, p. 1105 – 1111.

Legal Status of East Greenland (Denmark v. Norwegian), Permenent Court of International Justice, Series A. /B. 1933, p. 22 – 75.

Fisheries Case (The United Kingdom v. Norway), International Court of Justice Reports, 1951, p. 110 – 144.

The Minquiers and Ecrehos Case (France v. The United Kingdom), International Court of Justice Reports, 1953, p. 47 – 73.

Temple of Preah Vihear Case (Cambodia v. Thailand), International Court of Justice Reports, 1962, p. 6 - 38.

Argentine-Chile Frontier Case, United Nations Reports of International Arbitration Awards, 1966, Vol. 16, p. 109 - 182.

Case Concerning the Indo-Pakistan Western Boundary (Rann of Kutch), United Nations Reports of International Arbitration Awards, Vol. 17, 1968, p. 1 - 576.

Louisiana Boundary Case, 394 U. S. 11, 1969.

Western Sahara Advisory Opinion, International Court of Justice Reports, 1975, p. 12 - 69.

Aegean Sea Continental Shelf Case (Greece v. Turkey), International Court of Justice Reports, 1978, p. 3 - 46.

Continental Shelf Case (Tunisia v. Libyan Arab Jamahiriya), International Court of Justice Reports, 1982, p. 18 - 80.

Delimitation of the Maritime Boundary in the Gulf of Maine Area (Canada v. The U. S. A.), International Court of Justice Reports, 1984, p. 246 - 352.

Military and Paramilitary Activities in and against Nicaragua (Nicaragua v. U. S. A.), International Court of Justice Reports, 1984, p. 14 - 150.

Alabama and Mississippi Boundary Case, 470 U. S. 93, 1985.

Frontier Dispute Case (Burkina Faso v. Mali), International Court of Justice Reports, 1986, p. 554 - 651.

Land, Island and Maritime Frontier Dispute (El Salvador v. Honduras Nicaragua intervening), International Court of Justice Reports, 1992, p. 351 - 618.

Eritrea-Yemen Arbitration (First Stage), International Legal Materials, Vol. 40: 900, p. 900 - 982 (2001).

Eritrea-Yemen Arbitration (First Stage), International Legal Materials, Vol. 40: 900, p. 983 - 1019 (2001).

Land and Maritime Boundary between Cameroon and Nigeria (Cameroon v. Nigeria, Equatorial Guinea intervening), International Court of Justice Reports, 2002, p. 303 - 458.

Maritime Delimitation and Territorial Questions between Qatar and

Bahrain (Qatar v. Bahrain), International Court of Justice Reports, 2002, p. 40 – 118.

Sovereignty over Pulau Ligitan and Pulau Sipadan (Indonesia v. Malaysia), International Court of Justice Reports, 2002, p. 625 – 686.

Territorial and Maritime Dispute between Nicaragua and Honduras in the Caribbean Sea (Nicaragua v. Honduras), International Court of Justice Reports, 2007, p. 659 – 764.

Case Concerning Sovereignty over Pedra Branca/Pulau Batu Puteh, Middle Rocks and South Ledge (Malaysia v. Singapore), International Court of Justice Reports, 2008, p. 2 – 102.

Territorial and Maritime Dispute (Columbia v. Nicaragua), International Court of Justice Reports, 2012, p. 624 – 720.

(三) 著 作

John Bassett Moore, *A Digest of International Law*, Government Printing Office, 1906.

Philip C. Jessup, *The Law of Territorial Waters and Maritime Jurisdiction*, G. A. Jennings Co., Inc., 1927.

F. P. Walters, *A History of The League of Nations*, Oxford University Press, 1960.

Mitchell P. Strohl, *International Law of Bays*, Martinus Nijhoff, 1963.

R. Y. Jennings, *The Acquisition of Territory in International Law*, Manchester University Press, 1963.

L. J. Bouchez, *The Regime of Bays in International Law*, Sythoff, 1964.

Yehuda Z. Blum, *Historic Titles in International Law*, Martinus Nijhoff, 1965.

Charles de Visscher, *Théories et Réalités en Droit International Public*. 4th edition, Editions A. Pedone, 1970.

D. P. O'Connell, Edited by I. A. Shearer, *The International Law of the Sea*, Clarendon Press, 1982.

Malcolm Shaw, *Title to Territory in Africa*, Clarendon Press, 1986.

Óscar Vila Masot, *The Gulf of Venezuela: A Case Study of Historic*

Waters, Editorial Arte, 1991.

M. W. Clark Jr. , *Historical Bays and Waters, A Regime of Recent Beginning and Continued Usage*, Oceana Publication, 1994.

Unrya Suganuma, *Historical Justification on Sovereign Right over Territorial Space of Diaoyu/Senkaku Islands: Irredentism and Sino-Japanese Relations*, A Bell & Howell Information Company, 1996.

Surya P. Sharma, *Territorial Acquisition, Dispute and International Law*, Martinus Nijhoff Publishers, 1997.

R. R. Churchill, A. V. Lowe, *The Law of the Sea*, 3rd edtion, Manchester University Press, 1999.

Barbara Kwiatkowka, *Decisions of the World Court Relevant to the UN Convention on the Law of the Sea*, Kulwar Law International, 2002.

Jonathan I. Charney, Lewis M. Alexander, *International Maritime Boundaries*, Martinus Nijhoff, 2004.

Clive R. Symmons, *Historic Waters in the Law of the Sea, A Modern Re-Appraisal*, Martinus Nijhoff, 2008.

Ian Brownlie, *Principles of Public International Law 7th editon*, Oxford University Press, 2008.

John P. Grant, J. Craig Barker, *Harvard. Research in International Law: Original Materials*, W. S. Hein, 2008.

Pan Junwu, *Towards a New Framework for Peaceful Settlement of China's Territorial and Boundary Disputes*, Martinus Nijhoff, 2009.

Benedict Kingsbury, Benjamin Straumann, *The Roman Foundation of Law of Nations and Alberico Gentili and the Justice of Empire*, Oxford University Press, 2010.

Donald. R. Rothwell, Tim Stephens, *The International Law of the Sea*, Harting Publishing, 2010.

Max Planck Institute for Comparative Public Law and International Law, *Historic Titles*, Max Planck Encyclopedia of Public International Law. http://opil.ouplaw.com/view/10.1093/law:epil/9780199231690/law-9780199231690-e705? rskey=3CtvAW&result=1&prd=EPIL.

(四) 论 文

Philip C. Jessup, *The Palmas Island Arbitration*, American Journal of International Law, Vol. 22: 735, p. 735 – 752 (1928).

C. H. M. Waldock, *Disputed Sovereignties in the Falkland Islands Dependencies*, British Yearbook of International Law, Vol. 25: 311, p. 311 – 353 (1948).

D. H. N. Johnson, *Acquisitive Prescription in International Law*, British Yearbook of International Law, Vol. 27: 332, p. 332 – 354 (1950).

H. Lauterpacht, *Sovereignty over Submarine Area*, British Yearbook of International Law, Vol. 27: 377, p. 377 – 433 (1950).

Jens Evensen, *The Anglo-Norwegian Fisheries Case and its Legal Consequence*, American Journal of International Law, Vol. 45: 609, p. 609 – 630 (1951).

I. C. MacGibbon, *Some Observation on the Part of Protest in International Law*, British Yearbook of International Law, Vol. 30: 293, p. 293 – 319 (1953).

I. C. MacGibbon, *The Scope of Acquiescence in International Law*, British Yearbook of International Law, Vol. 31: 143, p. 143 – 186 (1954).

Gerald Fitzmaurice, *The Law and Procedure of International Court of Justice*, 1951 – 1954: *Points of Substantive Law*. Part II, British Yearbook of International Law, Vol. 32: 21, p. 21 – 96 (1955 – 1956).

D. H. N. Johnson, *Consolidation as a Root of Title in International Law*, Cambridge Law Journal, Vol. 3 (2): 215, p. 215 – 255 (1956).

Georg Schwarzenberger, *Title to Territory*, *Response to a Challenge*, American Journal of International Law, Vol. 51 (2): 308, p. 308 – 324 (1957).

Arthur H. Dean, *The Second Geneva Conference on the Law of the Sea*, American Journal of International Law, Vol. 54: 751, p. 751 – 789 (1960).

D. P. O'Connell, *International Law and Boundary Disputes*, Proceedings of the American Society of International Law at Its Annual Meeting (1921 – 1969), Vol. 54: 77, p. 77 – 84 (1960).

D. W. Bowett, *The Second United Nations Conference on the Law of the Sea*, International and Comparative Law Quarterly, Vol. 9: 415, p. 415 – 436 (1960).

L. F. E. Goldie, *The Critical Date*, International and Comparative Law Quarterly, Vol. 12: 1251, p. 1252 – 1284 (1963).

R. Y. Jennings, *Changing International Law of the Sea*, Cambridge Law Journal, Vol. 31 (1): 32, p. 32 – 49 (1972).

A. L. W. Munkman, *Adjudication and Adjustment-International Judicial Decision and the Settlement of Territorial and Boundary Disputes*, British Yearbook of International Law, Vol. 46: 1, p. 1 – 116 (1972 – 1973).

Chiu Hungdah, Choon-Ho Park, *Legal Status of the Paracel and Spratly Islands*, Ocean Development and International Law, Vol. 3 (1): 1, p. 1 – 28 (1974).

Kathleen L. Walz, *The United States Supreme Court & Article Ⅶ of the 1958 Convention on the Territorial Sea & Contiguous Zone*, University of San Francisco Law Review, Vol. 11: 1, p. 1 – 51 (1976 – 1977).

Carolyn Hudson, *Fishery and Economic Zones as Customary International Law*, San Diego Law Review, Vol. 17: 661, p. 661 – 689 (1979 – 1980).

T. O. Elas, *The Doctrine of Intertemporal Law*, American Journal of International Law, Vol. 74: 285, p. 285 – 307 (1980).

M. J. Jewett, *The Evolution of the Regime of Continental Shelf*, The Canadian Yearbook of International Law, Vol. 22: 153, p. 153 – 193 (1984).

James Michael Zimmerman, *The Doctrine of Historic Bays: Applying an Anachronism in Alabama and Mississippi Boundary Case*, San Diego Law Review, Vol. 23: 763, p. 763 – 790 (1986).

Oseph J. Darby, *Soviet Doctrine of the Closed Sea*, San Diego Law Review, Vol. 23: 685, p. 685 – 699 (1986).

Yehuda Z. Blum, *The Gulf of Sidra Incident*, American Journal of International Law, Vol. 80: 668, p. 668 – 677 (1986).

Mark Killas, *The Legality of Canada's Claims to the Waters of its Arctic Archipelago*, Ottawa Law Review, Vol. 19 (1): 95, p. 95 – 136 (1987).

Wang Tieya, *International Law in China: Historical and Contemporary* perspectives, in Hague Academy of International Law, *Hague Academy Collected Courses*, 1990, p. 199 – 369.

Chang Teh-Kuang, *China's Claim of Sovereignty over Spratly and Paracel Islands: A Historical and Legal Perspective*, Case Western Research Journal of International Law, Vol. 311: 403, p. 403 – 418 (1991).

Christopher C Joyner, *The Spratly Islands Dispute: Rethinking of Interplay of Law, Diplomacy, and Geo-Politics in the South China Sea*, International Journal of Marine and Coastal Law, Vol. 13: 193, p. 193 – 216 (1998).

Nuno Sérgio Marques Antunes, *The Eritrea-Yemen Arbitration: First Stage-the Law of Title to Territory Re-averred*, International and Comparative Law Quarterly, Vol. 48: 299, p. 299 – 344 (1999).

Shabtai Rosenne, *Historic Waters in the Third United Nations Conference on the Law of the Sea*, in Leo J. Bouchez, Terry D. Gill, Wybo P. Heere, *Reflection on Priciples and Practice of International Law: Essays in Honour of Leo J. Bouchez*, Martinus Nijhoff Publishers, 2000, p. 497 – 511.

Li Zhaojie, *Traditional Chinese World Order*, Chinese Journal of International Law, Vol. 1: 20, p. 20 – 58 (2002).

Steven Wei Su, *The Territorial Dispute over the Tiaoyu/Senkaku Islands: An Update*, Ocean Development and International Law, Vol. 36 (1): 45, p. 45 – 61 (2005).

Donat Pharand, *The Arctic Waters and the Northwest Passage: A Final Revisit*, Ocean Development and International Law, Vol. 38: 3, p. 3 – 69 (2007).

Lowell B, Bautista, *The Historical Context and Legal Basis of Philippine Treaty Limits*, Asian-Pacific Law and Policy Journal, Vol. (10) 1: 1, p. 1 – 31 (2008).

Nguyen Hong Thao, Amer. Ramses, *A New Legal Arrangement for the South China Sea?*, Ocean Development and International Law, Vol. 40: 333, p. 333 – 349 (2009).

Cornelis G. Roelofsen, *Treaties between Europeans and Non-European Powers in the Early Modern and Modern Times*, in Thilo Marauhn, Heinhard Steiger, *Universality and Continuity of International Law 1st edition*, Eleven International Publishing, 2011, p. 409 – 419.

Randolf Lesaffer, *Roman Law and Early Historiography of International Law*: *Wards, Wheaton, Hosack and Walker*, in Thilo Marauhn, Heinhard Steiger, *Universality and Continuity of International Law* 1st edition. Eleven International Publishing, 2011, p. 149 – 185.

Gao Zhiguo, Jia Bingbing, *The Nine Dash-Line in South China Sea*: *History, Status and Implications*, American Journal of International Law, Vol. 107: 98, p. 98 – 124 (2013).

附录　联合国秘书处关于包括历史性海湾在内的历史性水域法律制度的研究报告

JURIDICAL REGIME OF HISTORIC WATERS, INCLUDING HISTORIC BAYS*

DOCUMENT A/CN.4/143
Study prepared by the Secretariat

[*Original text: English*]
[*9 March 1962*]

CONTENTS

	Paragraphs
I. ORIGIN AND BACKGROUND OF THE STUDY	1—32
II. JURIDICAL RÉGIME OF HISTORIC WATERS, INCLUDING HISTORIC BAYS	
A. Preliminary explanation of the terms "historic waters" and "historic bays".	33—35
B. Concept of "historic waters"	
1. Background	36—41
2. Is the régime of "historic waters" an exceptional régime?	42—61
3. Is the title to "historic waters" a prescriptive right?	62—68
4. Relation of "historic waters" to "occupation"	69—71
5. "Historic waters" as an exception to rules laid down in a general convention	72—79
C. Elements of title to "historic waters"	80—148
1. Exercise of authority over the area claimed	84—100
(a) Scope of the authority exercised	85—88
(b) Acts by which the authority is exercised	89—97
(c) Effectiveness of authority exercised	98—100
2. Continuity of the exercise of authority: usage	101—105
3. Attitude of foreign States	106—133
4. Question of the vital interests of the coastal State in the area claimed	134—140
5. Question of "historic waters" the coasts of which belong to two or more States	141—148
D. Burden of proof	149—159
E. Legal status of the waters regarded as "historic waters"	160—167
F. Question of a list of "historic waters"	168—176
G. Settlement of disputes	177—181
III. CONCLUSIONS	182—192

* 注：该文献基本保留了原格式。

I. Origin and background of the study

1. The present study was prepared by the Codification Division of the Office of Legal Affairs at the request of the International Law Commission. The Commission's decision to initiate the study was taken at its twelfth session (1960), in pursuance of General Assembly resolution 1453 (XIV) of 7 December 1959. The Assembly resolution was prompted by a resolution on the matter taken by the United Nations Conference on the Law of the Sea held in 1958 at Geneva. A brief review of these resolutions and of their background will help to clarify the purpose of the study.

2. At its eighth session (1956) the International Law Commission completed the final draft of its articles concerning the Law of the Sea[1] and this draft was subsequently referred by the General Assembly to the above-mentioned United Nations Conference on the Law of the Sea. Article 7 of the draft dealt with bays; paragraphs 1 to 3 contained a definition of a bay and laid down rules for the delimitation of internal waters in a bay (the coasts of which belong to a single State), while paragraph 4 read in part as follows:

"4. The foregoing provisions shall not apply to so-called historic bays..."[2]

3. Although much attention was given in the reports of the Special Rapporteur and in the discussions of the Commission to the substantive provisions on bays in article 7 in its successive stages of development, there is little in the records of the Commission to shed light on the concept of "historic bays" referred to in paragraph 4 of the article.

4. A clause regarding "historic bays" did not appear in the first two reports on the territorial sea prepared by the Special Rapporteur. He submitted, however, at the fifth session of the Commission, an addendum[3] to his second report in which he presented redrafts of certain articles contained in the second report, among them the article on bays. These new drafts were to a large extent inspired by solutions proposed by a group of experts to a number of technical problems which had been referred to them by the Special Rapporteur. As redrafted, the article on bays, in its first paragraph, gave a definition of "a bay in the juridical sense" and thereafter stated:

"Historic bays are excepted; they shall be indicated as such on the maps."

In his third report,[4] submitted at the sixth session of the Commission, the Special Rapporteur transferred this clause regarding "historic bays" from the text of the

---

1 See chapter II of the Report of the International Law Commission covering the work of its eighth session, 23 April-4 July 1956, *Official Records of the General Assembly, Eleventh Session, Supplement No. 9* (A/3159).

2 *Ibid.*, pages 5 and 15.

3 A/CN.4/61/Add.l, the French text of which is printed in *Yearbook of the International Law Commission, 1953*, volume II, page 76.

4 A/CN.4/77, printed in French, in *Yearbook of the International Law Commission, 1954*, volume II, page 1.

article to the commentary. At the following session, he submitted a new redraft of the article on bays,[5] and in the text of that redraft the clause regarding "historic bays" reappeared. However, now the clause excepted "historic bays" not from the general definition of a bay but from the rules regarding the drawing of closing lines in bays. Another difference from the previous formulation of the clause was that the provision that "historic bays" should be marked on the maps, had been omitted.

5. In this form, i.e., as a proviso excepting "historic bays" from the rules regarding drawing closing lines in bays, the clause was included in article 7 (on bays) of the preliminary draft on the régime of the territorial sea which was adopted by the Commission at its seventh session and circulated to the Member States for observations.

6. In its reply[6] the Union of South Africa pointed out that the commentary accompanying the article seemed to indicate that the real intention of the Commission was to exempt "historic bays" not only from the rules on the drawing of closing lines but also from the other rules on bays laid down in the article. The Special Rapporteur and the Commission agreed, and the clause regarding "historic bays" was, consequently, in the final draft of the article formulated as set out above in paragraph 2 of this paper.

7. In the course of the discussions in the Commission of the article on bays in its successive formulations, only passing references were made to "historic bays". The debates, as a consequence, did not substantially contribute to the clarification of the concept.[7]

8. In order to provide the United Nations Conference on the Law of the Sea with material relating to "historic bays", a memorandum[8] on the subject was prepared by the Codification Division and circulated as a preparatory document of the Conference. It was pointed out in the memorandum that historic rights were claimed not only in respect of bays but also in respect of other maritime areas.

---

5 In A/CN.4/93, the French text of which is printed in *Yearbook of the International Law Commission, 1955*, volume II, page 5.

6 A/CN.4/99, *Yearbook of the International Law Commission, 1956*, volume II, page 77.

7 The question of bays was discussed at the fourth session in 1952, the seventh session in 1955, and the eighth session, in 1956; see, respectively, *Yearbook of the International Law Commission, 1952*, volume I, pages 188-190; *Yearbook, 1955*, volume I, pages 205-216, 251, 278, 279-80; and *Yearbook, 1956*, volume I, pages 190-193. In the 1955 discussion, Sir Gerald Fitzmaurice affirmed that the concept of "historic bays" formed part of international law (*Yearbook, 1955*, volume I, page 209), while Mr. García-Amador and Mr. Hsu (*ibid.*, pages 210 and 211) said that they had doubts about "historic bays". Mr. García-Amador contended that this concept only benefited old countries having a long history and that there were many comparative newcomers to the international community—countries in Latin America, the Middle East and the Far East—which could not claim such historic rights. The reference to "historic bays" in the relevant article was, however, adopted without any member voting against it (*ibid.*, page 214).

8 Historic Bays, Memorandum by the Secretariat of the United Nations (A/CONF.13/1), printed in *Official Records of the United Nations Conference on the Law of the Sea*, 1958, United Nations publication, Sales No.: 58.V.4, vol. I: Preparatory Documents, pages 1 *et seq.*

However, as the purpose of the memorandum was to shed light on the concept of "historic bays" referred to in the draft of the International Law Commission, the emphasis was on this latter concept, and historic claims to other waters were dealt with only incidentally. The content of the memorandum was succinctly set out in its paragraph 5 as follows:

"5. Part I describes the practice of States by reference to a few examples of bays which are considered to be historic or are claimed as such by the States concerned. Part I then proceeds to cite the various draft codifications which established the theory of "historic bays", and the opinions of learned authors and of Governments on this theory. Part II discusses the theory itself, inquiring into the legal status of the waters of bays regarded as historic bays, and setting forth the factors which have been relied on for the purpose of claiming bays as historic. The final section is intended to show that the theory does not apply to bays only but is more general in scope."[9]

9. The United Nations Conference on the Law of the Sea which met in Geneva on 24 February 1958 referred those articles of the International Law Commission draft dealing with the territorial sea and the contiguous zone, including article 7 on bays, to its First Committee. At the third meeting of the Committee, in connexion with the organization of the Committee's work, the representative of Panama proposed that the Committee should set up a sub-committee to examine the question of bays and in particular the problem of the legal status of "historic bays". The representative referred to the above-mentioned Secretariat memorandum and stated that it was

"essential that the international instruments to be drafted by the Conference should deal with such questions as the definition of historic bays, the rights of the coastal State or States, the procedure for declaring a bay 'historic', the conditions for recognition by other States, and the peaceful settlement of disputes arising from objections by other States".

The work of the First Committee with respect to these problems would, in the opinion of the representative, be considerably facilitated if it appointed a sub-committee specifically concerned with the law relating to bays.[10]

10. After a short discussion of the matter in the First Committee, the Chairman suggested that, as the forthcoming general debate in the Committee would probably make clear what other sub-committees would be needed, and it was desirable to consider the composition of all the sub-committees at the same time, the Panamanian proposal should be held over for the time being, on the understanding that he would bring it before the Committee at an early convenient date. The representative of Panama agreed to that procedure.

11. In the discussion at the third meeting and the general debate in the First

---

9 *Ibid.*, page 2.
10 *Official Records of the United Nations Conference on the Law of the Sea, Volume III, First Committee*, page 2.

Committee, the Panamanian proposal won support from several delegations, in particular the delegations of Saudi Arabia, Yemen,[11] El Salvador,[12] and Pakistan,[13] while the representative of the United Kingdom[14] expressed doubts regarding the usefulness of a study of the matter by a sub-committee. The representative of the Federal Republic of Germany[15] said that he thought that it would be difficult to establish general rules applicable to "historic bays". Mr. J. P. Å. François, the International Law Commission's special rapporteur on the law of the sea, who was present at the Conference as an expert to the Secretariat, also advised against setting up a subcommittee to deal with "historic bays". In his view, the Conference did not have at its disposal the material needed for a thorough study of the question, and the Conference might therefore

"merely use the term 'historic bays' and leave it to be construed, in case of dispute, by the Court, with due regard for all the features of the special case, which could not possibly be provided for in a general rule".

If necessary, he added, the International Law Commission

"could be instructed to study acquisition by prescription, with special reference to 'historic bays' ".[16]

12. When the Panamanian proposal was taken up for decision at the twenty-fifth meeting of the First Committee,[17] the representative of India stated that although his delegation was highly interested in the question of "historic bays", he felt that the Committee had neither the time nor the material available to deal with the matter properly. Each bay, he said, having its own particular characteristics, a mass of data would have to be sifted and collated before any general principles could be established. Instead of setting up a subcommittee, the Conference should therefore adopt a resolution recommending that the General Assembly make arrangements for further study of the question of "historic bays" by whatever body it might consider appropriate. The representative of Panama indicated willingness to accept this idea put forth by India and consequently to withdraw his own proposal. At the suggestion of the Chairman, the Committee thereafter agreed to postpone its decision until the text of a joint proposal by the delegations of India and Panama along these lines had been submitted.

13. In the meantime, the delegation of Japan submitted a proposal containing a definition of "historic bays". The delegation proposed that paragraph 4 of article 7, on bays, should be replaced by the following text:

"4. The foregoing provisions shall not apply to historic bays. The term 'historic bays' means those bays over which coastal State or States have effectively

---

11 *Ibid.*
12 Op. cit., page 48.
13 Op. cit., page 51.
14 Op. cit., page 9.
15 Op. cit., page 45.
16 Op. cit., page 69.
17 Op. cit., page 74.

exercised sovereign rights continuously for a period of long standing, with explicit or implicit recognition of such practice by foreign States."[18]

The representative of Japan explained that his delegation has submitted this proposal because the definition of "historic bays" was part of the task of codification and could not be left to arbitral tribunals or courts dealing with particular disputes regarding such bays.[19] The definition included in the proposal had been prepared with the aid of the Secretariat's memorandum on "historic bays" (A/CONF.13/1).

14. The representative of Thailand agreed with the Japanese delegation that the definition of the term "historic bays" should not be left to any court or tribunal, but on the other hand he considered that the definition included in the Japanese amendment was not precise enough. The representative of the Soviet Union urged that the Japanese amendment should not be considered until the Committee was ready to take up the Indian-Panamanian proposal referred to above.[20]

15. At its forty-eighth meeting the First Committee had before it both the Japanese amendment to article 7 and a draft resolution submitted jointly by India and Panama and reading as follows:[21]

"*The First Committee,*

"*Considering* that the International Law Commission has not provided for the régime of historic waters including historic bays,

"*Recognizing* the importance of the juridical status of such areas,

"*Decides* to request the Secretary-General of the United Nations to arrange for the study of the régime of historic waters including historic bays and the preparation of draft rules which may be submitted to a special conference."

16. As far as the records of the meeting[22] show, no explanation was given why the subject of the proposed study in the joint draft resolution was described as "historic waters including historic bays", not merely "historic bays" which was the term used in paragraph 4 of article 7 and also in the original Panamanian proposal to set up a sub-committee. When introducing the draft resolution, one of the sponsors used the term "historic waters" while the other used the term "historic bays", and in the debate some speakers used the former, others the latter, term.

17. The attention of the Committee was in fact focused on other aspects of the draft resolution. It was in particular pointed out that the resolution should rightly be in the name of the Conference not of the First Committee, and also that

---

18 A/CONF.13/C.l/L.104, op. cit.. page 241.
19 Op. cit. pages 145, 198.
20 Op. cit., pages 146, 198.
21 A/CONF.13/C.1/L.158, op. cit, page 252.
22 Op. cit., pages 147-1-18. It may be of interest in this respect to note that during the deliberations in the First Committee the question of an historic title to maritime areas came up not only in regard to bays but also in connexion with the problem of the delimitation of the territorial seas of two States whose coasts are opposite or adjacent to each other (article 12 of the Convention on the Territorial Sea and the Contiguous Zone); see op. cit., pages 187-193.

it was more seemly for the Conference to address itself to the General Assembly than to the Secretary-General. Both these points were admitted by the sponsor. Another change which was of more substantive importance was also accepted by the sponsors. Their attention was drawn to the possibility that the study might result in the conclusion that in view of the diversity of the particular cases of "historic waters, including historic bays" no general rules could be drawn up. The representative of India replied that no general rules could, of course, be drafted if it was clearly impossible to do so, and that it was precisely the object of the proposed study to determine whether such rules could be drafted.

18. In view of the various points brought up during the discussion, a decision on the draft resolution and on the Japanese amendment was further postponed.

19. The matter came before the First Committee again at its sixty-third meeting.[23] India and Panama now submitted a revised version of their draft resolution, reading as follows:[24]

"*The First Committee,*

"*Considering* that the International Law Commission has not provided for the régime of historic waters including historic bays,

"*Recognising* the importance of the juridical status of such areas,

"*Recommends* that the Conference should refer the matter to the General Assembly of the United Nations with the request that the General Assembly should make appropriate arrangements for the study of the juridical régime of historic waters including historic bays, and for the result of these studies to be sent to all Member States of the United Nations."

In this wording, the draft resolution was adopted by the First Committee. The delegation of Japan withdrew its amendment to article 7.

20. It might be useful to point out that in the revised draft resolution which was adopted, the word "juridical" had been inserted before the word "régime" so as to clarify the character of the study to be undertaken. The points made in discussion referred to above had also been taken into consideration in the revised version.

21. The resolution adopted by the First Committee was submitted to the Conference in the Committee's report on its work.[25] The resolution was adopted without discussion, by the Conference, at its twentieth plenary meeting.[26] The clause in the article on bays stating that the provisions of the article did not apply to "historic bays" was adopted in the wording proposed by the International Law Commission and quoted above in paragraph 2 of this paper.

22. In consequence, the following resolution dated 27 April 1958 was transmitted to the General Assembly:

---

23 Op. cit, pages 197-198.
24 A/CONF.13/C.l/L.158/Rev.l, op. cit., page 252.
25 *Official Records of the United Nations Conference on the Law of the Sea, Volume II, Plenary Meetings*, page 125.
26 Op. cit., page 68.

"*The United Nations Conference on the Law of the Sea,*
"*Considering* that the International Law Commission had not provided for the régime of historic waters, including historic bays,
"*Recognizing* the importance of the juridical status of such areas,
"*Decides* to request the General Assembly of the United Nations to arrange for the study of the juridical régime of historic waters, including historic bays, and for the communication of the results of such study to all States Members of the United Nations."

23. The General Assembly, at its 752nd plenary meeting on 22 September 1958, placed on the agenda of its thirteenth session the item "Question of initiating a study of the juridical régime of historic waters, including historic bays" and referred it to the Sixth Committee. After a short discussion, the Committee adopted and recommended to the General Assembly a draft resolution whereby the Assembly would postpone consideration of the question to its fourteenth session. This draft resolution was approved by the General Assembly at its 783rd plenary meeting, on 10 December 1958.[27]

24. At its fourteenth session, the General Assembly again referred the item to the Sixth Committee which discussed it at its 643rd to 646th meetings.[28] In the course of the debate some representatives discussed the substance of the question, but most of the speakers reserved their position on the substance and limited themselves to the problem of how the study of the question should be organized. In the end there was general agreement that the study of the question should be entrusted to the International Law Commission. The Sixth Committee unanimously adopted and submitted to the General Assembly a draft resolution to that effect, and at its 847th plenary meeting on 7 December 1959, the Assembly adopted the following resolution 1453 (XIV):

"*The General Assembly,*
"*Recalling* that, by a resolution adopted on 27 April 1958, the United Nations Conference on the Law of the Sea requested the General Assembly to arrange for the study of the juridical régime of historic waters, including historic bays, and for the communication of the results of the study to all States Members of the United Nations,
"*Requests* the International Law Commission, as soon as it considers it advisable, to undertake the study of the question of the juridical régime of historic waters, including historic bays, and to make such recommendations regarding the matter as the Commission deems appropriate."

25. General Assembly resolution 1453 (XIV) was included in the agenda of the twelfth session of the International Law Commission and discussed at its 544th

---

27　See *Official Records of the General Assembly, Thirteenth Session, Sixth Committee*, 597th and 598th meetings and annexes to agenda item 58.

28　Op. cit., *Fourteenth Session, Sixth Committee*, 643rd to 646th meetings and annexes to agenda item 58.

meeting on 20 May 1960.[29] As might be expected, the discussion mainly dealt with the methods of the study to be undertaken.

26. According to one school of thought which turned out to be the minority opinion, the Commission should invite the Member States to send to the Secretariat all available documentation concerning those historic waters, including historic bays, which were subject to their jurisdiction and to indicate the régime claimed by them for these waters. Only from such data provided by Governments could the Commission, according to this view, learn the rules of customary international law concerning historic waters. Although it was not the task of the Commission to decide on particular claims to these waters, nevertheless, it must discover what bays and other waters were claimed as historic and on what grounds, in order to be able to determine the principles governing the juridical régime of historic waters on the basis of existing international custom.

27. The majority of the members of the Commission, on the other hand, feared that if Governments were invited to specify their claims to historic waters they might be tempted, as a matter of prudence, to protect their position by advancing all their claims, including possibly some totally new ones. They might also thereby commit themselves to a rigid attitude which could make a solution of the problem more difficult in the future. Furthermore, possibly exaggerated claims would not be a suitable basis for the formulation of principles on the matter. Those members who held this opinion therefore felt that the Commission should first determine the principles governing the matter and then invite the Governments to comment on those principles. If the Governments so wished they could, of course, in their observations on the principles, refer to particular claims to historic waters.

28. While the majority of the members of the Commission were against requesting information from Governments at the present stage, they considered that in order to expedite the Commission's work in this field, some action should be undertaken forthwith. It was therefore decided to request the Secretariat to follow up the work begun by the preparation of the memorandum on "historic bays" mentioned above in paragraph 8. This decision was set out in paragraph 40 of the Commissions' report on its twelfth session (A/4425) as follows:

"... The Commisson requested the Secretariat to undertake a study of the juridical régime of historic waters, including historic bays, and to extend the scope of the preliminary study outlined in paragraph 8 of the memorandum on historic bays prepared by the Secretariat in connexion with the first United Nations Conference on the Law of the Sea..."

29. Paragraph 8 of the memorandum referred to in the quotation reads:

"8. As indicated in part II of this paper, the theory of historic bays is of general scope. Historic rights are claimed not only in respect of bays, but also in respect of maritime areas which do not constitute bays, such as the waters of archipelagos

---

29 *Yearbook of the International Law Commission, 1960*, volume I, pages 111-116.

and the water area lying between an archipelago and the neighbouring mainland; historic rights are also claimed in respect of straits, estuaries and other similar bodies of water. There is a growing tendency to describe these areas as 'historic waters', not as 'historic bays'. The present memorandum will leave out of account historic waters which are not also bays. It will, however, deal with certain maritime areas which, though not bays *stricto sensu*, are of particular interest in this context by reason of their special position or by reason of the discussion or decisions to which they have given rise."

30. It is apparent from what has been said above that the subject-matter of the study to be undertaken is wider in scope than the subject-matter of the memorandum on "historic bays" (A/CONF.13/1) prepared by the Secretariat with the purpose of shedding light on the clause exempting such bays from the provision of the article on bays contained in the International Law Commission's draft on the law of the sea. The subject-matter was widened to include also other "historic waters" than "historic bays". On the other hand, very little information can be gathered from the discussions related above as to the scope and meaning of the term "historic waters" or as to the relationship between that term and the term "historic bays". This was to be expected as the discussion was mainly concerned with methods and procedures for dealing with the matter. Moreover, as will be seen below, the question of the relationship between the terms "historic bays" and "historic waters" does not involve major problems.

31. Another point which clearly emerges from the foregoing is that the study at the present stage should not have as its purpose to attempt to establish a list of existing "historic bays" and other "historic waters". As far as "historic bays" are concerned, the previous Secretariat memorandum (A/CONF.13/1) contains a comprehensive enumeration of such bays and it would be difficult to make useful additions thereto without consulting the Governments.[30]

32. The purpose of the study should rather be to discuss the principles of international law governing the régime of "historic waters". The question then arises how these principles can be ascertained. The proper inductive method would be to study the particular cases of "historic waters" and see what common principles can be abstracted from them. This procedure would, however, seem to require that the first step should be to establish a collection of cases which would be as complete as possible. That would mean that the Governments must be approached with a request to provide information. On the other hand, if not every governmental claim to "historic waters" is to be accepted, some principles would be needed in the light of which the claims could be evaluated. Theoretically at least, there seems to be a dilemma here: in order to decide whether a claim to "historic waters" is rightful, it is necessary to have principles of international law by which the claims can be appraised, but in order not to be arbitrary these principles must

---

[30] The question of establishing a list of historic waters is discussed more extensively below in paragraphs 168-176.

be based on the actual practice of States in these matters. As usual the dilemma can be solved only in a pragmatic way. There is already available considerable material in the form of known claims to "historic waters", discussions of the subject in the literature of international law and previous attempts to establish and formulate the relevant principles. Most of the material has already been recorded in the Secretariat memorandum on "historic bays" (A/CONF.13/1). On this basis it is possible to analyse and discuss important aspects of the question and to arrive at certain tentative conclusions which can be further developed and where necessary modified in the light of information and observations received at a later stage from Governments. The present paper is conceived as a contribution to this initial or tentative discussion of the subject. Its purpose is to bring to light, analyse and discuss problems connected with the subject rather than to present complete solutions to these problems. In order to be useful and to advance the study of the relevant problems, the paper must go beyond the mere enumeration of the various opinions expressed in theory and practice. Without presuming to give judgements on these opinions, it will sometimes be necessary to point out difficulties which seem to be inherent in some of them and to express a preference for others.

II. Juridical régime of historic waters, including historic bays

A. PRELIMINARY EXPLANATION OF THE TERMS "HISTORIC WATERS" AND "HISTORIC BAYS"

33. It is hardly necessary to go deeply into the matter of "historic waters" to realize that this is a subject where superficial agreement among authors and among practitioners conceals several controversial problems as well as some obscurity or at least lack of precision. Nobody would contest that there are cases in which a State has a valid historic title to certain waters adjacent to its coasts, but when it comes to a more precise definition of this title, its relation to the rules of international law for the delimitation of the maritime territory of a State or the question of the circumstances in which the historic title may arise, agreement is far from complete. Although it would have been convenient to be able to give, at the outset, a definition of "historic waters", this is therefore not possible. Without an examination and discussion of the controversial problems involved, the presentation of a definition would be premature. Furthermore, as was said above, the purpose of the present preparatory study is not so much to provide ready-made solutions to the relevant problems as to indicate these problems and so to prepare the way for the International Law Commission's consideration of the matter. In other words, in the paper an attempt will be made to set forth, analyse and clarify a number of problems connected with the concept or theory of "historic waters", departing from the fact that it is universally recognized in the doctrine and practice of international law that States may under certain circumstances on historic grounds have valid claims to certain waters adjacent to their coasts.

34. One of the lesser problems which, at least in a preliminary way, should be clarified is the terminological question arising from the use in theory and practice rather indiscriminately of the terms "historic bays" and "historic waters". These two terms are obviously not synonymous; the latter term has a wider scope, as is also apparent from the expression used in the resolutions of the Conference on the Law of the Sea and the General Assembly, namely, "historic waters, including historic bays". It is a fact that the term "historic bays" is more frequently used or has until recent times been more frequently used than "historic waters". This circumstance cannot, however, be taken as evidence that the more general view is that only bays, not other waters, may be claimed by States on an historic basis. On the contrary, it can be said that all those authorities who have directed their attention to the problem seem to agree that historic title can apply also to waters other than bays, i.e., to straits, archipelagos and generally to all those waters which can be included in the maritime domain of a State. If the term "historic bays" has been used more frequently than "historic waters", this is mainly due to the fact that claims on an historic basis have been made more often with respect to what were called or considered to be bays than to other waters. In principle, as was said in the Secretariat memorandum (A/CONF.13/1). referred to above in paragraph 29, "the theory of historic bays is of general scope", i.e., it applies also to other maritime areas than bays. Sir Gerald Fitzmaurice no doubt expressed a generally held opinion when he stated that:

"... there seems to be no ground of principle for confining the concept of historic waters merely to the waters of a bay ... Even if the cases would in practice be fewer, a claim could equally be made on an historic basis to other waters ...".[31]

It may be of interest to note that in the *Fisheries* case between the United Kingdom and Norway, both parties agreed that the theory of "historic waters" was not limited to bays.[32] It will be seen below that the legal status of "historic bays" may be different from that of other "historic waters", but that circumstance obviously does not weaken the position that an historic title can exist to other waters than bays.

35. It is easily discernible that many of the problems and difficulties inherent in the theory of "historic waters" have their origin or are conditioned by the circumstances in which the theory arose and was developed. A short description of the background of the theory, in fact and in law, should therefore facilitate its understanding.

---

31 *British Year Book of International Law*, vol. 31 (1954), page 381; see also Gidel, *Droit international public de la mer*, vol. III (1934), page 651, and the Norwegian Counter-Memorial in the *Fisheries* case, paragraphs 539, 549 and 557-560; *International Court of Justice, Pleadings, Oral Arguments, Documents. Fisheries Case*, volume I, pages 548, 557 and 564-566, and British reply, paragraphs 471-472, op. cit. vol. II, pages 643-645; Cf. also the report of the Second Committee in *Acts of the Conference for the Codification of International Law (1930)*, vol. III, page 211.

32 Cf. op. cit, vol. II, page 643.

B. CONCEPT OF "HISTORIC WATERS"

1. Background

36. There are above all two factors which have contributed to the emergence and development of the concept of "historic waters". One important factor was the controversial status of the international legal rules relating to the delimitation of the maritime territory of the State. Without taking a position regarding the question whether or not there ever was a generally accepted maximum width of the territorial sea or a maximum breadth of the opening of bays, it can safely be said that these questions through the ages were enveloped in controversy and therefore appeared to both lawyers and laymen as subject to doubt. In these cir-cumstances it was natural that States laid claim to and exercised jurisdiction over such areas of the sea adjacent to their coasts as they considered to be vital to their security or to their economy. When a controversy arose after a State had for some time exercised jurisdiction over such an area of the sea, and the opponent State alleged that, according to the general rules of international law relating to the delimitation of territorial waters, the area in question was outside such waters, it was also natural for the defendant State to reply not only that it had a different opinion about the content of the applicable rule of general international law but also that by force of long usage it now had an historic title to the area. In the course of time there occurred quite a number of cases in which a State asserted its sovereignty, based on historic rights, over certain maritime areas, whether or not according to general international law rules such areas might be outside its maritime domain. No attempt will be made in this paper to enumerate these cases; an enumeration and description of many of them may be found in the Secretariat's memorandum on "historic bays" (A/CONF.13/1), pages 3 *et seq.*

37. The second important factor in the development of the concept and theory of "historic waters" was the attempts, official and unofficial, to substitute for the controversial and doubtful international law relating to the delimitation of territorial waters a set of clearcut, generally acceptable, written rules on the subject. For various such projects, reference may also be made to the aforementioned Secretariat memorandum (A/CONF.13/1), pages 14 *et seq.* As pointed out in that memorandum (pages 2-3), a codification of the international law rules relating to the delimitation of territorial waters and in particular regarding the delimitation of bays would in several cases have conflicted with existing situations. In other words, considerable maritime areas over which States claimed and exercised sovereignty would, if the codification were accepted, fall outside the jurisdiction of these States and belong instead to the high seas. It is obvious that a codification having such consequences would not commend itself to the States affected. The proposed rules would stand a better chance of being accepted if they included a clause excepting from its regulations waters to which a State had a historic title. As a consequence, the proposed codifications dealing with the delimitation of territorial waters generally contained such clauses in varying formulations. The concept of "historic

waters" came to be considered as an indispensable concept without which the task of establishing simple and general rules for the delimitation of maritime areas could not be carried out. Gidel expresses this thought when he says:

"The theory of 'historic waters', whatever name it is given, is a necessary theory; in the delimitation of maritime areas, it acts as a sort of safety valve; its rejection would mean the end of all possibility of devising general rules concerning this branch of public international law....".[33]

38. In summary, the concept of "historic waters" has its root in the historic fact that States through the ages claimed and maintained sovereignty over maritime areas which they considered vital to them without paying much attention to divergent and changing opinions about what general international law might prescribe with respect to the delimitation of the territorial sea. This fact had to be taken into consideration when attempts were made to codify the rules of international law in this field, i.e., to reduce the sometimes obscure and contested rules of customary law to clear and generally acceptable written rules. It was felt that States could not be expected to accept rules which would deprive them of considerable maritime areas over which they had hitherto had sovereignty. The Second Committee of the 1930 Hague Codification Conference said in its report:

"One difficulty which the Committee encountered in the course of its examination of several points of its agenda was that the establishment of general rules with regard to the belt of the territorial sea would, in theory at any rate, effect an inevitable change in the existing status of certain areas of water. In this connection, it is almost unnecessary to mention the bays known as 'historic bays'; and the problem is besides by no means confined to bays, but arises in the case of other areas of water also. The work of codification could not affect any rights which States may possess over certain parts of their coastal sea, and nothing, therefore, either in this report or in its appendices, can be open to that interpretation."[34]

39. The circumstance that the existence of historic rights to certain areas of the sea came to be of particular interest in connexion with the endeavour to formulate general rules of international law on the delimitation of the territorial sea had as a consequence a tendency to consider the juridical régime of "historic waters" as an exceptional régime. The protagonists of the codification of international law in this field understood that, as a practical matter, a long-standing exercise of sovereignty over an area of the sea could not suddenly be invalidated because it would not be in conformity with the general rules being formulated. On the other hand, as the purpose of the codification was the establishment of general rules it was natural to look upon these historic cases as exceptions from the rule. Gidel succinctly

---

33 Gidel, op. cit., page 651.

34 *Acts of the Conference for the Codification of International Law, Meetings of the Committee*, volume III: Minutes of the Second Committee (Series of League of Nations publications, V. Legal. l930.V.16), page 211.

expressed this view as follows:

"... while the theory of historic waters is a necessary theory, it is an exceptional theory ...".[35]

40. Whether or not the régime of "historic waters" is an exceptional régime may seem to be an academic question. In reality, it is of practical importance with respect to the question of what is needed to establish title to such waters. If the right to "historic waters" is an exceptional title which cannot be based on the general rules of international law or which may even be said to abrogate these rules in a particular case, it is obvious that the requirements with respect to proof of such title will be rigorous. In these circumstances the basis of the title will have to be exceptionally strong. The reasons for accepting the title must be persuasive; for how could one otherwise justify the disregarding of the general rule in the particular case? To quote Gidel again:

"The costal State which makes the claim of 'historic waters' is asking that they should be given exceptional treatment; such exceptional treatment must be justified by exceptional conditions."[36]

41. Both from the theoretical and from the practical point of view, it is therefore important to examine, analyse and clarify the notion that the régime of "historic waters" is an exceptional régime.

2. Is the régime of "historic waters" an exceptional régime?

42. It is probably true that, at least among the writers on the subject, the dominant opinion is that "historic waters" constitute an exception to the general rules of international law governing the delimitation of the maritime domain of a State. Gidel has been quoted above as an adherent of that opinion. His thoughts on the matter are expressed in greater detail in the following passage:

"An examination of the facts shows: (1) that certain States have claimed as part of their maritime domain waters which under the generally accepted rules applicable in principle to such areas would have had to be considered as part of the high seas, and (2) that such claims have often been recognized by other States.

"This state of affairs has given rise to a theory commonly referred to as the theory of 'historic bays': it has tried, with varying success, to identify a possible link between these different exceptional situations, whose only common feature appears to be their derogation from the generally accepted rules. Since it is necessary, if the general rule is not to be destroyed, to limit the claims of States tempted to nullify the generally recognized rules for determining areas that have a juridical status other than that of the high seas, the 'historic bays' theory has aimed at making such derogations subject to certain conditions, on which

---

35 Gidel, op. cit., page 651.
36 Gidel, op. cit., page 635.

agreement, both in the doctrine and in practice, appears not to be complete."[37] In this statement the exceptional character of "historic waters" is strongly emphasized as well as the necessity of limiting claims of this nature in order not to jeopardize the general rules regarding the delimitation of the maritime domain of States. It is also interesting to note that Gidel mentions two facts as bases of the concept of historic waters : a claim by a State to a maritime area which according to the general rules would be high seas, and the recognition by the other States of this exceptional claim. This indicates the connexion, according to this view, between the exceptional nature of the claim and a requirement that in order to be the basis of a valid title, the claim has to be combined with some form of recognition by the other States. We shall come back to this important proposition later. Here it is sufficient to point out the connexion as it appears in Gidel's statement.

43. A similar position is taken by another prominent authority on these matters. In an article discussing the law and procedure of the International Court of Justice, Sir Gerald Fitzmaurice says with reference to the *Fisheries* case between the United Kingdom and Norway:

"The Norwegian contention was essentially an attempt to remove from the conception of 'historicity' of given rights, the element of *prescription*, that is, in effect, the element of an *adverse* acquisition of rights in the face of existing law. Yet this element is of the essence of the matter, for a title or right based on historic considerations only becomes material when (and indeed assumes that) the actions involved are not or could not be justified according to the recognized rules, and can therefore be justified, if at all, only by reference to some special factor such as an historic right.

"As was suggested in the United Kingdom's written reply in the *Fisheries* case, this right takes the form essentially of a 'validation in the international legal order of a usage which is intrinsically invalid, by the continuance of the usage over a long period of time.'"[38]

Sir Gerald is here referring to the subsidiary issue in the *Fisheries* case whether Norway, even if the general rules of international law did not allow it to do so, had an historic right to delimit its waters in the manner provided by the Norwegian legislation and opposed by the United Kingdom. In his view, such an historic right would be an adverse acquisition of certain maritime areas, an acquisition on the basis of a title which in the particular case would constitute an exception to or an abrogation of the general rule. A similar thought is expressed in the following passage from another article of his on the law and procedure of the Court:

"It has for long been part of international law that, on a basis of long-continued use and treatment as part of the coastal domain, waters which would not otherwise have that character may be claimed as territorial or as internal

---

37 Gidel, op. cit, pp. 621-623.
38 *British Year Book of International Law,* vol. 30 (1953), pages 27-28.

waters...".[39]

44. In the opinion of Sir Gerald, the exceptional nature of the historic title also has as a consequence that some form of acquiescence on the part of other States isnecessary.[40] Further attention to this aspect of the problem will be given below.

45. Other authors who consider the régime of "historic waters" to be an exception to the general rules are, e.g., Westlake, Fauchille, Pitt-Cobbett, Higgins and Colombos, Balladore Pallieri and others. Pertinent quotations from their works are found in the Secretariat memorandum on "historic bays" (A/CONF.13/1), pages 18-20.

46. The view that "historic waters" constitute an exception to the generally valid rules regarding the delimitation of maritime areas was argued by the United Kingdom in the *Fisheries* case. A summary of its position is set out in the reply of the United Kingdom as follows:

"(i) A State is entitled to a belt of territorial waters of a certain breadth—the generally accepted limit is three miles—but Norway has an historic or prescriptive title to a belt of four miles.

"(ii) The belt of territorial waters must be measured from a base-line, which, subject to certain exceptions, must follow the low-water mark on the land.

"(iii) Where there are bays or similar indentations of the coast (whatever name these indentations have) which are of a certain character and where there are islands off the coast, there are rules of general international law which permit the base-line of territorial waters to cease to follow low-water mark on the land and to enclose as national waters certain areas of sea.

"(iv) A State can only establish a title to areas of sea which do not come within these general rules of international law on the basis of an historic or prescriptive title."[41]

47. In the opinion of the United Kingdom there were two essential elements in such an historic or prescriptive title, namely:

"(i) Actual exercise of authority by the claimant State;

"(ii) Acquiescence by other States."[42]

48. The connexion between the exceptional character of the claim to an historic title and the requirement of acquiescence by other States is clear from the following statement by the United Kingdom:

"...where the claim goes beyond what is accepted under general customary international law, it is the acquiescence of other States, express or implied from long usage, that sets the seal of legal validity upon the exceptional claim".[43]

---

39 Op. cit, vol. 31 (1954), page 381.
40 See op. cit., vol. 30 (1953), pages 27 *et seq.*
41 *International Court of Justice, Pleadings, Oral Arguments, Documents, Fisheries Case,* vol. II, page 302.
42 Op. cit., page 303.
43 Op. cit, page 621.

49. In contrast to this theory according to which the régime of "historic waters" is an exceptional régime, there is another opinion which denies that there exist general rules of international law regarding the delimitation of bays and other maritime areas from which the régime of "historic waters" could be an exception. In a study on "historic bays"[44] Bourquin has developed this line of thought. He says that:

"... Before taking a position on the theory of 'historic bays', one must ask oneself whether ordinary law subjects the delimitation of territorial bays to strict rules. The answer to this question cannot fail to influence the way in which one regards the practical importance and juridical function of historic titles.

"Is there a rule, valid for all States, which would limit the width of the opening of territorial bays to a given distance? More precisely, has the so-called ten-mile rule, generally advanced by those who favour a rigid delimitation, been consecrated by customary law?"[45]

50. After having reached the conclusion that no such fixed limitation of the opening of a bay exists in general international law and that in any case:

"The character of a bay depends on a combination of geographical, political, economic, historical and other circumstances ..."[46]

he continues:

"If it is agreed that the solution given by ordinary law to the problem of the territoriality of bays is not a matter of a mathematical limitation of their width but depends on an appreciation of the various elements that make up the character of the particular bay, the notion of 'historic titles' assumes a meaning that is quite different from that given it by those who favour the ten-mile rule. 'Historic title' no longer has the function of making an otherwise illegal situation legitimate. It is no longer a means whereby the coastal State can include a part of the high seas in its domain. It is no longer connected with the idea of usucapion. It is one element along with others characterizing a particular state of affairs, which must be considered as a whole and in its various aspects.

"Where long usage is invoked by a State, it is a ground additional to the other grounds on which its claim is based. In justification of its claim, it will be able to point not only to the configuration of the bay, to the bay's economic importance to it, to its need to control the bay in order to protect its territory, etc., but also to the fact that its acts with respect to the bay have always been those of the sovereign and that its rights are thus confirmed by historical tradition."[47]

51. As he does not consider the régime of historic bays as a deviation from general rules of international law, Bourquin is inclined to de-emphasize the importance of the acquiescence of other States. The historic title is for him "a

---

44 Bourquin, "Les baies historiques" in *Mélatnges Georges Sauser-Hall* (1952), pages 37-51.
45 Op. cit., page 39.
46 Op. cit., page 42.
47 Op. cit., pages 42-43.

juridical consolidation by the effect of time",[48] and such title is created by "the peaceful and continuous exercise of sovereignty".[49] Therefore,

"While it is wrong to say that the acquiescence of these States [foreign States] is required, it is true that if their reactions interfere with the peaceful and continuous exercise of sovereignty, no historic title can be formed."[50]

As said before, this question will be further analysed later on; the purpose of mentioning it here is to point out the connexion between the author's concept of "historic bays" and his attitude regarding the requirement of acquiescence on the part of foreign States.

52. In the *Fisheries* case, Norway took a similar position. The argument was, however, not limited to "historic bays" but referred to "historic waters" in general:

"In sum, it is not at all the function of an historic title, as conceived by the Norwegian Government and invoked in the present case, to legalize an otherwise illegal situation, but rather to confirm the validity of a situation.

"The Norwegian Government does not believe it necessary to discuss to what extent parts of the high seas may be included in the maritime domain of the State by virtue of an historic title, since the question does not arise in this case. It would only arise if the general rules which the United Kingdom Government alleges to be applicable to the delimitation of the maritime domain were really in force. But, the Norwegian Government has demonstrated that they are not and that they have never acquired the stability of customary rules...

"The Norwegian Government recognizes that the usage on which an historic title is based must be peaceful and continuous, and consequently that the reaction of foreign States constitutes an element to be taken into account in an appreciation of such title; but it completely rejects the thesis of the adverse Party that the aquiescence of other States is the only basis of an historic title, which would then be virtually indistinguishable from the juridical institution of recognition.

"The Norwegian Government considers that the absence of reaction by other States endows usage with the peaceful and continuous character it must have in order to give rise to an historic title.

"As to the consequences that must be deemed to ensue in this connexion from opposition by certain States, the Norwegian Government believes that it is a specific question, that each case must be judged in the light of its circumstances; that not all protests can be placed on the same footing; that, in any case, isolated opposition is incapable of preventing the creation of an historic title; and that in decisions in such matters one should bear in mind the wise counsel of the maxim

---

48 Op. cit., page 45.
49 Op. cit., page 46.
50 *Ibid.*

quieta non movere."[51]

53. Also Counsel for Norway said, as quoted by the Court in its judgement: "The Norwegian Government does not rely upon history to justify exceptional rights, to claim areas of sea which the general law would deny; it invokes history, together with other factors, to justify the way in which it applies the general law."[52]

54. Without passing judgement on these two opposing opinions, it may be pointed out that there seem to be certain difficulties inherent in the view that title to "historic waters" is an exception to the general rules of international law regarding the delimitation of the maritime domain of the State and that such title therefore must be based on some form of acquiescence on the part of the other States. If such general rules exist, and whatever their contents may be, they must obviously be customary rules. When the Geneva Convention on the Territorial Sea and the Contiguous Zone comes into force and is widely ratified, this situation will change to a certain extent.[53] For the present, however, the general rules in this field from which the régime of "historic waters" would be an exception could only be customary rules. This means that both the general rules and the title to "historic waters" would be based on usage. Why then should the latter be considered as exceptional and also inferior with regard to its validity, so that the acquiescence of the other States would be necessary to validate the title? The facts on which the title to "historic waters" are based belong to the usage in this field, no less than the facts on which the general customary rules would be based. And the *opinio juris* exists in the case of "historic waters" just as much as in the case of the so-called general rules.

55. If there are general rules in this field, the most that could be asserted is that, within the framework of customary international law, certain maximum limits for the territorial sea and the width of the opening of bays are generally applicable and that in certain cases there exists an historic title to waters which do not come within these limits. The so-called general rules would then be "general" in the sense only that they would be more generally applicable than the "exceptional" title to "historic waters". But they would not be "general" in the sense of having a superior validity in relation to the "exceptional" historic title. Both the general rules and the historic title would be part of customary international law, and there would be no grounds for claiming *a priori* that the historic title is valid only if based on the acquiescence of the other States.

56. However, it might be doubted whether it is even possible in this manner to distinguish within the framework of customary international law between a "general" régime and an "exceptional" régime based on an historic title. It may well be argued that a distinction between "general" and "exceptional" in this case would be wholly arbitrary. It could be said that only by *a priori* classifying certain cases

---

51 *International Court of Justice, Pleadings, Oral Arguments, Documents, Fisheries Case*, vol. III, pages 461-462.
52 *I.C.J. Reports, 1951*, page 133.
53 See below, paragraphs 72-79.

as exceptional, or by *a priori* classifying certain cases as normal, can one arrive at general customary rules regarding such questions as the limits of the territorial sea, bays, etc.

57. Furthermore, it may even be doubted whether there exist at present any general customary rules regarding the delimitation of the maritime domain of States. The fact is that through the ages many conflicting opinions have been expressed in the doctrine and in practice on these problems and that claims to maritime areas have been made by States on grounds which have varied greatly both within the same period of time and from one time to another. International doctrine and practice therefore present a rather confusing picture in this respect. It is to be expected that the Geneva Conventions will, when they come into force, bring more stability to this field, but as far as the customary law is concerned the situation is far from clear.

58. If that is true, the view that the régime of "historic waters" is an exceptional régime which deviates from certain precise general rules of customary international law becomes even more doubtful. If the rules of customary international law on fundamental questions such as the breadth of the territorial sea or the width of the opening of bays are in dispute between the States, where are the general rules from which the historic title would be an exception? In these circumstances, would not the most realistic view be not to relate the claim or right to "historic waters" to any general customary rules on the delimitation of maritime areas, as an exception or not an exception from such rules, but to consider the title to "historic waters" independently, on its own merits.[54]

59. It follows that also the problem of the elements constituting title to "historic waters" and the question of proof have to be considered independently and not on the assumption that the title to "historic waters" constitutes an exception to general international law. In particular, the question if, or to what extent, a claim by a State to "historic waters" is subject to the acquiescence of other States has to be studied without being prejudiced by the *a priori* postulate that this is an exceptional claim.

60. Some authors who consider that the régime of "historic waters" is an exception to the general rules of international law regarding the delimitation of bays and other maritime areas use the existence of "historic bays" as conclusive proof of the existence of such general rules. Gidel says:

"The simple existence of this category of 'historic bays', which is not questioned by anyone, is of itself enough to demonstrate conclusively the existence of customary international law in the matter."[55]

This argument seems based on a *petitio principii,* for only of it is already assumed that the régime of "historic bays" is an exception to certain general rules does the existence of "historic bays" imply the existence of such general rules. Sir Gerald

---

54 Cf. Jessup, *The Law of Territorial Waters and Maritime Jurisdiction* (1927), pages 355 *et seq.*
55 Gidel, op. cit., page 537. See also the reply of the United Kingdom in the *Fisheries* case, *International Court of Justice, Pleadings, Oral Arguments, Documents, Fisheries Case,* vol. II, page 607.

Fitzmaurice places the argument on a more practical level:

"... it must be assumed that the historic principle remains—and if this is admitted, it follows at once that international law, even if it does not impose a ten-mile limit [for bays], must still impose *some* limit, for if there were no legal limitation on the size of bays all reason for claiming a bay on historic grounds would disappear."[56]

There would, however, be a practical reason for claiming an historic title to bays or other maritime areas even if there is no generally accepted legal limitation on the size of bays or the breadth of the territorial sea. It is sufficient that the claiming State itself or other States *hold* that there is such a limitation to make it understandable that a State may wish to base its claim on historic grounds. Only if there existed general and absolute agreement among the States that there was no limitation, would it be pointless to claim a maritime area on historic grounds. It could even be asserted that it is the *uncertainty* of the legal situation, not the certainty that general rules of international law on the matter exist, which has given rise to the claims which form the factual basis of the theory of "historic waters".

61. Intimately connected with the view that the régime of "historic waters" forms an exception to general international law is the idea that the title to "historic waters" is a kind of prescriptive right. This thought is clearly expressed in some of the statements quoted above. It may therefore be of interest briefly to examine that idea.

3. Is the title to "historic waters" a prescriptive right?

62. There has been much debate regarding the existence of prescription in international law.[57] Of the two main forms of prescription, "extinctive prescription" (*prescription libératoire*), or loss of a claim by failure to prosecute it within a reasonable time, has no application in the present context. In connexion with "historic waters" it is the other form of prescription, namely "acquisitive prescription" (*prescription acquisitive*), which may be of interest.

63. "Acquisitive prescription" means that a title to something, e.g., a territory, is acquired by prescription, i.e., by the lapse of time under certain circumstances. Within the category of "acquisitive prescription" two sub-categories can be distinguished. One is acquisitive prescription based on "immemorial possession". In this case the original title is uncertain. It may have been a valid title or not; in any case the long lapse of time makes it impossible to establish what the original legal situation was. This uncertainty is cured and a valid title is considered to be acquired

---

56 *British Year Book of International Law, 1954*, page 416.

57 See, for instance, Oppenheim, *International Law*, vol. I, 8th ed. (1955), pages 575-578; Verykios, *La prescription en droit international public* (1934); Söressen in *Acta Scandinavica Juris Gentium*, vol. 3 (1932), pages 145-170; Johnson in *British Year Book of International Law*, vol. 27 (1950), pages 332-354; Pinto "La prescription en droit international", *in Recueil des Cours de l'Académie de Droit International*, vol. 87 (1955- I), pages 391-449.

by "immemorial possession". The existence in international law of this kind of "acquisitive prescription" does not seem to be disputed. More controversial is the question whether the other sub-category of "acquisitive prescription" has a place in international law. In this case, which is said to be akin to the *usucapio* of Roman law, the original title of the possessor is known to be defective. But because the possessor has enjoyed uninterrupted possession for a period of time under conditions which are considered to imply acquiescence (in any case tacit consent) on the part of the rightful title owner, the possessor is held to have acquired through prescription a full and complete title. Some authors have denied that this sort of acquisitive prescription exists in international law, because no fixed time for the necessary possession can be found there, in contrast to the situation in municipal law where precise time-limits are prescribed. The majority of writers, however, consider this to be a detail which should not prevent the acceptance in international law of this kind of prescription which they find necessary for the preservation of international order and stability. Some even think that no distinction should be made between the two sub-categories of "acquisitive prescription", because the "immemorial possession" cannot in practice be required to be literally "immemorial" and that therefore, as far as the lapse of time is concerned, the two sub-categories tend to merge.[58]

64. This argument for the assimilation of the two sub-categories is, however, hardly sufficient. There is another important difference between them, namely, a difference with respect to the original title. In one case the original title is uncertain, in the other case it is known to be defective. It would seem that the requirements for remedying uncertainty should be less stringent than those necessary to cure known illegality.

65. To what extent can the concept of prescription be applied to "historic waters"? This problem has to be approached with some circumspection, for although there seems to be no reason why prescription should not apply to maritime areas as well as to areas of land, that does not necessarily mean that acquisitive prescription in both its forms is applicable to "historic waters". If, for instance, there is a dispute between two States regarding the sovereignty over a certain area of water, it is thinkable that one of the parties to the dispute might base its case on a prescriptive right to the area. But that would hardly be a case of "historic waters". The theory of "historic waters" is not used to decide whether a maritime area belongs to one State or another. "Historic waters" are not waters which originally belonged to one State but now are claimed by another State on the basis of long possession. They are waters which one State claims to be part of its maritime territory while one or more other States may contend that they are part of the high seas. To what extent then is prescription applicable to this latter situation?

66. As far as the first form of acquisitive prescription is concerned, i.e., prescription based on "immemorial possession", this kind of prescriptive right does not seem to differ much from the historic title envisaged in the theory of "historic

---

58 Cf. Johnson, op. cit., pages 339-340.

waters". It refers to a situation where the original title is uncertain and is validated by long possession. It is approximately the same situation as in the case of "historic waters". If nothing more is implied in the term "prescriptive right", its application to "historic waters" seems innocuous, although not particularly useful.

67. If, on the other hand, the term "prescriptive right" refers to the second sub-category of acquisitive prescription, mentioned above, it is more difficult to accept the concept of prescription as applicable to "historic waters". In this case, prescription would mean that an originally *defective* or *invalid* title is cured by long possession. If applied to "historic waters" that would imply the assumption that according to the general rules of international law the waters were originally high seas, but that through the effect of time (in the proper circumstances) an exceptional historic title to the waters had emerged in favour of the coastal State. In other words, to consider the title to "historic waters" as a prescriptive right in this latter sense would really be to embrace the idea that the title to "historic waters" is an exception to the general rules of international law regarding the delimitation of maritime areas.

68. It is to be feared that this is usually what is implied when the term "prescriptive right" is used in connexion with "historic waters". In order to avoid that by the use of that term unwarranted assumptions are brought into the argument, it would therefore be preferable not to refer to the concept of prescription in connexion with the régime of "historic waters".

4. *Relation of "historic waters" to "occupation"*

69. Another term which is occasionally used in connexion with "historic waters" is "occupation", and it may therefore be useful briefly to examine whether there is a significant relation between these two concepts.

70. As is well known, occupation is an original mode of acquisition of territory. It is denned by Oppenheim as follows:

"Occupation is the act of appropriation by a State by which it intentionally acquires sovereignty over such territory as is at the time not under the sovereignty of another State."[59]

A similar definition is given by Fauchille:

"Generally speaking, occupation is the taking by a State, with the intention of acting as the owner, of something which does not belong to any other State but which is susceptible of sovereignty."[60]

Both authors agree that because of the freedom of the high seas, those seas cannot be the object of occupation.[61]

71. This doctrine that occupation is an original mode of acquisition of territory but one which is not applicable to the high seas seems to be generally accepted

---

59 Oppenheim, *International Law*, volume I, 8th ed. (1955), page 555.
60 Fauchille, *Traité de droit international public*, vol. 1, part 2, 8th ed. (1925), pages 680-681.
61 Oppenheim, op. cit., page 556; Fauchille, op. cit., page 702.

at the present time. A State could therefore hardly claim an area of water on the basis of occupation unless it affirmed that the occupation took place before the freedom of the high seas became part of international law. In that case the State would claim acquisition of the area by an occupation which took place long ago. Strictly speaking, the State would, however, not assert an historic title but rather an ancient title based on occupation as an original mode of acquisition of territory. The difference may be subtle but should in the interest of clarity not be overlooked: to base the title on occupation is to base it on a clear original title which is fortified by long usage.

5. *"Historic waters" as an exception to rules laid down in a general convention*

72. The difficulties inherent in the conception that the régime of "historic waters" is an exception to customary law have been discussed above. What is the situation when the customary rules of international law regarding the delimitation of the maritime domain of the State are codified? Does the régime of "historic waters" then become an exceptional régime in the sense that strict requirements regarding the establishment of an area as "historic waters" are justified? To give an answer, it is necessary to study the content of the codified rules, the circumstances in which the rules were adopted and the intention of the parties accepting them.

73. As the nearest approach to a codification of the rules of international law regarding the territorial sea, the 1958 Geneva Convention on the Territorial Sea and the Contiguous Zone is of particular interest. As mentioned above, references to historic title occur in articles 7 and 12 of that Convention. Article 7, which deals with bays the coasts of which belong to a single State, contains a final paragraph stating that the foregoing provisions of the article shall not apply to so-called "historic bays". In paragraph 1 of article 12, regarding the delimitation of the territorial seas of States whose coasts are opposite or adjacent, there is a clause saying that the provisions of the paragraph shall not apply where by reason of historic title it is necessary to delimit the territorial seas in a different manner.

74. It seems to be clear both from the texts and from the relevant discussions at the Conference, related above in the first section of this paper, that the purpose of these exception clauses in articles 7 and 12 was to maintain with respect to the historic titles mentioned the *status quo ante* the entry into force of the Convention. As was indicated previously in this paper, the Second Committee of the 1930 Hague Codification Conference took the position in its report that the proposed codification of the rules of international law regarding territorial waters should not affect the historic rights which States might possess over certain parts of their coastal sea. Articles 7 and 12 show that the 1958 Geneva Conference on the Law of the Sea took the same position regarding historic rights in relation to bays bordered by a single State or the delimitation of the territorial seas of States whose coasts are opposite or adjacent to each other.

75. The question arises, however, what the situation is in cases where the historic title has not been expressly reserved in the Convention. In principle, it seems that

the answer must be: if the provisions of an article should be found to conflict with an historic title to a maritime area, and no clause is included in the article safeguarding the historic title, the provisions of the article must prevail as between the parties to the Convention. This seems to follow *a contrario* from the fact that articles 7 and 12 have express clauses reserving historic rights; articles without such a clause must be considered not to admit an exception in favour of such rights.

76. Obviously the situation is different where a certain subject-matter has not been regulated by the Convention. Such is the case with respect to bays, the coasts of which belong to two or more States, and also in regard to the breadth of the territorial sea. Here the subject-matter is left completely untouched by the Convention; and as the Convention contains no relevant general rules, it would of course be pointless to reserve historic rights in this respect.[62]

77. Three hypotheses may therefore be envisaged:

(i) The historic title relates to maritime areas not dealt with by the Convention and the Convention has consequently no impact on the title;

(ii) The historic title relates to areas dealt with by the Convention but is expressly reserved by the Convention. Also in this case the Convention has no impact on the title;

(iii) The historic title is in conflict with a provision of the Convention and is not expressly reserved by the Convention. In that case, the historic title is superseded as between the parties to the Convention.

78. One can, of course, say in a certain sense that an historic title which is expressly reserved, as is the case in articles 7 and 12 of the Convention, thereby is implicitly qualified as an exception. But it must not be forgotten that the whole purpose of making the historic title an exception from the general rules contained in the main provisions of the relevant article is to *maintain* the historic title. It is not the intention, by excepting it, to subject the historic title to stricter requirements but to maintain the *status quo ante* with respect to the title. It would therefore be a fallacy if, from the fact that the Convention in certain cases excepts historic rights, one would draw the conclusion that the Convention requires stricter proof of the historic title than was the case before the conclusion of the Convention. In reality, the Convention simply leaves the matter, both regarding the existence of the title and the proof of the title, in the state in which it was at the entry into force of the Convention.

---

62 It may be interesting to note that while various proposals for regulating the breadth of the territorial sea were submitted at the two Geneva Conferences on the Law of the Sea, none of these proposals contained clauses reserving historic titles to certain areas of the sea. It was also fairly apparent from the discussion that the aim of the proposals was to arrive at rules which would have universal application. If any of the proposed regulations of the breadth of the territorial sea had been accepted, such regulation would then have prevailed over conflicting historic titles to maritime areas. In view of the fact that none of the proposals acquired the necessary majority, it might perhaps be worth while, if and when the question of the breadth of the territorial sea is again taken up for solution, to consider whether an agreement on a proposal might be facilitated if it contained a clause reserving historic rights.

79. The above discussion of the general aspects of the concept of "historic waters", its relation to general international law and to certain other concepts such as prescription and occupation, has cleared the way for a more concrete study of the juridical régime of "historic waters". The first problem to be taken up is the question, what conditions must be fulfilled in order that an historic title to water areas may arise or, in other words, the question of the elements constituting a title to "historic waters".

C. ELEMENTS OF TITLE TO "HISTORIC WATERS"

80. There seems to be fairly general agreement that at least three factors have to be taken into consideration in determining whether a State has acquired a historic title to a maritime area. These factors are: (1) the exercise of authority over the area by the State claiming the historic right; (2) the continuity of this exercise of authority; (3) the attitude of foreign States. First, the State must exercise authority over the area in question in order to acquire a historic title to it. Secondly, such exercise of authority must have continued for a considerable time; indeed it must have developed into a usage. More controversial is the third factor, the position which the foreign States may have taken towards this exercise of authority. Some writers assert that the acquiescence of other States is required for the emergence of an historic title; others think that absence of opposition by these States is sufficient.

81. Besides the three factors just referred to a fourth is sometimes mentioned. It has been suggested that attention should also be given to the question whether the claim can be justified on the basis of economic necessity, national security, vital interest or a similar ground. According to one view, such grounds should even be considered to form the fundamental basis for a right to "historic waters", so that they would be sufficient to sustain the right even if the historic element were lacking.

82. These various factors will be examined below. In order not to complicate the discussion unnecessarily, it is assumed that there is only one coastal State claiming historic title to the area. In a separate sub-section, the situation will thereafter be studied which arises when "historic waters" are bordered by two or more States.

83. The method to be used will be an analysis of problems and principles rather than a discussion of cases. For a more detailed presentation of both case law and opinions of writers reference may be made to the Secretariat memorandum on "historic bays" (A/CONF.13/1).

1. *Exercise of authority over the area claimed*

84. Various expressions are used in theory and practice to indicate the authority which a State must continuously exercise over a maritime area in order to be able validly to claim the area on the basis of an historic title. As examples may be mentioned: "exclusive authority", "jurisdiction", "dominion", "sovereign ownership", "sovereignty".[63] The abundance of terminology does not, however, mean that there

---

63　For other examples see pages 4-7, 14, 15, 16-20, 32-33 of the Secretariat memorandum on "historic bays" (A/CONF.13/1).

is a great and confusing divergence of opinion regarding the requirements which this exercise of authority would have to fulfil. On the contrary there seems to be rather general agreement as to the three main questions involved, namely, the scope of the authority, the acts by which it can be exercised and its effectiveness.

(a) *Scope of the authority exercised*

85. There can hardly be any doubt that the authority which a State must continuously exercise over a maritime area in order to be able to claim it validly as "historic waters" is sovereignty. An authority more limited in scope than sovereignty would not be sufficient to form a basis for a title to such waters. This view, which does not seem to be seriously disputed, is based on the assumption that a claim to an area as "historic waters" means a claim to the area as part of the maritime domain of the State. It is logical that the scope of the authority required to form a basis for a claim to "historic waters" will depend on the scope of the claim itself. If, therefore, as is the generally accepted view,[64] a claim to "historic waters" means a claim to a maritime area as part of the national domain, i.e., if the claim to "historic waters" is a claim to sovereignty over the area, then the authority exercised, which is a basis for the claim, must also be sovereignty.

86. This interrelationship between the scope of the claim and the scope of the authority which the claiming State must exercise, and also the soundness of the assumption that the claim to "historic waters" is a claim to sovereignty over the waters, may be illustrated by an example. Suppose that a State asserted, on a historical basis, a limited right related to a certain maritime area, such as the right for its citizens to fish in the area. This would not in itself be a claim to the area as "historic waters". Nor could the State, even if it so wanted, claim the area as its "historic waters" on the basis of the fact that its citizens had fished there for a long time. The claim would in such case not be commensurate with the factual activity of the State or its citizens in the area. Suppose on the other hand that the State has continuously asserted that its citizens had the exclusive right to fish in the area, and had, in accordance with this assertion, kept foreign fishermen away from the area or taken action against them. In that case the State in fact exercised sovereignty over the area, and its claim, on a historical basis, that it had the right to continue to do so would be a claim to the area as its "historic waters". The authority exercised by the State would be commensurate to the claim and would form a valid basis for the claim (without prejudice to the condition that the other requirements for the title must also be fulfilled).

87. The reasoning may be summarized as follows. A claim to "historic waters" is a claim by a State, based on an historic title, to a maritime area as part of its national domain; it is a claim to sovereignty over the area. The activities carried on by the State in the area or, in other words, the authority continuously exercised by the State in the area must be commensurate with the claim. The authority

---

64 See Gidel, op. cit, pages 625 *et seq.* and the Secretariat memorandum on "historic bays" (A/CONF.13/1), pages 21 *et seq.*

exercised must consequently be sovereignty, the State must have acted and act as the sovereign of the area.[65]

88. This does not mean, however, that the State must have exercised all the rights or duties which are included in the concept of sovereignty. The main consideration is that in the area and with respect to the area the State carried on activities which pertain to the sovereign of the area. Without venturing to present a catalogue of such activities, some examples may be given to illustrate the kind of acts by which the authority required as a basis for the claim might be established.

(b) *Acts by which the authority is exercised*

89. It may be useful to begin by quoting the opinions of some prominent writers on the subject. Gidel, in discussing what he calls the *actes d'appropriation* to which the claiming State must have proceeded, states as follows:

"It is hard to specify categorically what kind of acts of appropriation constitute sufficient evidence: the exclusion from these areas of foreign vessels or their subjection to rules imposed by the coastal State which exceed the normal scope of regulations made in the interests of navigation would obviously be acts affording convincing evidence of the State's intent. It would, however, be too strict to insist that only such acts constitute evidence. In the Grisbadarna dispute between Sweden and Norway, the judgement of 23 October 1909 mentions that 'Sweden has performed various acts ... owing to her conviction that these regions were Swedish, as, for instance, the placing of beacons, the measurement of the sea, and the installation of a light-boat, being acts which involved considerable expense and in doing which she not only thought that she was exercising her right but even more that she was performing her duty.'"[66]

90. Regarding the kind of acts mentioned in the first part of the above quotation, Bourquin is virtually in agreement with Gidel. Bourquin says:

"What acts under municipal law can be cited as expressing its desire to act as the sovereign? That is a matter very difficult, if not impossible, to determine *a priori*. There are some acts which are manifestly not open to any misunderstanding in this regard. The State which forbids foreign ships to penetrate the bay or to fish therein indisputably demonstrates by such action its desire to act as the sovereign."[67]

He is more doubtful or flexible with respect to the measures of assistance to navigation mentioned in the second part of Gidel's statement.

"There are, however, some borderline cases. Thus, the placing of lights or beacons may sometimes appear to be an act of sovereignty, while in other

---

65 Cf. Johnson, op. cit., pages 344-345 regarding the exercise of authority necessary as a basis for acquisitive prescription.

66 Gidel, op. cit., page 633.

67 Bourquin, op. cit., page 43.

circumstances it may have no such significance."[68]

91. Bustamante, in a draft convention prepared by him with a view to assisting the 1930 Hague Codification Conference, included an article relevant to the question now discussed. It reads as follows:

"There are expected from the provisions of the two foregoing articles, in regard to limits and distance, those bays or estuaries called historic, viz., those over which the coastal State or States, or their constituents, have traditionally exercised and maintained their sovereign ownership, either by provisions of internal legislation and jurisdiction, or by deeds or writs of the authorities."[69]

92. Substantially the same article was included in the "project" submitted in 1933 to the Seventh International Conference of American States by the American Institute of International Law.[70]

93. In the *Fisheries* case, Norway stated in its Counter-Memorial:

"It cannot seriously be questioned that, in the application of the theory of historic waters, acts under municipal law on the part of the coastal State are of the essence. Such acts are implicit in an historic title. It is the exercise of sovereignty that lies at the basis of the title. It is the peaceful and continuous exercise thereof over a prolonged period that assumes an international significance and becomes one of the elements of the international juridical order."[71]

And having asked how sovereignty is asserted, the Counter-Memorial replies:

"Above all, by action under municipal law (laws, regulations, administrative measures, judicial decisions, etc.)."[72]

94. The United Kingdom Government, while emphasizing that they were not in itself sufficient to establish the title, agreed that such acts by the State under municipal law (*actes d'ordre interne*) were essential to the establishment of an historic title to a maritime territory.[73]

95. These examples furnish some guidance as to the kind of acts which are required. In the first place the acts must emanate from the State or its organs. Acts of private individuals would not be sufficient —unless, in exceptional circumstances, they might be considered as ultimately expressing the authority of the State. As Sir Arnold McNair said in his dissenting opinion in the *Fisheries* case:

"Another rule of law that appears to me to be relevant to the question of

---

68 *Ibid.* See also the statements emanating from the Ministry of Foreign Affairs of the Netherlands in 1848 and quoted by Gidel, op. cit., page 633, footnote 3.

69 Bustamante, *The Territorial Sea* (1930), page 142.

70 See the Secretariat memorandum on "historic bays" (A/CONF.13/1), page 14.

71 *International Court of Justice, Pleadings, Oral Arguments, Documents, Fisheries Case*, vol.I, pages 567-568.

72 *Ibid.*, page 568.

73 Op. cit., vol. II, page 648. See also the Secretariat memorandum on "historic bays" (A/CONF.13/1), page 32.

historic title is that some proof is usually required of the exercise of State jurisdiction, and that the independent activity of private individuals is of little value unless it can be shown that they have acted in pursuance of a licence or some other authority received from their Governments or that in some other way their Governments have asserted jurisdiction through them."[74]

96. Furthermore, the acts must be public; they must be acts by which the State openly manifests its will to exercise authority over the territory. The acts must have the notoriety which is normal for acts of State. Secret acts could not form the basis of a historic title; the other State must have at least the opportunity of knowing what is going on.[75]

97. Another important requirement is that the acts must be such as to ensure that the exercise of authority is effective.

(c) *Effectiveness of authority exercised*

98. On this point there is full agreement in theory and practice. Bourquin expresses the general opinion in these words:

"Sovereignty must be effectively exercised; the intent of the State must be expressed by deeds and not merely by proclamations."[76]

99. This does not, however, imply that the State necessarily must have undertaken concrete action to enforce its relevant laws and regulations within or with respect to the area claimed. It is not impossible that these laws and regulations were respected without the State having to resort to particular acts of enforcement. It is, however, essential that, to the extent that action on the part of the State and its organs was necessary to maintain authority over the area, such action was undertaken.

100. The first requirement to be fulfilled in order to establish a basis for a title to "historic waters" can therefore be described as the effective exercise of sovereignty over the area by appropriate action on the part of the claiming State. We can now proceed to the second requirement, namely, that this exercise of sovereignty continued for a time sufficient to confer upon it the quality of usage.

2. *Continuity of the exercise of authority: usage*

101. A study of the extensive material included in the Secretariat memorandum on "historic bays" (A/ CON F.I 3/1) and drawn from State practice, arbitral and judicial cases, codification projects and opinions of learned authors, provides ample proof of the dominant view that usage is required for the establishment of title to "historic waters". This view seems natural and logical considering that the title

---

74 *I.C.J. Reports, 1951*, page 184. Cf. *Pleadings*, vol. II, page 657.

75 The question of knowledge on the part of foreign States is further discussed below in paragraph 125 *et seq.*

76 Op. cit., page 43.

to the area is an *historic* title.[77] A great variety of terms is used in describing and qualifying the usage required. A few of the terms employed in the codification projects mentioned in the memorandum[78] may illustrate this variety: "continuous usage of long standing" [*usage continu et séculaire*] (Institute of International Law 1894), "international usage" (Institute of International Law 1928), "established usage" (Harvard draft 1930), "continued and well-established usage" (American Institute of International Law 1925), "established usage generally recognized by the nations" (International Law Association 1926), "immemorial usage" (Japanese International Law Society 1926), "continuous and immemorial usage" (Schücking draft 1926).

102. The term "usage" is not wholly unambiguous. On the one hand it can mean a generalized pattern of behaviour, i.e., the fact that many persons behave in the same (or a similar) way. On the other hand it can mean the repetition by the same person of the same (or a similar) activity. It is important to distinguish between these two meanings or "usage", for while usage in the former sense may form the basis of a general rule of customary law, only usage in the latter sense can give rise to a historic title.

103. As was established above, a historic title to a maritime area must be based on the effective exercise of sovereignty over the area by the particular State claiming it. The activity from which the required usage must emerge is consequently a repeated or continued activity of this same State. The passage of time is therefore essential; the State must have kept up its exercise of sovereignty over the area for a considerable time.

104. On the other hand, no precise length of time can be indicated as necessary to build the usage on which the historic title must be based. It must remain a matter of judgement when sufficient time has elapsed for the usage to emerge. The addition of the adjective "immemorial" is of little assistance in this respect. Taken literally "immemorial" would be a wholly impractical notion;[79] the term "immemorial" could, therefore, at the utmost be understood as emphasizing, in a vague manner, the time-element contained in the concept of "usage". It will anyhow be a question of evaluation whether, considering the circumstances of the particular case, time has given rise to a usage.

105. Usage, in terms of a continued and effective exercise of sovereignty over the area by the State claiming it, is then a necessary requirement for the establishment of a historic title to the area by that State. But is usage in this sense also sufficient? There seems to be practically general agreement that besides this national usage, consideration must also be given to the international reaction to the said exercise of sovereignty. It is sometimes said that the national usage has to develop into an "international usage". This may be a way of underlining the importance of the

---

77 Regarding the opinion which pays less attention to the passage of time and lays more emphasis on the vital interests of the State claiming the area, see below paragraphs 134 *et seq.*
78 Pages 14-15.
79 Cf. Johnson, op. cit., page 339.

attitude of foreign States in the creation of an historic title; in any case, a full understanding of the matter requires an analysis of the question how and to what extent the reaction of foreign States influences the growth of such a title.

3. *Attitude of foreign States*

106. In essence, this is the problem of the so-called acquiescence of foreign States. As was indicated above, according to a widely held opinion acquiescence in the exercise of sovereignty by the coastal State over the area claimed is necessary for the emergence of an historic title to the area. The connexion between this requirement of acquiescence and the opinion that "historic waters" are an exception to the general rules of international law governing the delimitation of maritime areas was also pointed out above. It might be recalled that the argument was on the following lines. The State which claims "historic waters" in effect claims a maritime area which according to general international law belongs to the high seas. As the high seas are *res commnnis omnium* and not *res nullius,* title to the area cannot be obtained by occupation. The acquisition by historic title is "adverse acquisition", akin to acquisition by prescription, in other words, title to "historic waters" is obtained by a process through which the originally lawful owners, the community of States, are replaced by the coastal State. Title to "historic waters", therefore, has its origin in an illegal situation which was subsequently validated. This validation could not take place by the mere passage of time; it must be consummated by the acquiescence of the rightful owners.

107. The argument seems logically to imply that acquiescence is a form of consent. However, here a difficulty arises. If acquiescence is a form of consent, acquiescence would amount to *recognition* of the sovereignty of the coastal State over the area in question and reliance on a historic title would be superfluous. If the continued exercise of sovereignty during a length of time had to be validated by acquiescence in the meaning of consent by the foreign States concerned, the lapse of time, i.e., the historical element, would be immaterial.

108. Some of the defenders of the concept of acquiescence, on the one hand, desiring to avoid a confusion with recognition and, on the other hand, unwilling to concede that the continued exercise of sovereignty by the coastal State over the area claimed could in itself constitute a historic title to the area, have endeavoured to vindicate the idea of acquiescence by interpreting it as an essentially negative concept. The term "acquiescence" is said to "describe the inaction of a State which is faced with a situation constituting a threat to or infringement of its rights",[80] or to mean that the foreign States "have simply been inactive".[81] The historic title would then be based on the continued effective exercise of sovereignty by the coastal States over the area in question combined with the inaction of the other States. In this view,

---

[80] McGibbon, "The Scope of Acquiescence in International Law", in *British Year Book of International Law*, vol. 31 (1954), page 143.

[81] Fitzmaurice in *British Year Book of International Law*, vol. 30 (1953), page 29.

"the true role of the theory [of historic rights] is to compensate for the lack of any evidence of express or active consent by States, by creating a presumption of acquiescence arising from the facts of the case and from the inaction and toleration of States."[82]

109. It is interesting to note that the protagonists of the concept of acquiescence, if they reduce this concept to mean merely inaction or toleration, arrive at a position which is very near to the one taken by those who oppose the idea that the régime of "historic waters" is an exceptional régime and the consequent idea that the acquiescence of foreign States is necessary to acquire a title to historic waters. Bourquin, who as was seen above, is a spokesman for the latter opinion, states the following:

"While it is wrong to say that the acquiescence of these States is required, it is true that if their reactions interfere with the peaceful and continuous exercise of sovereignty, no historic title can be formed.

"In such cases the question to be asked is not whether the other States consented to the claims of the coastal State but whether they interfered with the action of that State to the point of divesting it of the two conditions required for the formation of an historic title.

"Obviously only acts of opposition can have that effect. So long as the behaviour of the riparian State causes no protest abroad, the exercise of sovereignty continues unimpeded ...

"The absence of any reaction by foreign States is sufficient."[83]

110. The similarity of the final positions arrived at, both by some of the proponents and some of the opponents of the notion of acquiescence is striking: both seem to agree that inaction on the part of foreign States is sufficient to permit the emergence of a historic right. This would seem to suggest that the term "acquiescence" is ambiguous. In these circumstances, it might perhaps be better, in the interest of clarity, not to use the term "acquiescence" in this context. The term seems at least *prima facie* to convey the idea of consent and its use can therefore result in the conclusion that a historic title can arise only if concurrence on the part of foreign States has been demonstrated in a positive way. If the proponents of the necessity of acquiescence really have in mind only the negative aspect, i.e., toleration on the part of the foreign States, it would be preferable to use the term "toleration" which better expresses their thoughts. Moreover, there should be no difficulty in dropping the term "acquiescence" once the dubious theory that title to "historic waters" constitutes an exception to general international law has been discarded.

111. "Toleration" is furthermore the expression used by the International Court of Justice in the *Fisheries* case when discussing Norway's historic title to the system of delimitation which was an issue in the dispute. The Court said, *inter alia*:

---

82 Fitzmaurice, *ibid.*, page 30.
83 Bourquin, op. cit., page 46. Bustamante is also against the idea of consent, see op. cit., page 100.

"In the light of these considerations, and in the absence of convincing evidence to the contrary, the Court is bound to hold that the Norwegian authorities applied their system of delimitation consistently and uninterruptedly from 1869 until the time when the dispute arose. From the standpoint of international law, it is now necessary to consider whether the application of the Norwegian system encountered any opposition from foreign States ...

"The general toleration of foreign States with regard to the Norwegian practice is an unchal-lenged fact."[84]

The Court continued further on in its judgement:

"The Court notes that in respect of a situation which could only be strengthened with the passage of time, the United Kingdom Government refrained from formulating reservations.

"The notoriety of the facts, the general toleration of the international community, Great Britain's position in the North Sea, her own interest in the question, and her prolonged abstention would in any case warrant Norway's enforcement of her system against the United Kingdom."[85]

In the Court's opinion, the consistent and prolonged application of the Norwegian system combined with the general toleration of foreign States gave rise to a historic right to apply the system. This opinion seems to correspond fairly well to the final positions taken both by the proponents and the opponents of the concept of "acquiescence", as set out in paragraphs 108 and 109.

112. However, even if it may be said that, whether the term "acquiescence" or the term "toleration" is used, there is substantial agreement that inaction on the part of foreign States is sufficient to permit an historic title to a maritime area to arise by effective and continued exercise of sovereignty over it by the coastal State during a considerable time, all difficulties in this respect are not solved. It is true, of course, that if there has been no reaction at any time from any foreign State, then there is no difficulty. But what happens if at any one time or another opposition from one or more foreign States occurred? Does any kind of opposition by any one State at any time preclude the historic title? It is *prima facie* highly improbable that the terms "inaction" or "toleration" would have to be interpreted so strictly. Before attempting a more precise answer, it would, however, be useful to examine more closely the three points which seem to be involved, namely, (i) what kind of opposition would prevent the historic title from emerging, (ii) how widespread in terms of the number of opposing States must the opposition be, and (iii) when must the opposition occur.

113. With regard to the first point, it is obvious that the opposition ending the inaction must be expressed in some kind of action. In the passage quoted above in paragraph 109, Bourquin states that:

"... if their reactions [i.e., of foreign States] prevent the peaceful and

---

84 Fisheries case, Judgement of 18 December 1951, *I.C.J. Reports, 1951*, page 138.

85 *Ibid.*, page 139.

continuous exercise of sovereignty, no historic title can be formed."[86]
Indeed, it is hardly doubtful that opposition by force on the part of foreign States would be a means of interrupting the process by which a historic title is formed. On the other hand it cannot be assumed that Bourquin, despite the use of the word *paisible*, would consider only opposition by force as effectively preventing the creation of a historic title. He also says in the passage quoted above that:

"... so long as the behaviour of the riparian State causes no protest abroad, the exercise of sovereignty continues unimpeded."[87]

This seems to imply also a protest could be a means of hindering the emergence of a historic right.

114. If that is so, Bourquin's view would not be far from the opinion expressed by Fitzmaurice in these words:

"Protest, in some shape or form or equivalent action, is necessary in order to stop the acquisition of a prescriptive right."[88]

In a footnote Fitzmaurice goes on to describe the action in question as follows:

"Apart from the ordinary case of a diplomatic protest, or a proposal for reference to adjudication, the same effect could be achieved by a public statement denying the prescribing country's right, by resistance to the *enforcement* of the claim, or by counter-action of some kind."[89]

115. These are some of the acts by which the opposition of foreign States could be expressed, and there are, no doubt, other means which could be used. More important than establishing a list of acts, is to emphasize that whatever the acts they must effectively express a sustained opposition to the exercise of sovereignty by the coastal State over the area in question. To quote Fitzmaurice again:

"Moreover the protest must be an effective one depending on what the circumstances require. A simple protest may suffice to begin with, but this may not be enough as time goes on."[90]

Should despite the protest the coastal State continue to exercise its sovereignty over the area, the opposition on the part of the foreign State must be maintained by renewed protests or some equivalent action.

116. The second point to be examined is how wide the opposition must be, to prevent the creation of a historic title. Is it sufficient that a single State effectively expresses its opposition? Hardly anybody would go as far as that. Gidel says on this point:

"A single objection formulated by a single State will not invalidate the usage; furthermore all objections cannot be placed on an equal footing, regardless of

---

86 Bourquin, op. cit, page 46.
87 *Ibid.*
88 *British Year Book of International Law*, vol. 30 (1953), page 42. A historic right to a maritime area is in Fitzmaurice's opinion a prescriptive right, see op. cit., pages 27-28
89 Op. cit., page 42, footnote 1.
90 Op. cit., page 42, see also pages 28-29.

their nature, the geographical or other situation of the objecting State."[91] Bourquin[92] agrees with Gidel that one opposing State would not be sufficient to invalidate the usage. This seems, moreover, to be a generally accepted opinion. If the total absence of opposition is not a necessary requirement for the emergence of a historic right, it would seem to be a matter of judgement, subject to the circumstances in the particular case, how widespread the opposition must be to prevent the historic title from materializing.

117. In this connexion it is interesting to note, in the above quotation, that Gidel is not willing to place all the opposing States on the same level. The opposition of one State may according to circumstances carry more weight than the opposition of another State. Fitzmaurice follows the same line of reasoning when he says:

"It is obvious that, depending on the circumstances, the acquiescence of certain States must be of far greater weight and moment in establishing the existence of a prescriptive or historic right than that of others. Thus the consent, either expressly given or reasonably to be inferred, of those States which, whether on account of geographical proximity, or commercial or other interest in the subject-matter, etc., are directly affected by the claim, may be almost enough in itself to legitimize it; while a clear absence of consent on the part of such States would certainly suffice to prevent the establishment of the right. Equally, acquiescence or refusal on the part of States whose interest in the matter, actual or potential, is non-existent, or only slight, may have little practical significance."[93]

118. The position, outlined in the passages quoted from Gidel and Fitzmaurice, that the same weight need not be accorded to the attitude of each State, seems to be reasonable and realistic. It may, perhaps, be pointed out, however, that this position is hardly consonant with the assumption that the right to "historic waters" is an exception to the general rules of international law. If that assumption were correct, if the State claiming "historic waters" were really claiming a part of the high seas, a part of a *res communis,* unless a historic title could be established, it would seem that any State, any member of the community of States, should be able to prevent by its opposition the emergence of the historic title. How could in such case some States be entitled to give away rights which belong to all States and how could in the matter of acquiescence or opposition greater weight be given to one State than to the other? On the other hand, if it is admitted that the legal situation regarding the delimitation of the maritime territory of States is not clear, that the customary international law in this respect is in doubt, and that it is against that background that the existence or non-existence of historic rights to particular areas has to be considered, then the view seems sensible and practical that this question of opposition is a question of appreciation, not a question of arithmetic, and that the

---

91 Gidel, op. cit., page 634.
92 Bourquin, op. cit., pages 47-48.
93 Fitzmaurice, op. cit., pages 31-32.

opposition of one State in view of the circumstances in the particular case may well be of greater importance than that of another State.

119. In this connexion, it may be useful to try to visualize how a dispute with respect to "historic waters" is most likely to arise. Although it is theoretically possible, it is not probable that a dispute will arise because all or most foreign States refuse to recognize the historic right of a coastal State to a certain maritime area. Many States may have no great interest in the question and would therefore have no reason to go out of their way to antagonize the coastal State. The dispute would be most likely to arise through the opposition of neighbouring States or of those States which have a particular interest in the area. It would therefore be only natural if the arbitrator or tribunal having to settle the dispute paid particular attention to the previous attitute of those States and, in determining the existence of an historic title, gave special weight to the fact that these States, in the formative period of the disputed title, had or had not effectively opposed the exercise of sovereignty by the coastal State over the area in question.

120. With regard to point two, relative to the question how wide-spread the opposition must be to preclude the emergence of an historic title, it may therefore be said that this is a matter of appreciation in the light of the circumstances in each case. How this appreciation may be made, can be illustrated by the last part of the statement of the International Court of Justice in the *Fisheries* case, referred to above in paragraph 111:

"The notoriety of the facts, the general toleration of the international community, Great Britain's position in the North Sea, her own interest in the question, and her prolonged abstention would in any case warrant Norway's enforcement of her system against the United Kingdom."[94]

121. It remains to deal with the third point, namely, the question at what time the opposition must occur in order to prevent the creation of an historic title. It is evident that the opposition must have been effectively expressed before the historic title came into being. After a State has exercised sovereignty over a maritime area during a considerable time under general toleration by the foreign States, and an historic right to the area has thus emerged, it is not possible for one or more States to reverse the process by coming forward with a protest against the accomplished fact. The historic title is already in existence and stands despite the belated opposition.

122. However, by this general and rather obvious statement the problem is not solved. There are in any case two questions which need to be discussed in this connexion. The first question is: how long is the considerable time during which sovereignty has to be exercised and tolerated? The second question is: from what moment does this time start to run?

123. Regarding the first question it can only be said that the length of time necessary for a historic right to emerge is a matter of judgement; no precise time

---

94 *I.C.J. Reports, 1951*, page 139.

can be indicated. However, as the exercise of sovereignty has to develop into a usage the length of time must be considerable. Reference may be made in that respect to the explanations given above in paragraphs 101-104.

124. The second question has several aspects. In the first place the time cannot begin to run until the exercise of sovereignty has begun. As was said above, the exercise of sovereignty must be effective and public and the time can therefore not begin to run until these two conditions have been fulfilled.

125. Here a problem arises: is it sufficient that the exercise of sovereignty is public or is it also necessary that the foreign States actually have knowledge of this exercise of sovereignty? In other words, can a foreign State offer as a valid excuse for its inaction, the fact that it had no actual knowledge of the situation, and demand that the time within which it must manifest its opposition should be construed to run only from the moment it received such knowledge?

126. Those who consider the right to "historic waters" to be an exception to general international law and therefore have a tendency to require at least tacit or presumed consent on the part of foreign States, are also inclined to require knowledge of the situation by these States, in order that absence of opposition may be held against them. For instance Fitzmaurice states:

"Clearly, absence of opposition is relevant only in so far as it implies consent, acquiescence or toleration on the part of the States concerned; but absence of opposition *per se* will not necessarily or always imply this. It depends on whether the circumstances are such that opposition is called for because the absence of it will cause consent or acquiescence to be presumed. The circumstances are not invariably of this character, particularly for instance where the practice or usage concerned has not been brought to the knowledge of other States, or at all events lacks the notoriety from which such knowledge might be presumed: or again, if the practice or usage concerned takes a form such that it is not reasonably possible for other States to infer what its true character is."[95]

127. The preference is evident in the quotation for a system according to which consent or acquiescence on the part of foreign States is required and consequently also their knowledge of the situation. On the other hand, the language used seems to indicate that also implied consent and presumed knowledge would be sufficient. The requirement of knowledge and consent seems to be more theoretical than real; in the end the author seems to be satisfied with notoriety from which knowledge may be presumed.

128. In any case, nobody seems to demand that the coastal State must formally notify each and all of the foreign States that it has assumed sovereignty over the area, before the time necessary to establish a usage will begin to run. If that is so, the notoriety of the situation, the public exercise of sovereignty over the area, would in reality be sufficient. It may, moreover, be recalled that in the *Fisheries* case, the International Court of Justice referred to

---

[95] *British Year Book of International Law*, vol. 30 (1935), page 33.

"the notoriety essential to provide the basis of an historic title."[96]

129. Against this opinion that notoriety is sufficient, the objection has been made that its effect would be to place an excessive burden of vigilance on States, as they would be forced to follow the activities of the legislative and executive organs of other States more closely than is usually the case.[97] It is, however, doubtful if this objection is justified. It may be argued that if a State had a real interest in a maritime area it would be natural for that State to follow closely what was going on there, and that the fact that the State was unaware of the situation was a good indication that its interest in the area was slight or non-existent. It might happen that at a later stage the State developed an interest in the area and so became aware of the circumstance that the coastal State for a long time had exercised sovereignty over it. If the newcomer State now found that this was against its interests, is it really a justifiable view to assert that this State could validly object to the coastal State's claim to an historic title to the area on the ground that it did not know until recently what was going on in the area?

130. In conclusion therefore, there seem to be strong reasons for holding that notoriety of the exercise of sovereignty, in other words, open and public exercise of sovereignty, is required rather than actual knowledge by the foreign States of the activities of the coastal States in the area.

131. Assuming now that the time necessary for the formation of a historic title has begun to run, sufficient opposition to block the title may not be forthcoming immediately. One or two States may protest, but still the over-all situation may be one of general toleration on the part of the foreign States. Opposition may build up successively and finally reach a stage where it no longer can be said that the exercise of sovereignty of the coastal State over the area is generally tolerated. Thereby the emergence of the historic title will be prevented, provided that this stage is not reached too late, i.e., at a time when the title has already come into existence because sufficient time under the condition of general toleration has already elapsed. There would therefore be a kind of race taking place between the lapse of time and the building up of the opposition. The outcome of the race is necessarily a matter of judgement as there are no precise criteria to be applied to either of the two competing factors. There is no precise time limit for the lapse of time necessary to allow the emergence of the historic right, and there is no precise measure for the amount of opposition which is necessary to exclude "general toleration".

132. This concludes the discussion of the three factors which according to the dominant opinion have to be taken into consideration in determining whether a right to "historic waters" has arisen. The result of the discussion would seem to be that for such a title to emerge, the coastal State must have effectively exercised sovereignty over the area continuously during a time sufficient to create a usage and have done so under the general toleration of the community of States.

133. It remains to study the fourth factor which is sometimes referred to, namely,

---

96 *I.C.J. Reports, 1951*, page 139.
97 Cf. *British Year Book of International Law*, vol. 30 (1953), page 42.

the question of the vital interests of the coastal State in the area.

4. *Question of the vital interests of the coastal State in the area claimed*

134. The Secretariat memorandum on "historic bays" (A/CONF.13/1), paragraphs 151 *et seq.*, describes a view taken by some authors and Governments, according to which a right to "historic bays" may be based not only on long usage, but also on other "particular circumstances" such as geographical configuration, requirements of self-defence or other vital interests of the coastal State. The origin of this idea is usually ascribed to Dr. Drago's dissenting opinion in the North Atlantic Coast Fisheries Arbitration (1910) where he stated that:

"a certain class of bays, which might be properly called the historical bays, such as Chesapeake Bay and Delaware Bay in North America and the great estuary of the River Plate in South America, form a class distinct and apart and undoubtedly belong to the littoral country, whatever be their depth of penetration and the width of their mouths, when such country has asserted its sovereignty over them, and particular circumstances such as geographical configuration, immemorial usage and above all, the requirements of self-defence, justify such a pretention."[98]

The basis for Dr. Drago's statement is evidently that in the classical cases of "historic bays" such as Chesapeake Bay and Delaware Bay, such "particular circumstances" were put forward in justification of the claims.

135. The significance of this line of thought is not so much that usage may have to be fortified by other reasons such as geographical configuration or vital interest in order to form a firm basis for a claim to "historic bays". It is rather that these other "particular circumstances" may justify the claim without the necessity of establishing also "immemorial usage". This is in any case the direction in which the idea developed, as may clearly be seen from the information given in the Secretariat memorandum.

136. Illuminating in this respect is article 7 of the draft international convention submitted at the Buenos Aires Conference of the International Law Association in 1922 by Captain Storny, reading as follows:

"A State may include within the limits of its territorial sea the estuaries, gulfs, bays or parts of the adjacent sea in which it has established its jurisdiction by continuous and immemorial usage or which, when these precedents do not exist, are unavoidably necessary according to the conception of article 2; that is to say, for the requirements of self-defence or neutrality or for ensuring the various navigation and coastal maritime police services."[99]

137. Also important is the statement of the Portuguese representative at the 1930 Hague Codification Conference:

"Moreover, if certain States have essential needs, I consider that those needs

---

[98] See quotation in A/CONF.13/1, paragraph 92.
[99] *Ibid.*, paragraph 152.

are as worthy of respect as usage itself, or even more so. Needs are imposed by modern social conditions, and if we respect agelong and immemorial usage which is the outcome of needs experienced by States in long past times, why should we not respect the needs which modern life, with all its improvements and its demands, imposes upon States."[100]

138. There is undoubtedly some justification for this view, and it is also understandable that it appeals to States which reached independence rather late and therefore are not able to base these claims on long usage.[101]

139. On the other hand it hardly seems appropriate to deal with the problem of these vital needs in the context of "historic bays". Bourquin, who otherwise appreciates the importance of the vital interests of the State with regard to bays, says in this respect:

"But why should this factor be considered strictly within the context of 'historic titles'? However widely the concept of a 'historic title' is construed, surely it cannot be claimed in circumstances where the historic element is wholly absent. The 'historic title' is one thing; the 'vital interest' is another."[102]

It is difficult to disagree with that opinion.

140. Attention may also be drawn to another aspect of the matter, which seems worth considering. In a convention on the territorial sea, it makes good sense to reserve the position of "historic bays". On the contrary, giving the parties the right to claim "vital bays" would come near to destroying the usefulness of any provision in the convention regarding the definition or delimitation of bays.

5. *Question of "historic waters" the coasts of which belong to two or more States*

141. In the foregoing discussion, it has been assumed that there was only one riparian State bordering the area in question and that therefore one State alone was interested in claiming it. What is the situation if there are two or more States bordering the area? Will that circumstance materially change the requirements discussed above for the emergence of an historic title to the area? Without pretending to deal with the matter exhaustively, a few considerations may be offered with respect to this problem.[103]

142. These questions may be discussed in regard to two different geographical settings both of which are in some way related to the 1958 Geneva Convention on the Territorial Sea and the Contiguous Zone.

143. Article 12 of the Convention deals with the situation where the coasts of two States are opposite or adjacent to each other, and paragraph 1 of the article provides as follows:

---

100 *Ibid.*, paragraph 155.

101 See the statement by Mr. García-Amador in the International Law Commission and referred to in the footnote to paragraph 7 above.

102 Bourquin, op. cit., page 51, quoted and translated in A/CONF.13/1, paragraph 158.

103 The question is also dealt with in the Secretariat memorandum on "historic bays" A/CONF.13/1, paras. 44-47 and 131-136.

"Where the coasts of two States are opposite or adjacent to each other, neither of the two States is entitled, failing agreement between them to the contrary, to extend its territorial sea beyond the median line every point of which is equidistant from the nearest points on the baselines from which the breadth of the territorial seas of each of the two States is measured. The provisions of this paragraph shall not apply, however, where it is necessary by reason of historic title or other special circumstances to delimit the territorial seas of the two States in a way which is at variance with this provision."[104]

144. It does not seem that in this case the fact that there is more than one coastal State would materially change the requirements for the establishment of an historic title. There is no doubt that an historic title can arise in that situation; at least this is assumed by the wording of the article. In other words, the emergence of an historic title for one of the coastal States is not prevented by the mere existence of another coastal State. On the other hand, in evaluating the attitude of the foreign States regarding the claim to an historic title,[105] it would seem reasonable to pay special attention to the attitude of the other coastal States.

145. The second geographical situation of relevance is the case of a bay bordered by two or more States.[106] This situation is related to the above-mentioned Geneva Convention in a negative way, as its article on bays (article 7) deals only with bays the coasts of which belong to a single State. The reason for this limitation on the scope of the article was that the International Law Commission, which prepared the text forming the basis of the Convention, considered that it did not have enough information regarding bays surrounded by two or more States to include provisions regarding them. The question of such bays was therefore left open as far as the Convention is concerned, and it would, indeed, seem to be a problem which could be discussed in depth only after additional information on the matter has been received from Governments. The few remarks which are made below in this paper are therefore of a very preliminary character.

146. Historic claims to a bay bordered by two or more States might be envisaged in two different circumstances. The claim may be made jointly by all the bordering States or it may be presented by one or more, but not all of these States.

147. If all the bordering States act jointly to claim historic title to a bay, it would seem that in principle what has been said above regarding a claim to historic title by a single State would apply to this group of States. One problem which might be raised in this connexion, without any attempt being made to solve it, is whether sovereignty over the bay must during the required period have been exercised by all the States claiming title or whether it is sufficient that during that period one or more of them exercised sovereignty over the bay.

148. The second hypothesis in which a claim to a bay bordered by two or more

---

104 *United Nations Conference on the Law of the Sea, Official Records*, vol. II, page 133.
105 Cf. above paragraphs 117-119.
106 Cf. Gidel, op. cit., pages 626-627.

States might be envisaged arises where only one or several of them jointly, but not all of them, claim the area. In this case, it is rather improbable that a historic title to the bay could ever arise in favour of the claiming State or States. For it must be expected that an attempt to exercise sovereignty over the bay on the part of one or some of the riparian States would cause immediate and strong opposition on the part of the other riparian State or States. It would therefore be difficult to imagine that the requirement of toleration by foreign States could in these circumstances be fulfilled. It must be emphasized in this connexion that, when it was said above that the opposition of one or two foreign States would not necessarily exclude the existence of a general toleration on the part of foreign States, this statement referred to waters bordered by a single coastal State. In the case of a bay surrounded by several States, the persistent opposition by one or more of the riparian States to the exercise of sovereignty over the bay by one or more of the other riparian States must naturally be of great if not decisive importance in evaluating whether or not the requirement of toleration had been fulfilled.

D. BURDEN OF PROOF

149. As the existence of a right to "historic waters" is to such a large extent a matter of judgement, the question of proof and in particular the problem of the burden of proof would seem to be of a rather secondary interest. The task of the parties to a dispute seems to be less to establish certain facts than to persuade the judges to follow their respective opinions regarding the evaluation of the facts. Still the question of the burden of proof cannot be ignored, in particular since it is one of the problems usually raised in connexion with the right to "historic waters".

150. In the memorandum of the Secretariat on "historic bays" (A/CONF.13/1), paragraphs 164-166, attention was drawn to certain significant statements in doctrine and practice regarding the onus of proof with respect to "historic waters". Gidel is quoted as follows:

"The onus of proof rests on the State which claims that certain maritime areas close to its coast possess the character of internal waters which they would not normally possess. The coastal State is the petitioner in this sort of action. Its claims constitute an encroachment on the high seas; and it would be inconsistent with the principle of the freedom of the high seas, which remains the essential basis of the whole public international law of the seas, to shift the onus of proof onto the States prejudiced by that reduction of the high seas which is the consequence of the appropriation of certain waters by the claimant State."[107]

151. Reference is also made to Basis of Discussion No. 8 submitted to the 1930 Hague Codification Conference and reading:

"The belt of territorial waters shall be measured from a straight line drawn across the entrance of a bay, whatever its breadth may be, if by usage the bay is subject to the exclusive authority of the coastal State; the onus of providing such

---

107 Gidel, op. cit., page 632.

usage is upon the coastal State."[108]

152. Finally it is pointed out that in the *Fisheries* case, the United Kingdom and Norway agreed that the onus of proof was on the State claiming a historic title, although they disagreed regarding the conditions and nature of the proof.

It may be interesting to quote the parties themselves in that respect. The Norwegian Government stated in its Counter-Memorial under the title "the proof of an historic title":

"The usage must be proved by the State which invokes it. Regarding this principle the Norwegian Government agrees with the United Kingdom Government. But it does not agree with it regarding the conditions of proof to be met and especially regarding the nature of the elements of proof to be produced."[109]

The United Kingdom Government said:

"The Norwegian Government... while disputing the contentions of the United Kingdom Government in regard to the conditions and nature of the proof of an historic title, agrees that the burden of proof lies upon the State which invokes the historic title. This admission that the burden of proof lies upon the claimant State was only to be expected in view of the abundant authority to that effect. The role of the historic element being to validate what is an exception to general rules and therefore intrinsically invalid, it is natural that the burden of proof should so emphatically be placed upon the coastal State..."[110]

153. There is doubt that there is abundant authority for the view that the burden of proof lies upon the claimant State. Some who hold that view are mainly influenced, as is evident from the statements of Gidel and of the United Kingdom, by their belief that the historic title is an exception to the general rules of international law and that "historic waters" is an encroachment on the freedom of the high seas. The difficulties involved in this line of reasoning have been referred to above and may be borne in mind also with respect to the question of the burden of proof. Others who say that the burden of proof lies upon the claimant may do so merely because it seems to restate a widely accepted procedural rule. It can, however, be doubted that the rule that the State claiming historic title has the burden of proof is equal to the procedural rule that the claimant must prove his case. The meaning of the former rule is evidently that the burden of proof lies on the State claiming the title whether that State is the claimant or the defendant in a dispute.

154. Moreover, the statement that the burden of proof is on the State claiming

---

108 *Acts of the Conference for the Codification of International Law*, vol. III: Meetings of the Second Committee, page 179; also cited in the aforesaid memorandum by the Secretariat (A/CONF.13/1), para.87.

109 *International Court of Justice, Pleadings, Oral Arguments, Documents, Fisheries Case*, vol. I, page 566.

110 Op. cit., vol. II, pages 645-646.

the historic title does not have a very precise meaning. It is significant in that respect that it could be accepted by both parties in the *Fisheries* case although they disagreed sharply as to what had to be proved and how. For the purpose of a useful discussion of the question, it is necessary to relate the burden of proof to the various factors which must be present to create an historic title to a maritime area.

155. As was pointed out above, the first requirement for the development of an historic right to a maritime area is the effective exercise of sovereignty over the area by the State claiming the right. There seems to be no doubt that the State claiming the area has to show that it has exercised the required sovereignty. To do that it would have to prove certain facts such as for instance that in certain instances it enforced its laws and regulations in or with respect to the area. These facts the State must prove to the satisfaction of the arbitrator (or Court or whoever has to decide whether the title exists or not). The opposing State (or States) might perhaps allege other facts intended to show that the required exercise of sovereignty did not take place, and the latter State must then show these facts to the satisfaction of the arbitrator. Each of the opponents therefore bears the burden of proof with respect to the facts on which they rely. On the basis of the facts which he considers to be proved, the arbitrator then decides whether it has been demonstrated that the required sovereignty was exercised. Obviously, this involves an evaluation not only of the evidence presented regarding the facts but also of the importance of these facts as signs of the alleged exercise of sovereignty. If the arbitrator finds that effective sovereignty has not been exercised, the State claiming the historic title loses this necessary basis for its claim. In that sense the burden of proof with respect to the exercise of sovereignty is undoubtedly on the State claiming the title.

156. In order to give rise to an historic title, the exercise of sovereignty, as was seen above, must not only be effective but also prolonged, continued. It must develop into a national usage. To persuade the arbitrator that this is the case, the State claiming title would again bring forward certain facts such as the fact that the enforcement of its laws and regulations had gone on for a number of years. These facts the State would have to prove. The opposing State (or States) might again allege other facts which in its opinion indicated that the claiming State had not been able to maintain its authority over the area uninterruptedly and that therefore, no prolonged, continued exercise of sovereignty had taken place. The opposing State would have to prove the facts on which its contentions were based. The arbitrator would then again have to evaluate the facts which he considers as established in order to decide whether or not an effective exercise of sovereignty by the State claiming title had taken place continuously during a sufficient period for a usage to have developed. If he finds that this was not the case, the State claiming title would have lost a necessary basis for its claim and in that sense it therefore carries the burden of proof regarding this point.

157. The third factor to take into consideration in relation to the emergence of an historic title is the attitude of the foreign States. The problem of the burden of proof is slightly more complicated with respect to this factor, because of the two

views opposing each other in this respect: one, that "acquiescence" in the meaning of tacit or presumed consent by the foreign States is required for the emergence of the historic title, and the other, that "general toleration" on the part of these States is sufficient. The general pattern of proof will, however, be the same as in regard to the previous factors. Whether the State claiming the title endeavours to prove "acquiescence" or "toleration", it will assert certain facts in support of its contention that "acquiescence" (or "toleration") existed, and these facts the State would have to prove to the satisfaction of the arbitrator. And similarly the opponent (or opponents) would bring forward certain facts in support of his assertion that "acquiescence" (or "toleration") did not exist; for these facts, the opponent would have the burden of proof. The facts upon which the claiming State and the opposing State (or States) rely may not be the same, if they attempt to prove (or disprove) "acquiescence" as if they attempt to prove (or disprove) "toleration", but in either case they have the burden of proof for the facts which they allege. Whether "acquiescence" or "toleration" is required is not a question of fact but a question of law, and each of the parties will no doubt try to persuade the arbitrator that its view in this respect is correct, but this is not a question of evidence. Finally the arbitrator will decide whether "acquiescence" or "toleration" is the necessary requirement and on the basis of the facts he will also decide whether the requirement of "acquiescence" (or "toleration") was fulfilled. If he comes to the conclusion that this was not the case, the State claiming title loses an indispensable basis for its claim of title, and in that sense it bears the burden of proof.

158. In summarizing this discussion of the problem of the burden of proof, it may be said that the general statement that the burden of proof is on the State claiming historic title to a maritime area is not of much value. If the statement means that, should the arbitrator (or whoever has to decide) not find that all the elements of the title (all the requirements for the existence of the title) are present, the State claiming the title will lose, then the statement simply asserts the obvious. The elements of the title have evidently to be proved to the satisfaction of the arbitrator, otherwise he will not accept the title. And this holds true whether or not the title is considered to be an exception to the general rules of international law, so that burden of proof is not *really* a logical consequence of the allegedly exceptional character of the title. In a dispute, each party has to prove the facts on which he relies, otherwise the arbitrator will not take these alleged facts into account. Furthermore, as regards the interpretation of the law and the evaluation of the facts in the light of this interpretation, each party will naturally try to persuade the arbitrator to adopt the party's views in this respect; to the extent that the party does not succeed in this, it will obviously have to bear the burden of his failure.

159. On the basis of what has just been said, it is submitted that it would be unnecessary, and possibly misleading, to include in a regulation of the régime of "historic waters" a general statement regarding the burden of proof. It would seem preferable to leave that question to be solved by the procedural rules which may be applicable in a particular case.

E. LEGAL STATUS OF THE WATERS REGARDED AS "HISTORIC WATERS"

160. The main question to be discussed in this section is whether "historic waters" are internal waters of the coastal State or are to be considered as part of its territorial sea. The importance of this problem lies in the fact that, according to the international law of the sea, the coastal State must allow the innocent passage of foreign ships through its territorial sea, but has no such obligation with respect to its internal waters.

161. As far as "historic bays" are concerned, the matter was dealt with in paragraphs 94-136 of the Secretariat memorandum on "historic bays" (A/CONF.13/1), and reference is made to the material and discussion which may be found there.

162. In paragraph 101 of the memorandum it is pointed out that, until the International Law Commission in its drafts on the law of the sea made a clear distinction between the "territorial sea" and "internal waters", the terminology used both in the doctrine and in State practice was ambiguous. "Territorial waters" could be used as a term comprehending both the "territorial sea" and "internal waters"; what is now known as "internal waters" was therefore often referred to as "territorial waters". In attempting to ascertain the opinions of authors and Governments in this field, one has therefore to take care not to be misled by the uncertain terminology used.

163. If allowance is made for this problem of terminology, the dominant opinion, as gathered from the statements assembled in the memorandum, seems to be that "historic bays" the coasts of which belong to a single State are internal waters. This was to be expected, for it is generally agreed that the waters inside the closing line of a bay are internal waters and that the territorial sea begins outside that line.

164. On the other hand, it should be recalled that the right to "historic bays" is based on the effective exercise of sovereignty over the area claimed, together with the general toleration of foreign States. The sovereignty exercised can be either sovereignty as over internal waters or sovereignty as over the territorial sea. In principle, the scope of the historic title emerging from the continued exercise of sovereignty should not be wider in scope than the scope of the sovereignty actually exercised. If the claimant State exercised sovereignty as over internal waters, the area claimed would be internal waters, and if the sovereignty exercised was sovereignty as over the territorial sea, the area would be territorial sea. For instance if the claimant State allowed the innocent passage of foreign ships through the waters claimed, it could not acquire an historic title to these waters as internal waters, only as territorial sea.

165. The seeming contradiction between the statement that "historic bays" are internal waters, and the conclusion that waters claimed on the basis of the exercise of sovereignty as over the territorial sea cannot be internal waters but only part of the territorial sea, is really one of terminology. In the latter case, it would be preferable not to speak of an "historic bay" but of "historic waters" of some other

kind.

166. What was said above refers to "historic waters", the coasts of which belong to a single State. The principle set out in paragraph 164 would, however, apply in the case of bays bordered by two or more States as well. Whether the waters of the bay are internal waters or territorial sea would depend on what kind of sovereignty was exercised by the coastal States in the formative period of the historic title to the bay.

167. The same principle also applies to "historic waters" other than "historic bays". These areas would be internal waters or territorial sea according to whether the sovereignty exercised over them in the course of the development of the historic title was sovereignty as over internal waters or sovereignty as over the territorial sea.

F. QUESTION OF A LIST OF "HISTORIC WATERS"

168. It is easy to see that claims to "historic waters" may be a source of considerable uncertainty regarding the delimitation of the maritime domain of States. As was shown above, the determination of the question whether or not such a claim is legitimate depends to a large extent on the evaluation of the circumstances in the particular case. Even if general agreement was reached on the principles involved, the application of these principles would not be without complications. The question how to avoid or reduce this uncertainty has held the attention of both authors and Governments, especially in connexion with the attempts to codify the rules of international law regarding the territorial sea.[111]

169. In the course of the preparatory work for the 1930 Hague Codification Conference, Schücking, the rapporteur of the sub-committee dealing with problems connected with the law of the territorial sea, suggested the establishment of an International Waters Office which would register rights possessed by the riparian States outside the proposed fixed zone of their territorial seas, including rights to "historic waters". Applications for registration of such rights could be made within a time limit and application could be opposed by other States within a time limit. A procedure was also provided for settling disputes arising in case of such opposition.[112] The idea of an International Waters Office was however later dropped by the rapporteur.[113]

170. Bustamante in his "project of convention", prepared in order to help the work of the 1930 Codification Conference, suggested a similar scheme, with the Secretariat of the League of Nations playing a role corresponding to that of the International Waters Office in the Schücking proposal.[114]

171. In the discussions at the 1930 Codification Conference, the representative of Greece stated that it would be useful to adopt Schücking's proposal

---

111 See for instance references in Gidel, op. cit., pages 636-638.

112 League of Nations document C.196.M.70.1927.V, pages 38-41 and 58.

113 *Ibid.*, page 72.

114 The relevant provisions of the Bustamante procedure may be found in the Secretariat memorandum on "historic waters", paragraph 209.

"that an international organ should be established to draw up in advance a list of historic bays".[115]

172. The representative of Great Britain said:

"May I add one other thing? It is quite clear that neither this Conference nor any Committee nor Sub-Committee of it could possibly undertake to draw up a list of historic bays. Yet the matter is one of great importance, and some machinery ought to be devised by which the various nations of the world can exchange views on this point, with the object ultimately of obtaining a list of historic bays agreed internationally.

"At a later stage, I shall propose that the Conference should suggest, before its work is completed, the setting up of some small body which might examine the claims of the various nations to historic bays with a view to making a report and possibly recommendations on the subject at a later date, to Geneva or elsewhere. The subject is one which has caused much friction and much dispute in the past and this seems to be a golden opportunity first of all to settle the principles on which the classification is to be based, and then, having settled the principles, to agree upon some list which will be binding for the future."[116]

173. Finally the representative of Portugal spoke in the same sense as follows:

"In the considerations it adduced today, the British delegation spoke of the establishment of an international organization. I venture to remind you that article 3 of Professor Schücking's draft speaks of the creation of an International Waters Office. After discussion by the Committee, Professor Schücking agreed to omit that article. I brought it forward again, but it was not taken into account either by the Committee of Experts or by the Preparatory Committee.

"This idea has now been put forward once again. On behalf of the Portuguese delegation, I wish to say that, from the general point of view, I am prepared to agree to the establishment of such an organization, provided that the character and functions with which it is endowed are satisfactory."[117]

174. The Second Committee of the Codification Conference in its report referred to the question of "historic waters" and, as was seen above, stated that the work of codification could not affect such rights. The Committee thereafter added:

"On the other hand, it must be recognized that no definite or concrete results can be obtained without determining and defining those rights. The Committee realizes that, in this matter too, the work of codification will encounter certain difficulties."[118]

175. While it no doubt would be convenient and desirable from the point of view of clarity and certainty to establish an agreed list of "historic waters", it is doubtful whether a practicable approach to the problem would be to ask

---

115 *Acts of the Conference for the Codification of International Law*, vol. III, page 105.
116 *Ibid.*, pages 104-105.
117 *Ibid.*, page 107.
118 *Ibid.*, page 211.

Governments to register their claims within a certain time and likewise request opponents of the claims to register their objections within a certain time. The advantage would, of course, be, after the expiration of the deadlines, that the unopposed claims would be considered as accepted, that no new claims could be made and that only the opposed claims would have to be settled. One weakness of such a scheme is, however, that it would be binding only on the States adhering to it, so that its effectiveness would depend upon how many and perhaps which States accepted it. Unless adherence by the totality of the States could be achieved, new claims could, in any case, not be excluded. Moreover, the scheme would involve the obvious danger that it might provoke a number of unnecessary disputes, as States would be tempted, in order to be on the safe side, to overstate both their claims and their objections. The net result might be less rather than more certainty.

176. It could therefore be argued that little advantage would be achieved by undertaking the rather formidable task of establishing a list of "historic waters". It might also be said that such an enterprise would be pointless as long as the question of the breadth of the territorial sea has not been settled. Under these circumstances the question is, whether it would not be preferable to limit the study to the principles of the matter and leave particular cases to be settled if and when they become the object of an actual dispute.

G. SETTLEMENT OF DISPUTES

177. Should a dispute arise, it would, however, be useful if means for the settlement of disputes were already agreed upon. It might therefore be desirable to supplement any agreement on substantive rules or principles relating to "historic waters" by provisions for the settlement of disputes regarding the interpretation or application of such rules or principles. As to the procedure to be followed in regard to such settlement, one might use as a pattern either the machinery set up by the 1958 Geneva Convention on Fishing and Conservation of the Living Resources of the High Seas[119] or the methods outlined in the Optional Protocols concerning the Compulsory Settlement of Disputes adopted at the 1958 Geneva Conference on the Law of the Sea[120] and at the 1961 Vienna Conference on Diplomatic Intercourse and Immunities.[121]

178. In the former case, disputes would be referred to a special commission, unless the parties agreed to seek a solution by another method of peaceful settlement, as provided for in Article 33 of the Charter of the United Nations. The members of the commission would be named by agreement between the States in dispute or, failing agreement, by the Secretary-General of the United Nations.

179. If on the other hand the pattern of the optional protocols is followed,

---

[119] *United Nations Conference on the Law of the Sea, Official Records*, United Nations publication, Sales No.: 58.V.4, vol. II, page 140.

[120] *Ibid.*, page 145.

[121] Document A/CONF.20/12, in *United Nations Conference on Diplomatic Intercourse and Immunities, Official Records*, United Nations publication, Sales No.: 62.X.1, vol. II, page 89.

disputes would be brought before the International Court of Justice by the application of one of the parties. The parties could agree to resort to an arbitral tribunal instead of the Court, and they could also agree to adopt a conciliation procedure before going to the Court.

180. The settlement of disputes regarding rights to "historic waters" is complicated by a peculiar difficulty. If the final decision in a dispute goes against the State claiming the area, it might be expected that the State would give up its claim and the matter would be settled once and for all. On the other hand, should the decision be in favour of the State claiming the area, this decision would bind only the other party to the dispute, and other States might later return to the charge and open up new disputes regarding the claim. The same could of course happen when the claiming State loses, if that State, while respecting the decision in its relations with the other party to the dispute continued to exercise sovereignty over the area in relation to other States or their citizens. In other words, although a dispute regarding an area of "historic waters" was finally settled between the State claiming the area and an opposing State, the matter whether this area is "historic waters" could be reopened by other States, which would not be bound by the first settlement. Even if the dispute was decided by the highest international court in existence, the International Court of Justice, its decision would be binding only on the parties to the dispute, as stipulated in Article 59 of its Statute. A third State would still be legally free to dispute the claim, and a final decision of the question whether an area is or is not "historic waters" would therefore be hard to obtain. Naturally, if in one dispute it decided that the area was "historic waters" of a certain State, the International Court of Justice in all probability would come to the same conclusion in another dispute; similarly, a decision by a special commission or an arbitral decision on the matter in one case would probably carry considerable weight in another case. Still, the question would not be legally settled once and for all, and the possibility of new disputes would remain.

181. The experience of the two above-mentioned conferences indicates that it would probably be practical to embody the provisions for the settlement of disputes in a separate optional protocol. Some States might be willing to accept certain substantive rules or principles on "historic waters", but not to submit themselves to a compulsory procedure for the settlement of disputes. By including the substantive and the procedural rules in separate instruments, these States would be able to adhere to the former although they could not subscribe to the latter.

III. Conclusions

182. The above discussion of the principles and rules of international law relating to "historic waters, including historic bays" would seem to justify a number of conclusions, provided that it is understood that some of these must necessarily be highly tentative and more in the nature of bases of discussion than results of an exhaustive investigation of the matter.

183. In the first place, while "historic bays" present the classic example of historic title

to maritime areas, there seems to be no doubt that, in principle, a historic title may exist also to other waters than bays, such as straits or archipelagos, or in general to all those waters which can form part of the maritime domain of a State.

184. On the other hand, the widely held opinion that the régime of "historic waters" constitutes an exception to the general rules of international law regarding the delimitation of the maritime domain of the State is debatable. The realistic view would seem to be not to relate "historic waters" to such rules as an exception or not an exception, but to consider the title to "historic waters" independently, on its own merits. As a consequence one should avoid, in discussing the theory of "historic waters", to base any proposed principles or rules on the alleged exceptional character of such waters.

185. In determining whether or not a title to "historic waters" exists, there are three factors which have to be taken into consideration, namely,

(i) The authority exercised over the area by the State claiming it as "historic waters";

(ii) The continuity of such exercise of authority;

(iii) The attitude of foreign States.

186. First, effective exercise of sovereignty over the area by the claiming State is a necessary requirement for title to the area as "historic waters" of that State. Secondly, such exercise of sovereignty must have continued during a considerable time so as to have developed into a usage. Thirdly, the attitude of foreign States to the activities of the claiming State in the area must have been such that it can be characterized as an attitude of general toleration. In this respect the same weight need not be given to the attitude of all States. Particularly, it would seem reasonable, in the case of a State (or States) claiming historic title to waters bordered by two or more States, to accord special importance to the attitude of the other riparian State (or States).

187. It is apparent from this description of the requirements which must be fulfilled for a title to "historic waters" to emerge, that the existence of such a title is to a large extent a matter of judgement. A large element of appreciation seems unavoidable in this matter, but it is possible that Government comments on the three factors listed above could yield a number of concrete examples which might serve as illustration and guidance.

188. The burden of proof of title to "historic waters" is on the State claiming such title, in the sense that, if the State is unable to prove to the satisfaction of whoever has to decide the matter that the requirements necessary for the title have been fulfilled, its claim to the title will be disallowed. In a dispute both parties will most probably allege facts in support of their respective contentions, and in accordance with general procedural rules each party has the burden of proof with respect to the facts on which he relies. It is therefore doubtful whether the general statement that the burden of proof is on the State claiming title to "historic waters", although widely accepted, is really useful as a definite criterion.

189. The legal status of "historic waters", i.e., the question whether they are to

be considered as internal waters or as part of the territorial sea, would in principle depend on whether the sovereignty exercised in the particular case over the area by the claiming State and forming a basis for the claim, was sovereignty as over internal waters or sovereignty as over the territorial sea. It seems logical that the sovereignty to be acquired should be commensurate with the sovereignty actually exercised.

190. The idea of establishing a definitive list of "historic waters" in order to diminish the uncertainty which claims to such waters might cause has serious drawbacks. An attempt to establish such a list might induce States to overstate both their claims and their opposition to the claims of other States, and so give rise to unnecessary disputes. Moreover, it would in any case be extremely difficult, not to say impossible, to arrive at a list which would be really final.

191. On the other hand, it would be desirable to establish a procedure for the obligatory settlement of disputes regarding claims to "historic waters". As a pattern for such a procedure one might use the relevant provisions of the 1958 Geneva Convention on Fishing and Conservation of the Living Resources of the High Seas; in that case disputes would be referred to a special commission, unless the parties agreed on another method of peaceful settlement. Or one could follow the optional protocols adopted at the 1958 Geneva Conference on the Law of the Sea and the 1961 Vienna Conference on Diplomatic Intercourse and Immunities; disputes would then lie within the compulsory jurisdiction of the International Court of Justice, subject to the possibility of having recourse also to a conciliation procedure or to arbitration.

192. For practical reasons, an agreement on the settlement of disputes might preferably be included in a protocol separate from any instrument containing substantive rules on "historic waters". In that way, States which would be unwilling to subscribe to a procedure for the compulsory settlement of disputes could adhere to the substantive rules agreed upon.

后　记

　　感谢自然资源部海洋发展战略研究所和知识产权出版社，为拙作提供面向更多读者的机会。

　　历史性所有权及其相关的历史性权利问题，是一个在中国语境中具有特殊意义的国际法问题。一方面，我国立法在这方面有明确规定，因而其成为维护国家领土主权和海洋权益的重要制度性工具；另一方面，又因其以"历史"作为权利前缀，容易产生望文生义的美好误解，以为有历史则必有权利。本书写作的初心，是希冀通过考察这一习惯法制度的形成脉络、要件构成和场景应用，搭建基于国际法实践的理论解释和分析框架，赋予广泛的历史事实以确切的国际法意涵，实现在历史事实和国际法基础上，通过谈判协商解决争端的外交政策目标。

　　本书论题始于2011年，彼时周边海洋权益争端尚未引起广泛关注，我的博士生指导老师清华大学贾兵兵教授以敏锐的学术洞察力，建议我将历史性所有权相关问题作为我博士阶段的研究方向，并逐章审读文稿，不断提出问题，修正研究方向。贾老师特别重视学术结论的严谨性，反复要求"有一分证据说一分话"。借此机会，对恩师一直以来的支持和关爱表示衷心感谢。

　　在我的写作过程中，同在导师门下学习的谈中正、闫晴、蒋超翊、邱雨桐等同学，他们对我的书稿或建议研究思路，或提供修改建议。雷筱璐、李任远、李扬、郑亦君等同辈学人对完善书稿提出许多建设性意见，李施安同学通读了全书文稿并协助编制参考文献和附录。此外，我在荷兰和平宫图书馆获得了大量开放的珍贵馆藏图书资料，图书馆还慷慨赠予我雅胡达·布鲁姆经典著作《国际法中的历史性权利》(*Historic Titles in International Law*)。之后，我在比利时荷语鲁汶大学访学期间，宽松舒适的研究环境为我的写作和构思提供了难得的条件。在此对大家的热情帮助致以诚挚谢意。

由于种种原因，本书出版一波三折，甚至一度产生了放弃出版的想法。幸得王宗来、李国强、贾宇、吴继陆等前辈学者审读书稿并给予较高的评价，肯定了出版本书对相关理论和实务确有裨益。特别是责任编辑庞从容老师多方奔走、坚持不懈，使得本书出版问世得以峰回路转。事不经历不知其难，对上述各位以及不便具名的领导同事们的热心襄助感念在心。

最后，感谢家人给我以包容，祝我的孩子幸福，成为一个他想成为的人。

是为记。

徐桥

2024 年 4 月 20 日于北京